*The Rebirth of the Missouri Pacific, 1956–1983*

**Missouri Pacific** corporate headquarters, 210 N. 13th St., Saint Louis.

# The Rebirth of the Missouri Pacific, 1956–1983

*By* H. CRAIG MINER

 *Texas A&M University Press*   COLLEGE STATION

Library of Congress Cataloging in Publication Data

Miner, H. Craig.
    The rebirth of the Missouri Pacific, 1956–1983.

    Bibliography: p.
    Includes index.
    1. Missouri Pacific Railroad—History.   I.  Title.
HE2791.M7593M55   1983      385′.065′78      83-45097
ISBN  0-89096-159-X

*Manufactured in the United States of America*

FIRST EDITION

*For all those I interviewed,*
*and who thus contributed to this history twice*

# Contents

# *Illustrations*

## MAPS

# *Preface*

SOMEHOW, with this project when planning came to execution it was always winter. The Christmas holidays were a time when no class schedules interfered with a trip to Saint Louis long enough to let me rummage through that entire line of boxes with the interesting labels I had noticed once before. In winter some exotic forms of public transport were not as reliable a means of reaching the operating centers of the system as a ride on its own freight-hauling diesel locomotives. Nasty winter days helped me feel that the basement of an office building might be for the moment a better place than the open air. So maybe it was portent more than accident that my first word about the writing of a history of the modern Missouri Pacific railroad came on a cold winter morning early in 1979.

The man I talked with by telephone was Harry Hammer, the railroad's assistant vice-president for public relations. We first met in 1969 when I was a graduate student writing a dissertation on the history of the Saint Louis–San Francisco. Since the MP and the Frisco were closely allied in the middle nineteenth century, I had reason to inquire at the Missouri Pacific building about the availability of minute books for several obscure companies of the 1860s. Mr. Hammer was as helpful and personable then as he is now, and, after consulting the company's well-organized archival inventory, he took me directly to the documents I sought. I did not fail to notice then or to recall ten years later that the volumes from which I took notes were part of an impressively vast array of company records. Volumes and boxes marked with dates from the 1850s to the present lined row after row of shelving and seemed to chide the economic historian who might imagine that the basic work in his field had been accomplished. What I did not know was that at the moment in 1969 when I gazed at the remnants of the MP's long tradition, the company was in the midst of perhaps its most revolutionary period, and that my future connection would involve not the handwritten leather-bound books I then perused, but typewritten records, many not then yet created. My subject was not in the basement vaults, but in the upstairs offices where men who smiled politely back from their desks at the historian seeking fragments of the nineteenth century filled their minds and challenged their spirits with the more "relevant" business of creating a thoroughly modern railroad. That their activity so soon would be history, too, was a thought far from their minds.

Could I come to Saint Louis in the next couple of days, Hammer asked that winter day in 1979? Downing Jenks, the chairman of the board, was interested in preserving the history of the company since its reorganization in 1956 and saw no reason to wait until memories grew stale and records were destroyed to begin. Jenks had read my earlier railroad book (a revision of the dissertation) and had liked it. He had a definite idea what he wanted. First, those who had made the recent company history should be interviewed before their unique insights were forever lost. Second, these interviews and research in the still voluminous company records for that period should form the basis of a narrative which, it was hoped, could clearly present a story so complex that even those who had directly experienced it found it difficult to explain. Jenks was decisive, Hammer told me, and a quick judge of people. He would run the history project just as he ran the railroad. If I were chosen to write the history, I would know quickly, and access to the company archives and personnel would be immediate and complete. And, no, neither Jenks nor others in the organization had any interest in mixing history and propaganda. Along with financial and administrative support would come entire freedom to use whatever methods and to reach whatever conclusions I felt the evidence justified. Two days later, with an agreement handwritten on a small sheet of memo paper, I began the research for *The Rebirth of the Missouri Pacific.*

Most of the relevant background to the recent history of the company came from an investigation of its situation in the Great Depression, for it was in the 1930s that the major difficulties originated that the management of the 1960s and 1970s so brilliantly solved. But there was a backdrop considerably deeper and always present—if not in the techniques at least in the attitudes of modern management. Who among them could forget that the MP was one of the oldest railroad companies west of the Mississippi, having its origin at the groundbreaking for the Pacific Railroad of Missouri on July 4, 1851? The company had been the tool of businessmen's most ambitious dreams several times before. First there was the goal of reaching the Pacific by connecting Saint Louis and San Francisco, so temptingly opposite each other, by a railroad that might penetrate the Rockies. Then, in the 1880s, the company was the headquarters corporation for Jay Gould's "Southwest System," which, through control of the St. Louis, Iron Mountain & Southern; Texas & Pacific; International Great Northern; and Missouri, Kansas & Texas lines, monopolized trade between Saint Louis and Texas. Like the thrust for the Pacific, Gould's plans eventually failed, but not before the southern connections were established that would be of major importance to the MP's traffic mix after World War II. Many subsidiaries were merged into the system during the early twentieth century, so the company which built a twenty-two-story office building in Saint Louis in 1928 could truly be described as one of the country's major rail systems.

Bankruptcy in 1933 stopped all the Missouri Pacific dreaming, including the latest by Cleveland's Van Sweringen brothers. And slowly, over the twenty-three years of legal wrangles in receivership, much of the public came to identify the company with hard times and with outdated technological, legal, and managerial strategems. Still, the potential was there: the track still went where dreamers had put it, and their hopes were built into the system map, waiting only for the right time—the time the earlier managers had mistakenly thought had come. The luck of a long history had not been all bad, and it left a great instrument which was bound to be picked up again and wielded by the future's deftest hands.

I leave these rich fields of the far past for others. My serious research began with the boxes of reorganization documents and hearings transcripts stored in abandoned salt mines at Hutchinson, Kansas, just an hour's drive from my home in Wichita. Of course I went to Hutchinson in winter and experienced the odd sensation of working in an entirely quiet and temperature-stabilized vault several hundred feet under the ground while an ice storm raged above.

Time spent among these records was important beyond the small amount of text in the final version of the book directly devoted to them because it allowed me accurately to re-create the situation in which the new management of 1961 found itself and to understand how heavily the burden of recent history and the actions of aggressive personalities of the 1930s, 1940s, and 1950s restricted the options of the railroad futurists who followed. Before the recapitalization of the MP in 1974, management played a chess game with elaborate rules for their side and sometimes no rules at all for the opposition. In the volatile atmosphere of rail industry change typical of the 1960s, management's situation was like that of brave knights going forth with lances and the pride they had inherited into an atomic battleground. But as players of less serious games understand, the most gifted practitioners seem almost to enjoy their handicaps and to use them to surprise and confound those who least expected an attack in that quarter. One respects the accomplishment of modern MP management more for each hour spent laboring literally in the salt mines over the records of the selfishness and acrimony built into the capital structure of the company they tried to defend and build.

My time in Saint Louis always began in the second-floor public relations office. It is just up a short flight of steps from the impressive vaulted hall which is the public entrance to the Missouri Pacific building. However, the office itself is a great contrast to the entryway. It is spartan and businesslike in appearance, with most employees sitting at undifferentiated desks among the copying machines and even the top officers of the department ensconced in cubicles that a professor might complain about. There is a little paneling in the offices of the chairman of the board and president on the top floor, but nowhere appear the expected trappings of executive power and prestige. The building on 13th Street downtown is a working headquarters, occupied by people running a no-nonsense railroad. The fountains, the oriental carpets, the colonial touches, and the double walnut doors are all at the Missouri Pacific Corporation headquarters on Clayton Road, the place where William Marbury used to plot his strategy when his Mississippi River Corporation first entered the railroad business.

Most of my work was downtown. There I would speak with Mr. Hammer about the next interview or the next set of records, and in the process he would always contribute some well-told and well-understood company history. After a hello to Wally Fussner, Jerry Brown, and Tim Hogan in their respective second-floor boxes, it was either up or down: up to the executive offices for interviews or down to the basement archives. More often it was down, rushing past the security guard, who could tell by my outfit that I did not belong, through a door at one side of that elegant first-floor hall and into Bobby Sponslor's catacombs. That was down-to-earth, indeed. Even the wall calendars were there replaced by steam pipes, while clacking sounds came not from typewriters but from the rolling of metal-wheeled document trucks over a cement floor supporting miles of nondescript shelving.

The labels on the boxes and the descriptions in the inventory were not always good guides to the contents. Therefore, nothing could be assumed without a good deal of laborious taking down of thirty-pound boxes of paper, always located on the top row. It was physical work for me and more so for the employees of the Records Management Department, but it yielded fine dividends of fresh history with its detail still full. One might ordinarily be glad for the survival of some testimony of company officers on a legal issue. Facing three hundred volumes of it, or fifteen boxes of exhibits and arguments, or, in the case of the final Union Pacific merger, an application that was forty-three hundred pages long, certainly did not allow for the medievalist's concern with watermarks and calligraphy. Speed reading might be a more appropriate skill. Also, as in studies of modern government, scholars working on recent corporate history must develop an eye for the salient amid a maze of either flat bureaucratic prose or subtle but purposeful obfuscation. Enough statistics are available to permanently cripple a reader's enthusiasm if they are used with abandon. But also, almost hidden at first, there is human drama as compelling as that in any period of time when people pursued goals just at the edge of their comprehension and abilities.

Working with the company archives gave me a special opportunity to balance the actual plans and perceptions of officers and employees against the speculations of the press. The MP was not unusually secretive, but it was standard industry practice, particularly during the merger wars of the 1960s, not to make informative public statements during delicate negotiations. Also, the focus of newspapers on the colorful and the briefly told concealed the complexity important to grasping that the company was not only playing for high stakes but also operating in an environment where action was always partly bluff and decision resembled striking out for a glimmer in a dense fog. The goal might prove illusory, or conditions could modify its desirability before the campaign to reach it peaked but after resources were diverted from other ends.

Yet while the archives provided bulk and depth, the interviews gave the book much of its life. In some ways the interview process became a personal model for interpreting the company's history. For one thing, the subjects of the interviews were the actors in the history. In talking with them I received direct and indirect information—special insights to be sure not written down anywhere, but also a feeling for the style and personality of the MP's people. Second, the entire history project was an example of how the management team operated together. Actually, being an academic loner, I started with a negative personal prejudice about teams, particularly corporate teams, which I pictured as consisting of relatively uncreative automatons carrying out the programmed tasks of some master plan while humming the company song. Not so; again and again I observed enormous and unique individual capabilities—which in several cases I could call nothing short of genius—combined with perfect group loyalty and completely enthusiastic participation in a discipline (in this case the history) not originally of their own choosing.

C. J. Maurer, the accountant, was quiet, almost withdrawn, while the statements of Mark Hennelly, the lawyer, could have been directed to a jury in a sizable courtroom, such was their style and volume. Thomas O'Leary was East Coast Ivy League —careful, fluent, precise, perfectly organized. One would have trusted him with money, and at Citibank and later at the railroad, many did. John Lloyd, on the other hand, lost nothing of Montana while attending the Wharton School of Finance. He is big, friendly, unassuming. He remembers names and spins yarns in a slow drawl. Guerdon Sines was West Coast—casual, healthy, innovative, and altogether modern. He could write a popular book on computers, as he speaks of them to the uninitiated with the entire familiarity and clarity of the master of the new electronics that he is. There is no question that he runs his division and is no more cowed by circuits and software than by the difficulties he uses them to solve. Wade Clutton, who spent a large amount of time teaching me about the computer's role in the MP's Transportation Control System, walked with me to the local stereo equipment shop one day to buy more tape for recording all he was telling me. I already had a couple of hours of his story, and I used the last of what tape I had while walking down the street. He talked in his office, he talked on the street, he brought things up on his terminal, and without question he *sold* me the TCS with the same manic involvement that must have been a factor in selling it to the management originally. Later I read Tracy Kidder's Pulitzer Prize–winning *The Soul of a New Machine*; when it spoke of the Data General team working often all night for months, driven only by pride, I thought of Wade Clutton.

These are some of the types, then. Joseph Austin of Traffic reminds one of Lloyd; John German, the motive power expert, of Sines. R. K. Davidson, a man in his thirties like me but already at the top in rail management, showed impressively the kind of model the MP management training program can produce. E. C. Pigean and Bob Rathert addressed me late one Friday afternoon in a fascinating and efficient dialogue chorus, putting into my head through their complementary style more information about inventory and stores than would have been thought possible in a brief time. Pigean was the matter-of-fact "old hand," savvy to personnel problems in implementing things. Rathert was intense, like Clutton. Maybe computers either create or attract these types, and in fact Rathert worked with computers on the MP in the late fifties, earlier than anyone else I talked with. A similar stereo experience came in Paul Morey's office when Morey and Ray Breedlove "trained" me about the company training program.

In New York City, I talked with John Tobin and Lauk Walton, who were attorneys for Alleghany Corporation during the MP stock battles of the 1960s and 1970s. Walton was mildly suspicious of me and of the project, I think, accustomed as he was to being the opposition attorney in the case. I believe he thought the story might turn out to be a whitewash of the MP, and I hope the final product, thanks in part to his contributions, pleases him as a balanced account. It speaks volumes about the professionalism of people on this level that Walton, the enemy, became fast friends with Hennelly at the MP during the stock fight and that when years later the MP chose an attorney to represent it in the MP/UP merger hearings, that attorney was Lauk Walton.

Also in New York City came fertile interviews with John Burns and Clifford Ramsdell of Alleghany Corporation. While I also spoke briefly with Walter Brown, who was actually one of the MP's reorganization managers in 1956, Ramsdell proved to be my finest living contact with the battles of the 1930s. As we sat and talked at the elegantly Victorian Player's Club, he had all the old fire in his eye and drama in his tone. I could easily sip my wine and conjure up near the next table the images of Robert Young, Allan Kirby, William Marbury, and other departed warriors of the fight whom Ramsdell knew so well.

Isabel Benham, who served on several crucial occasions as an analyst of MP security values, spent a number of hours with me in New York, both at her office and one of the little restaurants in the Citicorp building. She was one of the first of her sex to reach the upper echelons of the securities analysis field, and it is easy to see why. Benham is a completely remarkable woman in every way. She combines a subtle understanding of the most esoteric reaches of corporate finance with warmth, humanity, and the kind of empathetic understanding of past scenarios that a historian might envy. I have quoted her frequently, and not solely on the subject of bond values.

It is inevitable that I have omitted mention of many who gave me significant help, as the cooperation of all I met with was so ready and entire. For example, I did no formal interviews on my trip on MP freight trains through the heart of the system in December, 1979, but people I met that week taught me indispensible things. Dick Martin, road foreman of engines at Coffeyville, Kansas, started my mechanical education, while Tom Webster, whom I later met again in his role as student at Wichita State University, gave me an example of how a skilled engineer handles an ailing locomotive on a steep grade. Dennis Miller shepherded me most of the way through Arkansas, where one particularly memorable evening was spent aboard the U30C of Bill Wiley and Billy Joe Grove, who served me up a veritable feast of impressions of a railroad from the throttle end. Thanks to the Duke boys and their "Toyah Flash," to Jack Spurr, and to those unnamed for their own protection who let me feel what it was like to control eleven thousand horsepower for even just an hour of my life. For my MA in yard operation, I thank especially Ralph Ramsey at North Little Rock and David Barnes at Kansas City. And to the guys in the Little Rock hump tower, from one who specializes in language, my hat's off to you.

There at the beginning, there at the end, and the dominant force throughout the history project, as he was through the history it collected, was Downing Jenks himself. He is the quintessence of the corporate leader, combining in a single personality several seemingly incompatible, but all greatly desirable qualities. Obviously he pushes. Surely he gets excited and he drives. Yet to see him across a table, calmly puffing his pipe while spouting statistics or explaining strategy without a note outside his own brain, he looks as calm as the Buddha. An engineer by training, he is a dreamer by inclination and can not only get along with, but equally supercharge people so different that they likely actively hate each other. The technician as sage is irresistible. He can design his own vision and present specifications for the impossible.

I have no doubt that this history was one of the least difficult to execute among Jenks's ideas. But there are many corporate histories that have stalled for lack of material, more that are crippled by burdensome restrictions, and a good number that are confusing, dull, or both partly because those in a position to communicate the content or quality of the corporate past were either unwilling to do so or, alas, dead. That this history suffers from none of those defects, but only from those faults attributable to the historian's shortage of skill, is due in large measure to Downing Jenks. I am glad to count him as a benefactor and as a friend.

H. Craig Miner

*The Rebirth of the Missouri Pacific, 1956–1983*

# CHAPTER I

# *Out of the Depths*

---

THE officers, directors, and stockholders of the Missouri Pacific Railroad Company (MP) gathered at the Jefferson-Sheraton Hotel in Saint Louis on May 14, 1957, for what all expected would be one of the stormiest annual meetings ever held by a railroad that for over twenty years had been known to the public for controversy. There would be a proxy contest pitting Colonel Thomas Colburn Davis and his associates Thomas Shearman, Martin Watts, and John M. Balliet, all representing minority stockholders, against a slate of directors proposed by management. Management based its appeal on the strength of the company's performance in the brief time since it had emerged in 1956 from a twenty-three-year receivership, the longest in U.S. rail history.[1] Naturally, some believed this was not much to boast about.

The railroad's president, Paul J. Neff, confessed to knowing little about the "present purposes and ambitions" of the men mounting the proxy fight but was sure their animosity dated from the period of bankruptcy and reorganization. He saw no point "in reviving disagreements which were laid to rest barely a year ago" when through compromise the final reorganization plan had presumably satisfied the warring parties of security holders. He could not hide the fact, however, that those on the alternative directors' slate and many others in the room were "manifestly opposed to your Management."[2]

---

[1] P. J. Neff to stockholders, April 16, 1957, exhibit 4, Davis testimony, space 061012a, Missouri Pacific (MP) archives, Missouri Pacific Building, Saint Louis.

[2] Ibid.

T. C. Davis, the most colorful and outspoken of the maverick group, was already on the board as a reorganization director appointed by the court, but he could be displaced. Management in fact did not renominate him, and Davis in an open letter to the stockholders claimed that this action, combined with management's refusal to consider eliminating the staggered system of electing directors a few each year, was a sign it intended to "freeze out" the dissidents by diluting their legitimate powers. The independent MP could work, Davis thought, but not with the old guard at the helm, and not if it "continues along in the same lackadaisical manner as the prior management by Trustee."[3] The first stockholders' meeting of the reorganized, independent MP railroad would not and should not be business as usual. There was a new entity to be controlled and a new adventure in corporate diplomacy to be undertaken in the postdepression world.

President Neff was seriously ill at the time of the May, 1957, stockholders' meeting. Therefore, the fireworks were handled by former state senator Russell Dearmont, who had served as attorney for the company through its bankruptcy and had much influenced the final reorganization plan. Dearmont was shortly to be elected president of the board at a salary of $100,000 per year, and Neff moved to chairman of the board.[4] Senator Dearmont probably felt after two days of argument at the spring meeting that he had earned his entire year's salary before his term rightfully began.

T. E. Quisenberry, who had for years represented with tremendous tenacity one of the groups in the reorganization proceedings warmed at the 1957 meeting to an obstructionism that he was to develop in the next several years into a fine art. He took up over half the time in this meeting by raising parliamentary objections, asking for explanations, and in general trying the patience of all.[5] Former U.S. senator Burton K. Wheeler was

[3] T. C. Davis to stockholders, April 18, 1957, ibid.

[4] MP Railroad, directors' minutes, May 16, 1957, MP archives. Davis was the only director who voted no on both the creation of the office of chairman of the board and the election of Dearmont as president of the railroad.

[5] MP Railroad, transcript of stockholders' meeting, microfilm, May 14, 1957, MP

also there to add oratory and to contribute accounts of his struggles during the Great Depression to save the MP's common stockholders from disinheritance by the court. T. C. Davis lent the opposition his fearless irascibility and unflappable bluntness.

The meeting proceeded calmly for a few minutes. Then a stockholder interrupted the routine by objecting to the process used in qualifying referees for the balloting. He began quoting at some length from Interstate Commerce Commission (ICC) Finance Docket 9918, the multivolume document that contained the history of the bankruptcy. The record showed, he said, that the officers of the bankruptcy trustee "had a dirty hold and added to the stockholders' burden." These men now had no right "to represent or be in the employ of the company." Dearmont tried to put this line of questioning aside by saying that neither he nor other officers would oppose the interests of any security holder. But Burton Wheeler rose and again quoted the ICC record to show that Paul Neff once said during hearings that his first interest was in the bondholders. Did not Neff and Dearmont hold private conferences with the staff of the ICC? Did not the trustee try to manipulate the outcome of the proceedings to freeze out common stockholders? "No, no," Dearmont replied. The officers helped formulate a plan after 1954 at the request of the ICC but were neutral and testified only when asked. Wheeler shot back: were not the common and preferred stockholders' interests wiped out entirely in the reorganization plans of 1940 and 1944? Dearmont admitted that. Wheeler went on: "Colonel Davis was fighting constantly to have the preferred stock and the common stock recognized." Dearmont: "There will be some question about that." Wheeler: "There will be no question about that." Dearmont: "In my mind, if not in yours." Wheeler then launched into a long dissertation on the history of the reorganization. He droned on until a stockholder not interested in history who had come a long way to vote for the 1957 directors said he could not understand what this had to do with the current order of business. "If this is a nominating speech for

---

archives. See ibid., May 12, 1959, pp. 17–18, for revealing exchanges between Dearmont and Quisenberry on wasting time.

Mr. Davis, I didn't realize the Chairman had called for nominations as yet."[6]

Actually, nothing was more relevant to the current interests and future prospects of the railroad than the curious financial structure arising from the company's history in bankruptcy since it first filed under Section 77 of the Bankruptcy Act in 1933. The MP was the first railroad to file under this new legislation and the last one to be reorganized under its terms. In the interim it got great attention from the press and public because of its potential and because of the dramatic dreams of some of those battling for its control.[7]

In 1930 the attention centered on the Van Sweringen brothers, Otis Paxton and Mantis James. From humble origins in Wooster, Ohio, these two created one of the largest rail empires of the twentieth century. They formed Alleghany Corporation in 1929 as a holding company for their diverse purchases and the next year used its fund-raising power to buy a controlling interest in the MP for $100 million. The brothers later lost control despite a $75 million loan from the Reconstruction Finance Corporation, then gained it back in a marvelous auction, only to be cheated at last by death. In 1937 Alleghany, with its large interest in MP common stock, was purchased by a syndicate of Frank Kolbe, Allan Kirby, and Robert Young. Kirby in a quiet way and Young in a flamboyant fashion were equal to the Van Sweringens as attention-getters, and they kept the railroad in the public limelight.[8]

The struggles of Alleghany to preserve the common stock, usually wiped out in Section 77 proceedings, were what made

[6] Ibid., May 14, 1957.

[7] For a summary of the receivership, see *New York Times*, March 2, 1956, pp. 31 and 34.

[8] The best treatment of the development of the Van Sweringen empire overall is Ian S. Haberman, *The Van Swearingens of Cleveland: The Biography of an Empire* (Cleveland: The Western Reserve Historical Society, 1979). See also Joseph Borkin, *Robert R. Young, the Populist of Wall Street* (New York: Harper & Row, 1969), pp. 28–35, and "The Van Swearingen Pyramid" in Alex Groner, *The American Heritage History of American Business & Industry* (New York: American Heritage, 1972), pp. 282–83.

the reorganization of the MP such a long and vociferous process. After twenty years of debate and several rejected plans, the so-called Agreed System Plan got the company out of the control of the trustee. The price of agreement was the creation of A and B stock. The former controlled management but was limited to a $5 dividend. The latter had almost no power at the start but incorporated in its contingent privileges the hope of Alleghany and other former common stockholders that they could someday realize dividends and again control the equity as the railroad prospered. The stock scheme was admittedly a hybrid one, and the leverage of Alleghany Corporation, left as it was with little voice in the management of a railroad it once controlled, insured there would be no calm while such a stock arrangement lasted. It may be said with no fear of contradiction that the history of the MP, from 1956 until its recapitalization in 1974 eliminated the A and B stock quandary, was dominated by the shadow of the collapsing Van Sweringen empire and by its corporate incarnation, Alleghany Corporation.

The minority dissidents of the 1950s were, with the exception of Alleghany, largely latecomers to investment in the company and could be charged with being more interested in a speculation on the value of the B stock than the true interests of the corporation. Also, their alignment with Alleghany as the major B stockholder might seem a liability. However, Alleghany's reputation underwent a change during the years just before the MP reorganization. Once it had been seen as the corrupt instrument of the most ruthless of robber barons and had come under attack in the early 1930s by none other than Senator Burton K. Wheeler —a fact Wheeler's enemies in the MP of the 1950s delighted to emphasize.[9] However, Robert Young was a master populist publicist, and economic reverses changed his company's public image from instrument of corporate moguls to pleader for widows, orphans, and other beleaguered common stockholders who were, like itself, threatened with loss of an investment. The

[9] Borkin, *Robert R. Young*, pp. 42–43; MP Railroad transcript of stockholders' meeting, May 14, 1957, pp. 22–23, MP archives.

American sympathy for the underdog worked in Alleghany's favor. Wheeler became its supporter.[10] So did Davis, Quisenberry, and other sophisticated investors who saw the B as a gamble, but one with great promise if the MP ever realized the potential of its location and traffic. These types made the early stockholders' meetings of the reorganized road hectic. Management was no more fond of them than they were of management.

At the 1957 stockholders' meeting Davis won a director's seat, receiving more votes than any other candidate. The rest of the board, however, consisted of the management slate: Robert Craft, James Johnson, James Kemper, and Abe Wattner.[11] Davis demanded a recount of the ballots, and that was only one of the actions that indicated what the tone of the near future was to be. Once, a stockholder, returning after an absence of several hours, inquired where the opposition was. Dearmont, practicing the courtesy with a barb that was to mark relations between the MP cliques for the next fifteen years, answered, "They're here and very agreeable. I'm sure they are just resting on their—well, they are just here interested." There followed worried laughter.[12]

The long struggle over the reorganization had a dramatic effect on the way the MP management thought in 1956 and for years following. For one thing, there was the sheer volume of management time taken by legal work rather than operations, and a consequent tendency for managers to be persons, like Dearmont, with more legal than rail-operating background. Second, the fight with Alleghany and the B stockholders, who would gain power relative to the A holders as the railroad earned more, led managers to be conservative in their accounting, their projections, and perhaps even their operating decisions.

That the tenacity of the old common stockholders in demanding recognition would create special mountains of bureaucratic paper was evident early. By June, 1937, the correspondence in the railroad's files from security holders inquiring about

[10] District Court, No. 6935, transcript of hearings, June 25, 1951, p. 81, box 746, space 9340303c, Underground Storage, Hutchinson.

[11] MP Railroad, transcript of stockholders' meeting, May 15, 1957, p. 1, MP archives.

[12] Ibid., p. 12.

the reorganization filled seven pressboard boxes, each ten inches high.[13] The job of mailing out information on the first reorganization plan to 25,000 people took forty women a week.[14] And the 1936 plan was easy compared with what came later. By 1941 there were 50,000 names in the card file at Saint Louis. The company sent out 70,000 copies of a 352-page booklet in 1947 and paid $16,501 for printing.[15] Woe to the envelope stuffers who had to deal with the 281 sacks of mail delivered to the Saint Louis post office by the MP in May, 1955. That mailing weighed 21,447 pounds![16]

But this was only a part of the piles of paper. ICC Finance Docket 9918, entitled "Missouri Pacific Railroad Company Reorganization," consisted eventually of an original report, issued in January, 1940, and eight supplemental reports. The last of the ICC reports, issued in 1955, was 266 pages long, and the combined printed record on the 1940 plan and its modifications totaled 2,400 pages.[17] There were documents issued by the company to security holders each time a vote occurred and printed reports by the district court. All these were minuscule, however, compared with the verbatim transcripts of the hearings before the ICC and the district court. Before 1950 the ICC had examined 1,034 exhibits and recorded 6,564 pages of testimony concerning the most recent MP plan. The collected court records to 1950 were 28,955 pages. Total hearing transcripts fill eight large boxes at the MP storage section in the salt mines at Hutchinson, Kansas; assorted exhibits and correspondence con-

[13] Wm. Wyer to R. Dearmont, June 24, 1937, correspondence file on reorganization, box 1a, space 1030602, MP archives.

[14] A. T. Cole to Wm. Wyer, Dec. 1, 1938, ibid.

[15] Memo, Martin Stotler, June 17, 1941; Con. P. Curran to Missouri Pacific Railroad Company, May 12, 1947, both in ibid.

[16] Memo to J. H. Ketson to Mr. Runge, May 10, 1955, ibid.

[17] The major ICC reports are 239 ICC 7 (original report), 240 ICC 15 (first supplemental), 257 ICC 479 (second supplemental), 257 ICC 745 (third supplemental), 257 ICC 59 (fourth supplemental), 275 ICC 203 (fifth supplemental), 282 ICC 629 (sixth supplemental), 290 ICC 477 (seventh supplemental), 290 ICC 674 (eighth supplemental). The principal court reports are found in 39 Fed. Supp. 436, 64 Fed. Supp. 64, 93 Fed. Supp. 832, 129 Fed. Supp. 329, 135 Fed. Supp. 102. The statistics come from Russell Dearmont, *Brief of Trustee for Debtor Companies* . . . , June 15, 1955, box 697, space 9040202a, Underground Storage, Hutchinson.

cerning the reorganization overflow fifteen more. Attorneys expected to be paid for their contributions to this bulk, and over one hundred different ones were involved, filing 150 briefs.[18] The proceedings became, as one politician put it, "a lawyer's paradise, and a security holder's nightmare."[19]

Naturally, as the hearings dragged on, economic conditions changed and previous plans became outdated. This required "shuttling" of plans back and forth between the ICC and the court as the world outside was changed by World War II, growing citrus and chemical traffic on the MP, postwar inflation, the Korean conflict, and a seemingly permanent quantum jump in government spending.[20] During the Depression years, delays were in the interest of Alleghany Corporation, whose common-stock interest would have been wiped out entirely under any capitalization remotely appropriate to earnings of the MP in the 1930s. Alleghany's attorneys and the attorneys for the junior bondholders slowed the reorganization walk to a crawl.

For a time, rail managers seemed to enjoy the respite from the demands of interest-due dates that bankruptcy gave them, and they rested comfortably in the arms of the court. Eventually, however, they became restive. The court allowed adequate maintenance of the road. For example, dieselization was entirely accomplished during the bankruptcy protectorate, and some later charged the line was "gold plated" in those years. Still, it seemed management had too much to do with lawyers and too little with the railroad's operation. C. D. Peet, the MP chief financial officer, felt that as other roads emerged from receivership and were able to concentrate on implementing advances in accounting, financing, taxes, and the study of regulatory agencies, the MP would be left behind.[21]

Representatives of Alleghany claimed that these same frustrated officers became "doomsayers" just at the time when the

[18] Charles Mahaffie, transcript of hearings before U.S. Senate Committee on Interstate and Foreign Commerce, April 13, 1950, p. 241, box 742, space 9340204a, Underground Storage, Hutchinson.

[19] *Congressional Record*, 83rd Cong., 2d Sess., June 9, 1954, C. pt. 6, p. 7903.

[20] Interview with Walter Brown, March 12, 1980, New York City.

[21] District Court, No. 6935, transcript of hearings, Dec. 16, 1957, p. 195, box 743, space 9340203c, Underground Storage, Hutchinson.

economic picture brightened. When in hearing of a judge, congressman, or interstate commerce commissioner, they made dire predictions of disaster. MP president Neff and others arguing in the hearings for the expulsion of the common stockholders from the new capitalization emphasized the possibly temporary nature of the boom during and following World War II and pointed out that the cost of labor and equipment on railways was rising in the inflationary climate.[22] It was awkward for officers to balance interests so oddly aligned. Worse was that what had been thought a temporary problem passed out of the hands of the court, Congress, and the ICC, to fall directly into the laps of confused rail officers when the B holders gained permanent if contingent status in the road's capitalization in the Agreed System reorganization plan.

MP officers felt certain the delay in the reorganization had been Alleghany's doing, but there were charges in the press and in Congress that the real cause was a "conspiracy" on the part of the officers themselves. During the hearings on Senate Resolution 241, introduced in 1950 after intensive lobbying by T. C. Davis, MP managers were charged with bad faith and even collusion with bankers and insurance companies who had investments in MP bonds and did not wish common stockholders to have any rights at their expense. Senators said that "good men" could have brought the road out of receivership earlier "if they had the will to do it." When Dearmont noted that it might not be proper for the Senate to look into that question or others concerning the MP while the issue was before the courts and the ICC, he was criticized by those who felt that the Senate had an unlimited right to investigate anything it chose. That body had a mandate from the people to defend them against railway czars and money kings on the eastern seaboard. Concluded one senator, speaking as much to his constituents as to those assembled: "It is a very trying picture for the public in general for a great railroad concern to be in receivership 17 years. People live, die and pass out and don't know whether they have an estate or not, or whether it has all gone to the four winds, and there is this

---

[22] For an example of Neff's 1949 thinking contrasted with that of Alleghany witnesses, see 275 ICC 98–101 (F. D. 9918, Fourth Supplemental Report).

interminable delay. . . . It is tragic. Don't you see that people are completely disgusted with the *modus operandi* on the receivership?"[23] It appeared that officers in the future would have to be better at public relations, not to mention legal and financial maneuver. Then, of course, there was a railway to run.

The public pressure the representatives of the MP common stockholders generated ultimately had its effect. Several ICC commissioners began in 1950 to dissent from the majority opinion, which denied the common stock any part, and congressmen kept up a barrage against the plutocrat bondholders.

Yet for some time the ICC majority, led by Commissioner Charles Mahaffie, held out against this line of thinking on the grounds that it was unsound economics. Mahaffie told the Senate Committee on Interstate and Foreign Commerce that people like Burton K. Wheeler (who was sitting in the room at the time) were simply wrong about the strength of the economy and self-serving in thinking an A-B hybrid stock setup would ever work smoothly to advance the railroad. Mahaffie only stated the obvious in saying that, given the multiplicity of conflicting points of view in the case, no plan the ICC might devise could expect unanimous support—at least no practical plan.[24]

In the bargaining that followed these hearings the animosities were evident. At the stockholders' meeting in 1954, Colonel T. C. Davis spoke of the "violent" disagreement between himself and others in the management on the question of the amount of money being spent on the maintenance of the property. He said that the road was being "gold-plated" and that its percentage of maintenance charges was much higher than other railroads' and "just entirely out of line."[25] Still, there was slow but certain progress. Economic conditions made it possible to recognize the common stockholders in a way more solid than the warrants (redeemable only under certain conditions) that had

[23]Transcript of hearings on Sen. Res. 241, April 15, 1950, pp. 307–8, 331, box 747, space 9340102c, Underground Storage, Hutchinson.

[24]Mahaffie testimony, ICC, F.D. 9918, transcript of hearings, July 18, 1950, pp. 1–12.

[25]MP Railroad, transcript of stockholders' meeting, May 11, 1954, pp. 15–18, Davis deposition, exhibit 1, space 0610102a, MP archives.

been offered in the immediate past. The Agreed System Plan, presented to the ICC in 1954, proposed a capitalization for the MP of over $800 million and offered the common stockholders just over $4 million in class B stock in a reorganized company. This was in return for a claim by them of $81 million—or an exchange of about one new B share for twenty of the old common shares. Alleghany and other holders of the common stock found this less than ideal, especially since the small issue would almost eliminate any general market for the B stock, but they agreed not to press objections provided the ICC would follow the Agreed System Plan precisely.[26]

The approval of the Agreed System Plan, while by no means automatic, was indeed accomplished. During the hearings before the ICC in 1954 all the experts were once again brought forward and the familiar arguments heard, though this time advanced with less fervor in the hope that at last the line might emerge on its own, however hybrid the capitalization. The pattern was familiar. There came a representative from the rail management with a tale of possible future woes and a plea for a relatively low capitalization, followed on the stand by the cheery economists drawing their fees from Alleghany.

The ICC tended to accept the more conservative projections. This was understandable in the wake of a depression that had made mincemeat of all the conventional economic wisdom and left the professors on the defensive about their credibility. Also, the commission had testimony from a number of experts in the marketing of bonds, including Charles Bergmann, to the effect that the coupon rates on the bonds for the reorganized railroad were too low (the commission raised them slightly) and that any deference to the arguments of the Alleghany people in rewarding the common stockholders at the expense of the bondholders would make the new MP bonds unmarketable. Bergmann testified that there could be no hope of success unless the railroad could obtain low-cost capital. No derogatory comments

[26] For a tabular breakdown of the Agreed System capitalization, see Appendix J of the ICC Seventh Supplemental Report, 290 ICC 477. Throughout this report are discussions concerning how the Agreed System compromise was arrived at.

about the robber-baron tendencies of the institutional investors group he represented could hide that fact of economic life.[27]

Judge George Moore at the district court was also convinced that the Agreed System Plan was the best that Alleghany and other dissenters from previous plans could hope for. He did not feel that it should be rejected simply because it was a compromise that completely satisfied no one, but on the contrary thought this was, under the circumstances, its most attractive characteristic. The judge had written in 1945 that "in view of the extremely complicated and contentious nature of a railway reorganization proceeding, and its tendency to drag on over the years, compromise plans are to be favored rather than criticized, when they tend to expedite reorganizations and allow greater security to those not so securely situated." Moore wrote that he thought the commission had examined the question of capitalization "with painstaking care" and that there was no further reason to believe it was unfair to anyone or unrealistic in a world that lacked working crystal balls.[28]

The final days of what would stretch to a twenty-three-year receivership were characterized by an optimism so cautious it was perhaps not altogether deserving of the name. T. C. Davis was jubilant that justice had prevailed but sorry that the common stockholders were "subjected to a reverse split and their voting rights drastically reduced." His hope was that the B stock's claim to the equity of the railroad after the maximum $5 dividend was paid to the A might eventually be a commodity worth having. He recognized also that in the light of prior reorganizations it was "little short of miraculous" that the common stock had maintained any participation at all in the new company.[29]

Charles Mahaffie, however, was not so certain that the compromise resulting in the creation of the stock classes was some-

[27] 290 ICC 545–50. Isabel Benham, now a well-known rail stock analyst in New York, worked with Bergmann on the statistics for this testimony as one of her first projects. She remembers that people thought it was a miracle that Bergmann was able to get the interest on some classes of bonds raised by ¼% and attributed it partly to her quantitative analysis. Interview with Isabel Benham, March 11, 1980, New York City.

[28] Judge Moore, Feb. 25, 1955, 129 Fed. Supp. 398.

[29] T. C. Davis to stockholders, Feb. 23, 1955, Davis exhibit 2, Davis deposition, space 0610102a, MP archives.

thing that boded well for the future of the railroad. Mahaffie voted with the majority on the ICC to approve the Agreed System Plan only with the gravest of misgivings. He recognized that it was an absolute necessity to bring the road out of receivership somehow, and this seemed to be the only plan that would do it. He did not feel, however, that it was sound in the long run for so much representation to go to creditors and so little to stock. The Depression had led to what Mahaffie called "a national policy to put a premium on debt as against an equity interest in such properties," and this policy created unsound capital structures. However, Mahaffie though that rewarding the MP common stockholders by creating the class B stock was a dangerous defect of the plan. To give the B only a small part of the present value but to make it a residual beneficiary of any future prosperity would make this stock "a token for speculation" and insure that its relation to the A stock and the bonds of the railroad would "cause trouble" in the future. The B stock could control nothing directly, but it had a "nuisance value" in vetoing moves, such as merger, that might require a vote by classes of stock.[30] Certainly Davis realized this when he told his companions in 1955 that in the B stock they had a "very virile entity."[31]

During the final hearings before the court there were clear intimations that Mahaffie's predictions of trouble between A and B interests need not wait for realization. Russell Dearmont objected to the court's allowing for the expenses of T. C. Davis during the long reorganization proceedings, claiming that Davis had been paid $200,000 by Alleghany. Dearmont charged that Davis, while chairman of the MP board, had been a close comrade of Alleghany's Robert R. Young, and that through Davis, Alleghany managed to exercise control over the railroad during reorganization and might do so even after the road emerged from it. Trustee Guy Thompson said that he did not especially like Davis personally, nor did much of the rest of the management.[32]

[30] 290 ICC 624–25.

[31] Transcript of stockholders' meeting, May 10, 1955, Davis exhibit 3, Davis deposition, space 0610102a, MP archives.

[32] For the argument over Davis, see District Court, No. 6935, transcript of hearings, April 8, 1955, pp. 19–37, 43, box 747, space 9340102c, Underground Storage, Hutchinson.

Judge Moore liked Davis least of all. Moore was incensed about an ad placed by Alleghany Corporation in the 1951 *New York Times* entitled "Congress be Damned." This was one of Robert Young's typically flamboyant productions, arranged by Clifford Ramsdell and signed by Allan Kirby, Robert Young, and T. C. Davis. In it, there was mention that Judge Moore had appointed Guy Thompson and his brother as trustees of two competing railroads, the MP and the Frisco, and that the judge had been a collector of Internal Revenue. The former statement suggested malpractice, while the latter was damning at the time when the entire Internal Revenue Service was under investigation for massive fraud. Another ad, entitled "The Captain's Obligation is the Highest," said that the MP bondholders were "first into the life boat" during the reorganization hearings, leaving "trampled behind, naked and helpless, the tens of thousands of men, women and children who hold some 13 other Missouri Pacific security issues that can only be scuttled by your callous desertion of them." Moore questioned Davis intensively about his role in the placing of the ads and could get no direct answer. Therefore, the judge stated during the court hearings in 1955 that he did not want to appoint Davis a reorganization manager for the transition period to private control, as was recommended in the plan. "I want to say about Col. Davis . . . that the Court, this Court is not especially impressed favorably by Col. Davis . . . Mr. Davis is not a man that this court would ever think of reaching out to appoint to a place of responsibility certainly, and I would rather imagine that the trustee would not be much more favorably impressed by him." Told that Davis was the only representative acceptable to the B interests, Moore responded, "Don't they [Alleghany] have some other hireling they could send here, some other hireling a little more reputable than this man?"[33] Davis became a reorganization manager despite this rhetoric.

[33] Ibid. There is a good account of the placement of the newspaper ads in Borkin, *Robert R. Young*, pp. 135–36. Davis remained close to the Alleghany management until after the death of Young in 1958. He then joined with the Murchison brothers in their attempt to take control of Alleghany from Allan Kirby and was, after Kirby's return to power, persona non grata at Alleghany thereafter. In fact, he was one of the directors

In 1956 there were summary hearings before both the ICC and the court to listen to the last objections and to give final approval to the plan to bring the MP railroad out of the longest receivership on record. Russell Dearmont commented at the court session that it had been twenty years ago April Fool's day that he had entered the case, and he had dealt with it weekly since. The judge had been involved even longer. Judge Moore did not claim that he had enjoyed all the experiences of the receivership but said it had been a "very, very interesting experience." "I have seen various types and you learn to distinguish between those who have some sense of responsibility and some regard for the public interest and those who only want to grasp the last possible dime that can be squeezed under some circumstances." The MP case had both kinds, and the bills for the honest and dishonest together came to over $1 million.[34]

At 12:01 A.M. March 1, 1956, the reorganized Missouri Pacific Railroad Company took control of its 9,710 miles of mainline track as a private company. A few days later the Board of Reorganization Managers elected Paul J. Neff president and began the not-so-simple task of leaving its recent past behind.[35]

---

named in that company's lawsuit against the MP in the 1960s. Interview with Clifford Ramsdell, March 11, 1980, New York City.

[34] District Court, No. 6935, transcript of hearings, March 1, 1956, pp. 43–44, box 747, space 9340102c, Underground Storage, Hutchinson.

[35] *New York Times*, March 2, 1956, p. 31, col. 1.

# CHAPTER II

# The Eagle Turns

WHEN the news of the successful reorganization was announced, the mood along the line of the Missouri Pacific, from the river banks of Missouri to the plains of Texas, was hopeful. In hundreds of small-town cafes and city buildings, and maybe in thousands of tail-finned cars rolling along new highways on nineteen-cent-a-gallon gasoline, rail employees and town boosters discussed the future that an independent MP would be capable of bringing to themselves and their region. Most of these folks understood little of the labyrinthine course taken by the reorganization hearings, and less of the legal technicalities that had so long kept "their" railroad ensnared. But they did have great loyalty to the MP company. It had served their region in the time of their grandfathers, and there were three and sometimes four generations of MP employees in many families, sharing the folklore and the pride that went along with being a hogger or a fireman or with turning brake wheels in the wind and snow of the middle plains. This did not change because slide valves disappeared and traction motors came, nor did it lessen because attorneys in Saint Louis and New York made changes in capital structure. It was a vague but strong feeling in the blood. It endured, and upon it everything else ultimately depended.

Paul Neff knew many of his employees and their families personally, and he recognized the importance of esprit de corps. He said in 1954, when the Agreed System Plan was first put forward, that "there has inevitably crept into their minds a consuming fear that these proceedings will never end and that the system will be dismembered and they don't understand or sympathize with further disagreement of the parties." The employees sensed that the system, created in the corporate struggles of the nineteenth century, would suffer if it were divided now. Shippers looked upon the MP, the Texas & Pacific, the New Orleans, Texas & Mexico, and others of the twenty-one companies that made up the system before 1956 as part of a single empire —functionally if not legally, in the understanding of generations if not in articles of incorporation, in the flesh where corporate power came to freight and engines and rail. Neff said that the employees sensed that their personal fortunes were at stake in the decision whether they would work for one of three or so weak railroads, or for a single strong one; whether they would be in the forefront or the backwash of the coming rail consolidation movement. "They believe and I believe it also," Neff intoned, "that this is indeed the last chance for the system reorganization and that it would be fantastic to believe the system could ever be reorganized as such if it can't be done under the Agreed System Plan."[1] It could be done, if barely, and it was. The sigh of relief across six states was the first breath of a wind of change.

The company paid immediate attention to keeping the loyalty of its work force by raising salaries. In 1956 there was a 5-percent raise for everyone, from the engine cabs to the executive suites. Individual elective officers found themselves finally with salaries comparable to those of other supposed profit-making organizations. President Paul Neff, for example, would now receive $110,000 a year. A more liberal group insurance policy came from Sun Life of Canada, with a major contribution made by the company toward paying the premiums of young managers.[2] There was hope that these actions would mean that when the old guard, which had carried the road through the Depression, came to retirement age the company might attract the best of the next generation of managerial talent.

The feeling of largesse, however, did not mask concern about the productivity of the employees. Through the 1950s

[1] Paul J. Neff testimony, District Court, No. 6935, Dec. 15, 1954, pp. 113–16, box 746, space 9340303c, Underground Storage, Hutchinson, Kansas.

[2] MP Railroad, directors' minutes, April 11, 1956, pp. 3–4, 9, microfilm, MP archives.

there was a study of ways to reduce the 30,000-person payroll through some combination of technology, organization, and lobbying for repeal of certain union rules and federal and state legislation. Russell Dearmont told the directors in 1959 that the industry was "absolutely loaded down with feather-bedding," much to the chagrin of those wishing to reduce train crews in the age of the diesel and the sixty-mile-per-hour freight train. There were operating employees who operated no more than twenty hours a week; the average in 1960 was thirty-three hours a week, while pay was based upon a work week of sixty-three to sixty-seven hours. One engineer made over $11,000 a year and averaged ten days' work a month. Reports came in that some engineers had second jobs or owned small businesses. The run on the double-track line between Poplar Bluff, Missouri, and Little Rock, Arkansas—180 miles—took the diesels an average of two hours, thirty-five minutes. The union pay scale, however, based as it was on steam operations in the days before centralized dispatching and automatic signals, required a day's pay for each 100 miles negotiated. This meant almost two full days' pay for the two-and-a-half-hour run through the Arkansas countryside.[3]

But the extra time paid for the run from Poplar Bluff to Little Rock was not the most galling thing to management about entering Arkansas. That dubious honor was reserved for the Arkansas full-crew law, which required that an extra man join the train crew in that state. The stockholders heard that in Arkansas they were paying over $1 million a year to give a "free ride" to a man who often curled up in the second unit and slept.[4] Repeal of this law was a priority, though it was not accomplished for a decade.

Naturally, it was hard to convince the men switching cars and rolling freights down the line that many of them were excess baggage. Railroading in the mid-twentieth century, for all its technical advances, had not been reduced to a series of office jobs. It was yet dangerous and physically demanding. Boiler explosions were not a danger, and freezing to the brake wheel was

[3] MP Railroad, transcript of stockholders' meeting, May 12, 1959, p. 51, MP archives; ibid., May 10, 1960, pp. 51–52.
[4] Ibid., May 12, 1959, p. 52.

no longer likely, but air-braking on a long and heavy train was anything but an automatic technique, and the speed and close siding passes demanded by the modern signal system required an alertness equal to the best of the past. It was as cold in winter and as hot in summer as it ever was, and the items a brakeman or maintenance-of-way employee might be asked to pick up and carry had not gotten any lighter over the years. Engineers and road foremen needed now to have knowledge of electronic systems, while the office people at stations and yards dealt with card sorters and would very soon feel the effects of computers. The engineer whose single decision whether a hazard ahead justified throwing the brakes into emergency could in seconds gain or lose the company the equivalent of his lifetime salary did not feel he was overpaid.[5]

If direct reductions in employee benefits were impossible or inappropriate, reductions in numbers of employees through application of technology was nonetheless certain. The president told the MP directors in April, 1956, that the road's expenditures for capital improvements during its first independent year would be $15 million. This was dictated by the terms of the reorganization plan, but managers felt such investments would yield great returns.[6]

The MP motive power fleet was all diesel by 1955, but the mix was not efficient. John Lloyd remembers that when he arrived in the early 1960s, the company used "everything but a Maytag washing machine" to pull trains. Lloyd thought the late-1950s management must have been reluctant to turn down any salesman for engines; certainly the company did its part in that period to keep a number of locomotive manufacturers in business.[7] The MP bought two NC2 900-h.p. switchers from the infant Electro-Motive Corporation in 1937 and continued to patronize that company when it became General Motors Electro-Motive Division (EMD) and produced a variety of E and F

---

[5] Information on the thinking of road crews was gleaned from talking about the past and present with numerous crews on the MP during a trip over the line in the lead units in late December, 1979.

[6] MP Railroad, directors' minutes, April 11, 1956, p. 11, MP archives.

[7] Interview with John Lloyd, July 12, 1979, Saint Louis.

units. But alongside the E-8s, F-7s, GP7s, and GP9s from EMD ran passenger PAs from the American Locomotive Company (Alco), freight units and switchers from the same company, and a stable of equipment from Baldwin, General Electric, and several others.[8] To save money, the company sometimes combined parts from these brands. In 1959, for instance, the trucks and traction motors from twelve retired Baldwins were reconditioned and installed in Alcos.[9]

It was difficult to keep parts on hand for all these makes, and there could not be, as there were later, centralized service procedures at all shops. In the 1950s each shop was a service empire of its own—individualistic, colorful, and inefficient. The same was true of yards. The car supply was chaotic. Cars could be traced by cards physically attached to them, but an executive in Saint Louis could not learn the pattern of cars at the Little Rock yards until several days after the situation had entirely changed. The yardmaster ruled his domain and got cars when and how he was able. As for the situation on the railroad overall, extending across ten thousand miles of territory, either it was regulated by some "invisible hand" that made the interests of each region work for the good of all, or car and engine supply was largely an accident. Those familiar with the operation, including shippers trying to get or locate cars, favored the latter view.

Important steps were taken to remedy this during the 1950s. Officers of the MP decided to build two large electronically controlled hump yards, one at Kansas City and one at North Little Rock. These were organized around a large classification "bowl" (eventually there were two at Kansas City) with departure and receiving yards on either side. Trains were pushed over a hill, or hump, and rolled into the bowl by gravity. An analog computer threw the proper switches and directed the cars to the proper classification tracks to be made into blocks for outbound destinations. The computer operated retarders, which slowed the car to

[8] The best study of recent MP motive power is John Eagan, *1975–1976 Missouri Pacific Annual* (Danvers, Mass.: Prototype Modeler, 1976). The introduction, pp. 4–7, treats the 1950s.

[9] MP Railroad, directors' minutes, Sept. 10, 1959, pp. 5–6, MP archives.

a speed that made it strike the cars already on that track at the prescribed four miles per hour.

The system was amazing but expensive. The estimated cost in 1956 for the Kansas City yard was $11.5 million. The company spent $8.5 million in 1959 and $6.6 million in 1960 on the construction of the Little Rock yard.[10] But the system was effective. When the eastbound unit of the Paul J. Neff Yard in Kansas City began operation in March, 1959, it was estimated it would save $2 million a year and speed car movement through Kansas City by nine to ten hours. When the west unit was completed in November, results were better than that. In the first year, savings were $2.7 million in payroll savings alone attributable to the reduction in manual switching the computer allowed.[11] The return on investment at the Kansas City yard was over 18 percent.

Russell Dearmont, whose strength was the law rather than operations, nevertheless grasped early the importance of this yard technology and pressed hard for it. Though he seldom took inspection trips, he took one in 1960 to examine the yards and reported back to the directors.[12] Telling of the gentle touches of cars coming through the retarders, Dearmont remembered a boyhood trip he took on the MP to accompany the shipment of his horse. During one switching operation their car was hit so hard Dearmont fell down under the horse. Times had now changed for the shipper at last. "We can't be as rough on them as they were on me way back there when I was a little boy."[13]

Other innovations of the 1950s, while not as dramatic as the hump yards, made a difference also in the way the railroad operated. For example, there was the matter of specialized cars. In the nineteenth century, a railroad told shippers that if something could not move on a flatcar or boxcar, it could not move on the railroad. Large markets in petroleum and meats eventually led to the tank and refrigerator car, and during the 1930s the MP

[10] Ibid., June 18, 1956, p. 5; ibid., Nov. 23, 1959, p. 4.

[11] MP Railroad, transcript of stockholders' meeting, May 12, 1959, p. 47, MP archives; ibid., May 10, 1960, pp. 19–20.

[12] Interview with Downing Jenks, March 13, 1979, Saint Louis.

[13] MP Railroad, transcript of stockholders' meeting, May 10, 1960, pp. 20–22, MP archives.

experimented with specialized means of carrying automobiles.[14] In the 1950s came piggyback service.

In 1956 the MP invested in Trailer Train Company, which made available special flatcars and movable cranes used for the direct loading of truck trailers.[15] This allowed the railroad to take advantage of the boom in truck traffic occasioned by the building of interstate highways, and it opened the possibility of interchanging with ships and airplanes. It dawned on managers also that containerization by all transportation, use of piggyback service by the railroads, and use by all of communicating computers might one day result in truly coordinated shipments, with a single bill of lading nationally and internationally. In 1960 the MP handled 25,000 container loads of general merchandise and 4,000 of set-up automobiles.[16]

The first interest in computers for aiding with office and management functions was tentative. But any step toward the use of "electronic machines," as Dearmont called them, in this traditional realm was a large one for a road just out of receivership and dominated by officers near retirement. The initial discussion of electronic data processing was at the MP board of directors' meeting of June 10, 1957. There had been talk about using computers to reduce the cost of paperwork, but no one in the railroad understood the new machines sufficiently to know whether this would justify the $35,000 a month it then cost to rent the Univac or IBM 705. The board therefore authorized Dearmont to engage Price-Waterhouse Company for $245,000 to make an extensive study of the question in conjunction with an administrative methods group of railroad people.[17]

One year later H. S. Sawin of the Price-Waterhouse Management Advisory Services Department summarized for the directors the conclusions of this study. First, there should be greater centralization of accounting activity. Second, the speed of electronic equipment would aid in several areas. Third, there

[14] W. Lloyd Kitchel to Edward J. White, Sept. 30, 1935 in file 17, space 9640401a, Underground Storage, Hutchinson.

[15] MP Railroad, directors' minutes, April 11, 1956, pp. 11–12, MP archives.

[16] MP Railroad, transcript of stockholders' minutes, May 10, 1960, p. 16, MP archives.

[17] MP Railroad, directors' minutes, June 10, 1957, pp. 16–17, MP archives.

was need for more effective integration and coordination of short- and long-term management planning. Fourth, there was not enough use of cost and budgetary control procedures. Fifth, mathematical techniques, aided by the computer, could be used to improve inventory controls, reduce clerical effort, and solve complex operating problems.[18]

On the basis of this study the board authorized the company to lease a large data processing system, which it was estimated would pay for itself in savings.[19] Initially, most of the use was by the comptroller. Accounting procedures were speeded up (for example, a conversion deck could be run to translate internal accounting figures into those needed for reports to various government agencies) but not revolutionized in approach. The real revolution, only dimly glimpsed in 1958, was to be in what was called transportaion or operations control, a technique that would make basic changes in the way cars had been distributed and located on railroads for a hundred years.[20]

Amid this modernization, the railroad continued to deal with one legacy of the past that it was reluctant to jettison—the passenger business. Although the blue-and-white passenger Eagles had not made money for some years, there was pride in the spit and polish and the good meals aboard the "varnish," and the trains were thought of as good public relations. The company's bus line, the Missouri Pacific Transportation Company, was sold in 1956 in order to concentrate highway efforts on the trucking subsidiary, but tradition made it more difficult to face the balance sheet on the streamliners.[21] In fact, the company innovated in more economical meal service and thriftier sleeping accommodations in hopes of upping patronage.[22] As late as 1956 it was purchasing new passenger equipment.[23]

[18] Ibid., June 12, 1958, p. 3.

[19] Information on the accounting uses of the early equipment is from interview with C. J. Maurer, March 12, 1979, Saint Louis. The cost figures are from MP Railroad, directors' minutes, June 12, 1958, pp. 3–4, MP archives.

[20] Interview with C. J. Maurer, March 12, 1979, Saint Louis.

[21] MP Railroad, directors' minutes, April 11, 1956, p. 7, MP archives.

[22] MP Railroad, *News Reel*, March, 1958, and Jan., 1959. This paper was published by the MP public relations department, and files of it are available at the Saint Louis office.

[23] MP Railroad, directors' minutes, March 2, 1956, p. 53, MP archives.

Dearmont gave an impassioned address to the stockholders in May, 1959, on the theme of the passenger business, which he said was "dear to my heart." To him, passenger trains were not necessary evils, but an essential part of a railroad. He advised company officers and stockholders to ride the trains and to take their wives and children along to experience the country as it was meant to be seen. Airplanes were fine, he said, if you were in a great hurry and had a long way to go. But, "It's really a sort of an inconvenient way to travel. You have to buckle yourself into your seat real tightly. You look out the window and down at the fleecy clouds that get monotonous. And I say fleecy clouds advisedly, because if they are not fleecy, Lord help you. It's all right. It isn't so comfortable. You have attractive hostesses. But you can bring your own personally selected hostess on a Missouri Pacific train."[24]

Whenever Dearmont looked at a Pullman car and saw only a few passengers, he "felt sick." But with his retirement in the early 1960s there was internal pressure to phase out the passenger trains. The route's eagle logo changed. The slightly Egyptian stylized bird, blandly breasting the breeze with wings outstretched around the fronts of streamlined F units pulling blue-and-white pin-striped passenger cars designed by Raymond Loewy, was replaced by a fierce, squat bird decorating the slab sides of solid blue GP35s with safety stripes on the nose and a heavy drag of freight behind. One after another the Eagle trains disappeared, lonely and out of place on a railroad intent on moving freight.

Certain of the railroad's problems of the 1950s were political. There yet existed a 10-percent tax on passenger fares and a 3-percent tax on freight imposed during wartime. And there was the longstanding problem of what rail management considered overregulation of its industry and oversubsidization of competitors by the federal government. In 1957 and 1958 Dearmont went to Washington. He pointed out that too many truckers were allowed to operate commercially without regulation. He

[24] MP Railroad, transcript of stockholders' meeting, May 12, 1959, pp. 54–57, MP archives.

proposed amendments to the Commerce Act to free agricultural products from regulation, and he lobbied for bills to permit railroads to establish construction reserve funds that would be deductible from federal income tax.[25] Most galling to Dearmont and his successors was the unfair advantage given to the railroad's highway and waterway competition. Railroads had significant advantages in use of manpower and fuel over trucks carrying similar tonnage and over waterways with their circuitous routes. But any advantage was negated if these means of transport were only partially regulated while railroads were regulated "from soup to nuts."[26] Rail management wanted regulatory equality so it could be free to make maximum use of its technology.

If such freedom were forthcoming, visions of the future could be bright. It would be possible for the MP to acquire and operate a much larger system and to integrate its rail operations with wholly-owned airline, truck, and barge subsidiaries. Was not the government's special fear of rail diversification something antique, left over from the last century when there was no viable transport alternative?[27]

While "one package" transportation represented long-range thinking when applied nationally or to separate modes of transport, it was one of the MP's immediate internal goals. There could be better control of cars and shipments along the line and at interchanges with other lines, and the application of standardized practices to independent but family lines like the Texas & Pacific. These goals could also be advanced through advantageous mergers, provided they were not blocked by the B stockholders, or through cash purchases of complementary systems.

There was no doubt the MP had to add to its system in order to gain connections with more important shipping centers and to take full advantage of its strategic entry into Saint Louis. Stock analyst Isabel Benham, who studied the road carefully

[25] MP Railroad, *News Reel*, March, 1957, May, June, 1959; MP Railroad, transcript of stockholders' meeting, May 13, 1958, p. 46, MP archives.

[26] MP Railroad, transcript of stockholders' meeting, May 13, 1958, p. 46, MP archives.

[27] Association of American Railroads, quoted in MP Railroad, *News Reel*, June, 1959.

during this period, put it well: "It just sprawled out nowhere. The heart of the system was nothing. It had nothing to look forward to. It went to Kansas. Who wanted to go to Kansas? It was nothing but a dust bowl. . . . The big problem has been that the Missouri Pacific went nowhere. It began in St. Louis and it didn't get to the Pacific coast; it didn't get anywhere."[28]

The advantages of controlling the Texas & Pacific had been recognized for a long time. Not until 1956, however, was the MP able to begin systematic purchases of Texas & Pacific stock with the goal of getting the 80-percent control required to consolidate the tax returns of the two companies. Before the end of the year, the MP had purchased 4,000 shares at $622,000. Then 12,000 Texas & Pacific shares became available from the estate of Frank Gould. The MP purchased them with the $2 million from the sale of its bus line.[29] By the end of 1957 the MP held 76.9 percent of Texas & Pacific, and there were internal discussions of a formal merger.[30]

During the early months of 1958 a large study was done of the practicality of fully merging the Texas & Pacific with the MP. In June the study committee, headed by Texas & Pacific chairman J. T. Suggs, presented a two-volume printed report recommending, surprising many, that the merger not be undertaken.[31] Projected losses due to merger could outdistance savings by $5.5 million a year. Texas was proud of having a local railroad that seemed under regional control, and the committee reasoned that the two separate strong concerns could secure more traffic than a single corporation joining them. This was why the Southern Pacific maintained the Cotton Belt (St. Louis Southwestern) and the Frisco the Quanah, Acme & Pacific. It was why General Motors kept Buick and Oldsmobile separate, though there was overlap in their products. Since the MP had actual

[28] Interview of March 11, 1980, New York City.
[29] MP Railroad, directors' minutes, April 1, 1956, p. 10, Sept. 17, 1956, p. 3, Dec. 17, 1956, pp. 6–7, MP archives.
[30] *Forbes* (Dec. 1, 1957) in Alleghany clippings file, MP public relations office.
[31] *Report of Special Committee Appointed to Study Consolidation of Missouri Pacific Railroad Company and the Texas and Pacific Railway Company* (2 vols.), space 0610102a, MP archives.

control of the Texas line anyway, the committee felt it was better business to leave the two legally separate.[32]

This conclusion was controversial enough to require considerable documentation. Advantages of a merger would include: increased influence over traffic through the southern gateways, a better competitive position against the Southern Pacific at New Orleans, longer hauls on westbound interchange shipments between the Southern Pacific and MP, improvements in shipper service and car tracing within the system, better utilization of cars, and longer hauls on business originating and terminating on the system. Against these were set the drawbacks. There would be resistance among competing lines to giving the system the long haul. They would cooperate to deny the enlarged MP business, whereas they presently helped the Texas & Pacific get business they hoped to pick up later. Shippers were reluctant to specify junctions in bills of lading, and this would result in short hauling of the consolidated line on some of the eastbound traffic coming from the Southern Pacific or Santa Fe. National firms allocated their business on a basis other than mileage, usually according to a "fair share" system, so much to each railroad. The consolidated system would get one share, while the two present railroads got two. There were reciprocity advantages in relations with firms along the line. The railroad bought supplies from them and they shipped on the railroad. Local loyalty might be diminished by consolidation. Also, the consolidated system might lose voting power in the traffic bureaus. The Texas & Pacific had several advantageous special rate schedules and divisions agreements that could not survive the merger, and certainly its status as a "home town institution" in Texas, for all that meant, would be compromised.[33]

Quite apart from these traffic considerations, a merger would face serious internal legal difficulties. A strong group of Texas & Pacific minority holders would object to any but the most generous valuation of their interests if stock were exchanged. More frightening was the prospect of escalating an al-

[32] Ibid., pp. 1–8.
[33] Ibid., pp. 10–29.

ready warm struggle between the A and B stockholders of MP by a merger that would change the relative positions of these groups in a larger company.[34] George Holmes of the legal department wrote Suggs in March, 1958, that "no matter how the T&P minority stock is satisfied on exchange, it is bound to have some effect on the very delicate Missouri Pacific stock structure, and I certainly think that we can anticipate some trouble from our stocks and the B stock in particular." Holmes advised that the merger would be a good opportunity to recapitalize the MP, getting rid of the "muddled" A and B stock situation by having all shares exchanged for a new issue with single classes of preferred and common stock in the traditional manner.[35] The Suggs committee considered this but considered it too risky. Its report concluded that "such a reorganization with its obvious possibility for intracorporate controversy so soon after the road's emergence from its prolonged trusteeship would hardly seem desirable."[36]

The Suggs report led to a decision not to merge with the Texas & Pacific. However, the MP continued open-market purchases of the Texas company's stock and in November, 1958, achieved 80 percent control.[37] This was definitely not the end of the question either of a Texas & Pacific merger or a recapitalization of the MP.

In fact, there was extensive investigation of other means of recapitalizing the railroad even while the Texas & Pacific studies were proceeding. The MP law department in August, 1957, composed a memo suggesting that merger was not the only possibility for recapitalizing, or even the best one. "It is not known," said the memo, "whether the Interstate Commerce Commission would look favorably on a proceeding which was patently a recapitalization and only cast in the form of a merger." It would perhaps be better to take advantage of provisions in the Interstate Commerce Act allowing railroads to alter their financial

[34] Ibid., p. 42.
[35] George W. Holmes to J. T. Suggs, March 26, 1958, Bates 3077, space 1150005b, MP archives.
[36] Suggs report, p. 43, space 0610102a, MP archives.
[37] MP Railroad, directors' minutes, Nov. 18, 1958, pp. 2–3, MP archives.

structure with the consent of 75 percent of the security holders and to "cram down" the plan with the recalcitrant minority. There were also possibilities using the Mahaffie Act. The difficulty here was that proceedings would be held before the same Interstate Commerce Commission that had just approved a reorganization plan and might feel offended to be asked for a change so soon.[38] In short, it seemed that the A and B stock interests would be struggling for a time yet and the MP could only hope that the national merger movement would go slowly until the company could place itself in a better position to attract a partner.

The arguments of the late 1950s between the A and B stockholders did not turn much on dividends but, rather, concentrated on board representation. There were some dividends paid on the A stock in this period: $2.00 a share in 1956 and $3.50 in 1957. This was important, as the total stock dividends paid by the company since 1917 on its preferred stock were only $23.75 and there had been none since 1931.[39] However, the amount was not yet near the $5.00 a share required before the B stock could expect any dividend payments, and there seemed little prospect it soon would be.

The B stockholders presented a proposition each year, usually offered by Donald Wilson of Oak Park, Illinois, at the stockholders' meeting, to eliminate staggered elections to the MP board. This would dilute the A vote sufficiently that the B people could elect one director by uniting on a single candidate. Management felt that the plan was illegal because it would remove present directors before their terms expired.[40] Some thought eliminating the staggered system would make the board less efficient. One stockholder said at the 1958 meeting that "you don't build a railroad and you don't build the type of railroad that we have with a new slate being swept into office at one particular meeting by some group that may have selfish interests

[38] "Memo RE: Modification of Missouri Pacific Railroad Company's Capital Stock Structure," Aug. 15, 1957, Bates 1570, sec. H. space 1150803b, MP archives.

[39] MP Railroad, directors' minutes, April 11, 1956, p. 2, March 12, 1957, p. 3, MP archives.

[40] Ibid., March 11, 1958, p. 6.

or some group who may desire to take over."[41] The vote on changing the election system consistently boiled down to the A versus the B, and each year the proposal failed.

It was not desirable that things long remain in such strained equilibrium. Rail mergers were a trend of the next decade and the MP would have to find means of making offensive and defensive mergers through stock exchange or be damaged by larger and stronger systems. Current management was near retirement, though one director in 1959 claimed that at seventy he could still outshoot, outwalk, and outdrink anyone present. The successor management might be less successful in throttling the internal feuding.[42]

Most recognized that change in control and/or management would come very soon. Some thought it would take the form of a move by Alleghany Corporation to protect its investment in the B stock by taking control of the A. Alleghany, however, was much involved in the New York Central and could not control two railroads without running afoul of antitrust laws. Also, after Robert Young's suicide in 1958 the management of Alleghany had other things to worry about, including an attempt by the Murchison brothers of Texas to wrest control of the holding company from the Kirby family.

Few observers, maybe none, had an idea of the actual scenario that would unfold. It would have seemed incredible to those watching the company in the late 1950s that by 1961 the A stock would be controlled, not by Alleghany or by the New York investment houses that had been interested in it for years, but by a Saint Louis natural gas pipeline company with assets only one-eighth those of the MP and no prior experience with rail investment. But those who failed to predict it badly missed the significance of the election to the MP board of a little-known financial wizard named William Marbury.

[41] MP Railroad, transcript of stockholders' meeting, May 13, 1958, p. 13, MP archives.

[42] Ibid., May 12, 1959, p. 80.

# CHAPTER III

# William Marbury

$I$N the first years of the reorganized Missouri Pacific William Marbury was occupied with the financial affairs of the Mississippi River Fuel Company of Saint Louis (MRFC). But the study of finance was a hobby as well as an avocation with him, and he did not limit his intellectual curiosity to the economics of pipeline companies. He knew enough about the MP to recognize that it had financial potential greater than it had realized. It had a large debt, but it was a debt of a special kind, much of it contingent upon earnings and with distant maturity dates. Handled correctly, the leverage could be attractive.[1] He therefore kept an eye on the MP, as he did on several other potential opportunities for giving his talents a sufficiently broad base on which to build his dreams of eventual empire.

William Marbury could claim to be "just a country lawyer," but at the same time he was a self-made financial genius whose flexibility and audacity were shortly to be the subject of anecdotes in high places. He was the eighth child of a lawyer in the small town of Farmington in southeast Missouri, and he learned early to stand firmly for his rights against his siblings. He proceeded from there to Fayette, Missouri, to attend college but lost his father's financial support over their disagreements about how much time should be allotted to studies rather than girls,

---

[1] John Burns of Alleghany, who during this period was working on Wall Street for Goldman, Sachs, said an analyst once told him that the MP was the only good railroad in the U.S. that was properly capitalized and leveraged. In times of rapid inflation proper leverage in the debt structure was a big corporate asset. Interview with John Burns, March 10, 1980, New York City.

boxing, and football. Young Marbury boxed so aggressively that he damaged one eye and afterward wore a glass replacement. Undiscouraged, he went to Saint Louis to continue his education at Washington University, supporting himself through a job as night dispatcher for the MRFC. Soon he transferred to Saint Louis University, which had a more lenient policy about accepting IOUs for housing, and stayed there until he earned a law degree in 1937. He served for a time in both the state auditor's and governor's office before entering private practice in Saint Louis.[2]

Marbury did some legal work for the MP during the reorganization proceedings (as did most Missouri attorneys), but his first break came from contacts with the MRFC, his employer in college.[3] While working for the state he insisted on the payment of a state sales tax by MRFC, much to the annoyance of its management. His relations with the same company became more pleasant, however, when he joined the law firm of Jones, Hocker, Gladney, & Grand of Saint Louis in 1939. MRFC was one of the firm's clients and Marbury took its business as a specialty. The officers there were much impressed over the next several years by the sometimes brilliant and always unusual methodology of the young attorney with the sandy hair and the deep tanned complexion of a farmer.[4] In 1945 Marbury joined the company as assistant to president Ben Comfort and by 1949 was president himself.[5] As Marbury put it, he was "one of those fellows with a lot of energy."[6]

MRFC operated a 1,500-mile gas pipeline extending from source fields in Louisiana to Saint Louis, where it sold its output to LaClede Gas Company. It was formed in 1928 by a group of oil companies, including Standard Oil of New Jersey, as a means of getting into the pipeline business. However, legislation passed

[2] *St. Louis Post Dispatch*, June 3, 1976, in DBJ clippings, vol. 3, MP public relations office; *Wall Street Journal*, Oct. 11, 1966, MRC clippings, ibid. Marbury left Washington University because he could not pay $32 owed for housing. Later, his companies gave large contributions to Saint Louis University and noticeably less to that other Saint Louis institution, which Marbury had long ago been forced to leave.

[3] *Wall Street Journal*, Oct. 11, 1956, MRC clippings, MP public relations office.

[4] *New York Times*, Aug. 14, 1966, ibid.

[5] *St. Louis Post Dispatch*, June 4, 1976, DBJ clippings, vol. 3, ibid.

[6] *New York Times*, Oct. 29, 1961, ibid.

in the late 1930s restricting oil company activities in the natural gas business. In 1949, just as Marbury took the presidency of MRFC, the founding companies divested themselves of interest in it and the corporation went public.[7]

Actually, Marbury's appointment as Comfort's successor was partly accidental. He had been brought into the company originally when Comfort blurted out his name suddenly at a board meeting and suggested "that young lawyer who's been working with us" be made an officer.[8] Thus began the association that led to the presidency when Comfort fell ill in 1949. Yet, even then Marbury was not at first considered, but rather appointed by the board to find a replacement for Comfort. He did such a good job lining up prospects and preparing reports that the directors decided he was a better prospect than anyone he was recommending.[9] No amount of careful planning, however, would have yielded a wiser choice. Marbury at the time was thirty-seven years old, with just the right combination of experience and vigor, and MRFC was just beginning its career as a public company capable of diversification. Seldom have a man, an instrument, and a situation been better matched.

Marbury was not happy with the restricted range of MRFC's operations and was very annoyed at the inhibitions inherent in federal regulation of energy companies. He was outspoken on the subject of the Federal Power Commission (FPC), which he said had "strangled the pipelines by injecting itself too much into management, discouraging gas exploration, failing to show proper concern for the investing public and encouraging too much debt."[10] To a man for whom even the fastest changing corporate techniques were overtraditional, the "mass of bureaucratic red tape and government regulation" imposed by the FPC was anathema. MRFC was organized originally to serve industrial companies but had been pressured by the FPC to allocate more supply to utility customers where the agency could impose price restrictions. MRFC was not allowed any return on its 1929

[7] Interview with C. J. Maurer, March 12, 1979, Saint Louis.
[8] *Wall Street Journal*, Oct. 11, 1966, MRC clippings, MP public relations office.
[9] *New York Times*, Aug. 14, 1966, ibid.
[10] Ibid.

pipeline because it was fully depreciated.[11] Facts of this sort made Marbury feel that the pipeline company had exhausted itself as a money-making proposition, and he began looking for other fields to enter. Meanwhile, however, he ranted at the FPC and in 1951 punched an FPC rate division chief. This cost the former boxer $6,000 in damages and brought him his first national attention.[12]

Regarding diversification, it was Marbury's philosophy that "it doesn't pay to play penny ante." His first project was to try to gain more control over Saint Louis gas distribution by buying LaClede Gas, the utility to which MRFC sold its supply. Between 1949 and 1952 MRFC bought 8 percent of LaClede's stock, but bitter proxy fights limited it to one seat on the utility's board. Marbury did manage to influence LaClede to build large underground gas storage facilities at Saint Louis so that the pipeline would bear a less heavy share of responsibility for maintaining the city's winter supply. However, such small potatoes did not suit his style. One afternoon at the bar at the Missouri Athletic Club in Saint Louis, Marbury swapped MRFC's stock in LaClede for four compressor stations that the FPC said he had to buy rather than lease, and he turned his attention thereafter to other things.[13]

At this time Marbury was still thinking of directing his company's attention to the energy field. There is in fact evidence that his earliest interest in the MP hinged in part on an idea he had about running a pipeline to the Gulf along its right-of-way. In 1951 MRFC diversified by becoming involved in exploration and drilling through the Natural Gas and Oil Company headquartered at Shreveport, Louisiana. This company among other activities operated one offshore oil rig.[14] In 1956 MRFC added the oil field supply business through the reorganization of two small drilling supply companies as Milwhite Mud Sales. MRFC boasted an average exploration cost of 75 cents a barrel, com-

[11] "Magnate of Mid-America," *Forbes*, June 15, 1963, p. 21.
[12] *St. Louis Post Dispatch*, June 4, 1976, DBJ clippings, vol. 3, MP public relations office.
[13] *Wall Street Journal*, Oct. 11, 1966, MRC clippings, ibid.
[14] Interview with Maurer, March 12, 1979, Saint Louis.

pared with an industry average of $1.25. "It's a long-range project," Marbury commented, "but it's like money in the bank."[15]

Other diversification attempts were less successful. Marbury failed to get control of Missouri Portland Cement because of an abrupt change in management. MRFC backed Arkansas industrialist Witt Stephens in his bid for control of Arkansas-Louisiana Gas Company, but later sold its interest and took no active role. Marbury created Mississippi River Chemical from scratch to convert natural gas into anhydrous ammonia fertilizer for the wholesale market. However, success there came to involve getting into the retail trade and Marbury was not interested in that.[16]

Even with his relative failures, Marbury had a knack of salvaging his money if not his grand idea. When the potential merger with Missouri Portland Cement fell through, MRFC sold its stock for $1.6 million, a 75-percent profit on its investment. Marbury found a way to use energy in a manufacturing operation in the experiments with Mississippi River Chemical and also a way to use part of a 4,500-acre riverfront estate he had purchased to entertain guests. He sold the chemical business to Armour in 1959 at a profit of $1.5 million. Milwhite Mud Sales, successful but a dead end, was third in its industry when sold for $3.5 million in profit. The Arkansas-Louisiana Gas venture netted MRFC $2 million, and it was to represent stock held by Witt Stephens, his associate in that adventure, that Marbury first came to the board of the MP railroad and was introduced to his greatest challenge.[17]

According to C. J. Maurer, who worked with Marbury at the time, he succeeded by being flexible and pragmatic enough to change direction entirely within a few weeks. No elaborate plan for his future inhibited him from grasping opportunities wherever they came.[18] "We learned something out of these other businesses," Marbury told a reporter in 1963. "We got into

[15]"Magnate of Mid-America," p. 22.

[16]Ibid.; *Wall Street Journal*, Oct. 11, 1966, MRC clippings, MP public relations office.

[17]Ibid.; interview with Maurer, March 12, 1979, Saint Louis.

[18]Interview with Maurer.

some that were too small, and we realized that we had to go into something big if we wanted to make a real contribution to our stockholders."[19]

The "something big" turned out to be a railroad. Marbury became a director of the MP in May, 1958. Jackson T. (Witt) Stephens, the chairman of Arkansas-Louisiana Gas and president of Stephens, Inc. of Little Rock, was the largest holder of MP stock, with 60,000 shares of class A. Stephens was on the board himself but was entitled to more than one director. He therefore called upon Marbury, who was seated despite objections from a few that the company should not "reach down in to the depths" for directors who had no financial interest in the railroad.[20] Dearmont defended Marbury on the grounds that such men as he could attract much business to the railroad, but perhaps the criticism struck home anyway.[21] At least, director Marbury did not remain without MP stock holdings for long.

Marbury later said that his interest in the railroad's A stock was "love at second sight."[22] His associate Robert Craft recalled later that Marbury liked the MP debt structure and "said it was an unusual debt structure, that it had certain attributes . . . despite its topheaviness."[23] But, arrayed against advantages like the 1990 earliest maturity date on bond issues, much contingent interest debt, and a property that had good operating statistics, there were problems. The sheer size of the debt load was one. The MP debt of $500 million was as large as that of the Pennsylvania road, but revenues were only one-third as large. It was three times the debt of some comparable western railroads. Interest payments and mandatory sinking and capital expenditure funds absorbed a much larger than usual percentage of revenues, leaving little income available for dividends to the A stock, not to mention the frustrated holders of the B. "That big debt doesn't scare me," Marbury said. "I know it as a technician and

[19] "Magnate of Mid-America," p. 22.
[20] MP Railroad, transcript of stockholders' meeting, May 13, 1958, pp. 2, 6–8, MP archives.
[21] *New York Times*, Aug. 14, 1966, MRC clippings, MP public relations office.
[22] *Wall Street Journal*, Oct. 11, 1966, MRC clippings, MP public relations office.
[23] Testimony of Robert Craft, June 27, 1972, p. 102, space 0610102a, MP archives.

it's the most beautiful debt structure I've ever seen."[24] But privately, at least in 1958, he must have had doubts. There was the possibility that the stock structure could be radically altered, and Marbury could find no convenient lever to gain quick and large influence in the company. Craft at least felt that some of the public persona of Marbury was bluff and bravado. "Marbury was given to platitudes, and I didn't pay much attention to what he said most of the time."[25]

There was activity in MP stock as Marbury came to the board, and the feeling was general that, although Dearmont held out for a merger, it was more likely that a recapitalization would come first.[26] Naturally, the key to the situation was Alleghany.

Alleghany had an offer to buy its B stock for $300 a share, which, with a cost basis of $1,000 a share, it could not afford to accept. The offer, however, piqued the interest of Alleghany's David Wallace in negotiating a recapitalization plan with the railroad to free his company of its B stock. Estimates of a fair exchange ratio between A and B stock ranged from 30 to 1 to Wallace's own figure of 10 to 1.[27] Kidder, Peabody & Company was retained by Alleghany to study the situation and noted that although Alleghany's B stock was worth $2.8 million against a cost basis of $24.5 million, some tax advantage could come by offsetting the loss in a sale against unrealized capital gains then being generated by the Alleghany-controlled Investors Diversified Services (IDS). True, in theory the B stock had great value if simply held until the railroad made larger profits. But the A holders controlled management and, knowing their stock was

[24] "Magnate of Mid-America," p. 23.

[25] Testimony of Robert Craft, June 27, 1972, p. 103, space 0610102a, MP archives.

[26] Testimony of Robert Craft, June 27, pp. 112, 115, space 0610102a, MP archives.

[27] W. H. Hernstadt to Charles Ireland et al., Dec. 20, 1963, doc. 00211, 19(r), index Alleghany discovery documents, space 0610102a, MP archives; Memo from David Wallace, n.d., doc. 00147, 19(v), ibid.; William Eppler to Allan Kirby, Jan. 16, 1958, doc. 00126, 19(v), ibid. These documents from the Alleghany files were copied during a later lawsuit concerning dividends on the B stock. Some of the copies survive, but many have been lost and I have depended upon the abstract of their contents in the index made in connection with the lawsuit. When complete copies are cited, they will be referenced to the MP law department files rather than to this space in the archives.

limited to a $5 a share dividend, they might "gold plate" the railroad with high capital expenditures to avoid paying dividends to the B and thus keep B values low even in good times. Kidder, Peabody therefore advised that the A interests buy out the B at a ratio reflecting the increase in the value of the B that should occur with each small future improvement in the railway's operating ratio.[28]

Serious negotiations between Alleghany and the MP took place in 1959. T. C. Davis tried to enter these as a representative of Alleghany, but his services were refused by that company.[29] Instead, Wallace worked closely with Gustave Levy and commissioned a Goldman, Sachs study which in January, 1959, recommended a 15-to-1 ratio.[30] This interested Witt Stephens enough that he recommended such an exchange to the MP board, which declined to consider it.[31] Thereafter, Levy corresponded with Dearmont concerning some trade at between 10 to 1 and 15 to 1. Both the MP and Alleghany stockholders became increasingly less interested in recapitalization, however, as Marbury began to invest in MP stock and the Murchison brothers in Alleghany. Brokers still advised that 10 to 1 was the best trade the B holders could hope for, but by 1960 minority B holders were writing Alleghany that they would not accept an exchange at a ratio of less than 50 to 1.[32]

With this impasse came Marbury's opportunity. Witt Stephens died in 1959, leaving his 60,000-share block of A stock available for purchase. The A was then selling at an attractive price, and its ownership was so diverse that it might be possible to control MP management with a relatively small percentage of

[28] "Alleghany Corporation's Stake in MoPac," research memo from Kidder, Peabody, June 19, 1958, ibid.

[29] Allan Kirby to T. C. Davis, Oct. 9, 1958, doc. 00135, 19(v), ibid.

[30] Memo, David Wallace to Edward Beaugard, Jan. 19, 1959, doc. 00137, 19(v), ibid.

[31] W. H. Hernstadt to Charles Ireland et al., Dec. 20, 1963, doc. 00211, 19(r), ibid.

[32] For suggestions of settlement at about 10 to 1, see Edward Beaugard to Allan Kirby, Jan. 29, 1959, doc. 00142, 19(v); Research release, Kidder, Peabody & Co., March 24, 1960, doc. 00122, 19(p); Edgar Houpt to William Rabe, Aug. 18, 1960, doc. 800549, 19(v); Memo from T. C. Davis, Aug. 23, 1960, doc. 800548, 19(v), all ibid. The 50-to-1 minimum is suggested in Albert Redpath to Allan Kirby, Aug. 23, 1960, doc. 00146, 19(v), ibid.

it.[33] Marbury asked the MRFC directors to use $12 million in "free" treasury cash to purchase Stephens's MP stock as an investment.[34] Some doubted the wisdom of entering such an unfamiliar field as railroads, but the availability of such a fund of cash was itself evidence of Marbury's prior success in experimental ventures. They agreed.

What was Marbury's thinking? There was high risk, after all, in involving a medium-sized pipeline company in the affairs of an unstable and marginally profitable railroad, and for a man disillusioned with government regulation, going from the gas supply into the rail business was a jump from the frying pan into the fire. Probably Marbury at this point had no fixed idea about controlling the railroad, and the talk about building a liquid petroleum gas pipeline to Saint Louis from the Gulf along the railroad's right-of-way was at most contingency planning.[35] His own explanation was that the MP was a good railroad, its A stock was underpriced, and it seemed a good place to invest MRFC's spare cash. Those who knew Marbury knew that he could move for control if the right opportunity came, but he could also quickly withdraw completely, probably with a profit, if things took an unfavorable turn. After the Stephens purchase, MRFC continued to buy A stock on the open market, while Marbury kept close track of the direction of the corporate wind.

In 1960 MRFC's holdings approached 25 percent of the A stock, and understandably there was interest on Wall Street and in Saint Louis in Marbury and his plans. Those who inquired about Mr. Marbury learned that his friends found him loyal, hard-working, and generous, while his enemies described him as "aloof, obstinate, and ruthless."[36] The same man who anonymously gave away thousands to poor blacks he met in Saint Louis could take on the aspect of a corporate Captain Kidd in certain business situations.[37] The talk on Wall Street was typical of the opinion of strangers. One analyst remembers: "Mr. Mar-

[33] Interview with Maurer, March 12, 1979, Saint Louis.
[34] *New York Times*, Oct. 29, 1961, DBJ clippings, vol. 1, MP public relations office.
[35] MP Railroad, directors' minutes, March 11, 1958, MP archives.
[36] *Wall Street Journal*, Oct. 11, 1966, MRC clippings, MP public relations office.
[37] Interview with Harry Hammer, July 12, 1979, Saint Louis.

bury was considered a very strong, very ruthless, very dynamic maverick type guy. He would force a bag of corn down the mouth of a two pound goose if he thought it was good for him."[38]

To the Saint Louis establishment, Marbury was something of a pariah. His southern Democratic political views and his bluntness offended some business leaders.[39] Also, Marbury liked to do his banking in New York City, where he could centralize the financing of the large projects he favored. Saint Louis bankers interpreted this and Marbury's refusal to serve on the boards of any local banks as disloyalty to the community where his business was located.[40] A few Saint Louis eyebrows were raised too at his lifestyle. In 1953 he bought a 4,500-acre site along the Mississippi River near the town of Festus, complete with a pre–Civil War plantation house known as Selma Hall. Local wags called it "Marbury's Castle" and thought that spending $450,000 for a place with a swimming pool and fishing lake to entertain business guests was not in the Saint Louis manner. More annoying yet to his critics was that Marbury did not seem to care what they thought of him. He once observed: "The status quo is very important in Saint Louis. People don't like to be moved and I came in from the country and started stirring things up. This is a provincial town and they didn't like it."[41]

There were a number of questions from the floor at the 1960 MP stockholders' meeting concerning Marbury's intentions. Dearmont answered that when he asked Marbury why MRFC was investing in the railroad, Marbury replied: "They liked to make money." "What will be the effect on the railroad's stock structure?" someone asked. Dearmont did not pretend to know but stated that MRFC was cooperative, it served the same territory as the railroad, and had made no attempt to interfere with detailed day-to-day management. "We love to ship their pipe," Dearmont concluded, ". . . and personally I have complete confidence in Mr. Marbury and his associates."[42]

[38] Interview with John Burns, March 10, 1980, New York City.
[39] *Wall Street Journal*, Oct. 11, 1966, MRC clippings, MP public relations office.
[40] Interview with Thomas O'Leary, July 9, 1979, Saint Louis; *Saint Louis Post-Dispatch*, June 4, 1976, DBJ clippings, vol. 3, MP public relations office.
[41] *Wall Street Journal*, Oct. 11, 1966, MRC clippings, MP public relations office.
[42] MP Railroad, transcript of stockholders' meeting, May 10, 1960, pp. 55–56, MP

Marbury himself then gave a short address. He emphasized that MRFC had no intention of controlling the MP: "We bought it to make money, it's just that simple. Very few people believe it, but that's true." The discourse continued with some praise for the future of America and the area served by the road and statistics to indicate it could be profitable. "Now, it's not a quickie, we don't expect to make a lot of money this year, but in time. In time we will make a lot of money."[43]

An observer at the 1960 meeting might have sensed in Marbury's comments and actions on other topics a feeling on his part that the railroad was more than just another investment. It was a surprise, for example, when T. E. Quisenberry rose and said he had talked with Marbury, and Marbury supported Quisenberry and Wilson's annual proposal to eliminate the staggered system of electing directors. Marbury then spoke personally in favor of such a change. He said that the company stock was no longer in the hands of short-term speculators, the stockholders and directors had become a "much more harmonious group" than formerly, and therefore all stock should get full voting representation when the board was appointed.[44] This was the argument that had always been made by the B stock and had regularly been rejected. Why should Marbury join the B holders now when it was known he had a low opinion of the value of that security?

The answer surely was that Marbury found himself in a minority position within the group of A stockholders similar to that of the B holders in the overall capitalization. The staggered system prevented MRFC from being able to elect a director or two by concentrating its votes on one or two people while the rest of the stock was diluted over thirteen or fourteen. Marbury denied thinking of control, but he was certainly thinking of representation and direct input by MRFC on rail policy decisions. The staggered system of elections was not changed until May, 1963,

---

archives. There was some discussion with Dearmont about the possibility of running a pipeline along the railroad right-of-way. He said that experts were not sure this would be feasible.

[43] Ibid., pp. 59–60.
[44] Ibid., pp. 8–10.

when MRFC was firmly in control of the A stock, but by late 1960 other events confirmed Marbury's drift.[45] In September, 1960, William Marbury was elected chairman of the board of the MP, an office that had been vacant since Paul Neff had occupied it for a month just before his death in 1957.[46] Raymond Terry, an MRFC vice-president, was elected to the MP board at the same time.[47]

Some may have felt that Marbury's executive status was temporary, a stopgap measure after the heart attack Russell Dearmont suffered that fall. But, as shall be seen, Marbury entered quickly and aggressively into direction of railroad policy by reversing Dearmont's decision on an important merger negotiation.[48] Over the next two years MRFC's activity in buying A stock on the open market and organizing a major tender offer for stock it could not acquire in that way left no doubt that, whatever Marbury's ideas had been in 1959 or early 1960, by 1961 and 1962 he did seek control of the A stock and therefore of the management of the railroad. One of the things prominently on his mind during this period was insuring that the MP replaced its retiring officers with young and imaginative people who would give it a competitive edge as the future came rapidly on.

[45] *New Orleans Times Picayune*, May 15, 1963, DBJ clippings, vol. 1, MP public relations office.

[46] *St. Louis Globe Democrat*, Sept. 11, 1960, MRC clippings, ibid.

[47] *Wall Street Journal*, Aug. 27, 1962, ibid.

[48] The negotiations were with the C&EI and shall be discussed in a later chapter.

# CHAPTER IV

# Downing Jenks

O NE of the brightest young managers mentioned to Marbury when he inquired where he could find talent was Downing Jenks. Usually, however, praise was followed by the comment that it was unlikely Jenks would be available to the Missouri Pacific. He was president of the Rock Island, having reached that office at an age (forty) unprecedented among major railroad chief officers, and he had no reason to believe in 1960 that his company had less of a future than the MP. He was aware of the MP and of the MRFC. But he admitted to thinking the corporate title of the latter sounded too much like the name of a barge company for it to amount to much in the railroad field. A man who was already at the top in his forties might be expected to rest on his laurels. But Jenks would not have gone so far so early had he not been willing to take chances and had he not had grand ambitions. And all his ambitions had to do with railroads.

Born in Portland, Oregon, in 1915, Jenks was a model railroad buff as a boy and breathed the atmosphere of a family that was railroad to the core. His grandfather, Cyrus H. Jenks, was a superintendent on James J. Hill's Great Northern. When Downing Jenks later worked for that company, it had a passenger car named "Cyrus Jenks," as though to remind the younger Jenks of his special destiny. C. O. Jenks, Downing's father, was general manager of the Spokane, Portland & Seattle at the time of his son's birth, and later (1921–47) vice-president of operations for the Great Northern. His maternal grandfather, W. O. Downing (for whom he was named), was a Missouri state senator and an

attorney for the Burlington and the Great Northern.[1] In Downing Jenks's mind it was not enough just to follow in these foot-
steps. He wished to build upon the family tradition to influence
rail history.

He brought to that ambition a fine combination of theoreti-
cal understanding and practical know-how. While both Jenks
and his right-hand man at the Rock Island, John Lloyd, culti-
vated a folksy manner, both were most capable of confronting
academics on their own turf. Jenks had a B.S. in engineering
from Yale and Lloyd a degree in finance from the Wharton
School at the University of Pennsylvania. In addition to education and intuition, however, Jenks drew largely upon personal
experience. His first rail work was as a chainman on the Spokane,
Portland & Seattle. Later, he worked in the engineering department of the Pennsylvania and then was roadmaster, division engineer, trainmaster, and superintendent on various divisions of
the Great Northern. During World War II he served with the
704th Railway Grand Division in Africa and Europe, and rose
from first lieutenant to lieutenant colonel. In 1948 Jenks went to
the Chicago & Eastern Illinois railroad as general manager and
soon became vice-president. In 1950 he joined the Rock Island
as assistant operating vice-president and became vice-president
for operations in 1951, executive vice-president in 1953, and
president in 1956.[2]

Jenks liked the job of superintendent best and was proud
enough of it to need to repeat to himself his grandfather's warn-
ing to his father. "If you wore a 7⅛ hat as an assistant superintendent," Cyrus told C. O., "don't increase the size now that you
are superintendent."[3] He might have added in Downing's case,
not when you are president or chairman of the board, either.
But the lesson was in the younger Jenks's blood. All the operating positions he had held taught him to avoid the smoke-filled

[1] Interview with John Lloyd, July 12, 1979, Saint Louis; *Kansas City Star*, Feb. 19, 1961, DBJ clippings, vol. 1, MP public relations office.

[2] Jenks deposition, Jan. 22, 1973, in "Recapitalization, Mississippi River Corporation, Related Tender Offer, 1972–74"; *San Antonio Light*, Jan. 22, 1961, DBJ clippings, vol. 1, both in ibid.

[3] *Sedalia Democrat*, April 9, 1961, ibid.

rooms of corporate headquarters and be much out on the line, no matter what his title. He learned in his early thirties while superintendent of a thousand miles of the Great Northern that there is a pulse to a railroad operation, and it is found by traveling up and down the line, poking at ties, sighting down rails, and talking to the employees. "You've got to get out and see the property," he said, "see what's going on, talk to people." That "rugged way to make a living" appealed most when the challenge was the greatest—when there were cars buried in flood waters or a line paralyzed by snow. This empathy and "feel" for the railroad was the only special talent Jenks would ever freely admit to. But he surely had also determination and iron discipline. "I just started early," he told a reporter, "and knew what I wanted to do."[4]

William Marbury also knew what he wanted to do, and a good part of that in 1960 was to find new management for the MP to replace the outgoing Dearmont group. Jenks's name was mentioned, but no one thought to ask him since it seemed likely he would refuse. Marbury spoke to Gus Aydelot, president of the Denver & Rio Grande Western, but he was not interested. D. W. Brosnan, executive vice-president of the Southern, was highly recommended, but he would not even talk with Marbury about a job with a struggling midwestern railroad. "I saw a whole gang of men for the job," Marbury recalled later. "The ones I thought were well suited for it by reputation were more than satisfied with what they had."[5]

Alleghany Corporation agreed with Marbury that the management situation was critical to MRFC's future with the MP. Allan Kirby of Alleghany received a report on MRFC strategy in the MP in July, 1960. His investigators concluded that MRFC was a good company but "lacked speculative appeal" because its growth prospects were limited. The investment in the MP might change that, but the "intriguing" debt structure of the railroad would not do investors any good in the long run unless new management could keep it out of receivership in the short run.

[4] *Kansas City Star*, Feb. 19, 1961, ibid.
[5] *New York Times*, Oct. 29, 1961, ibid.

An Alleghany source on the MRFC board reported that all the "kick" in the fuel company lay in the future of the MP and surmised that, despite Marbury's statement that "the good things take care of themselves," he would quickly withdraw from railroading if stock values dropped sharply. The informant wryly commented that "Bill Marbury is a very resourceful fellow and did not want to just concentrate on the pipe line business and sit back and amortize debt, felt that his daughter could do that just as well as he could."[6]

Just then came a fortunate accident. Early in November, 1960, Downing Jenks arrived in Saint Louis to talk with Marbury about the possibility of merging the Rock Island with the MP.

The Rock had fallen on hard times, due largely to the fact that it was a granger railroad without good connections outside an agricultural service area that was no longer very profitable. Jenks wanted to make a good alliance and had favored one with the Milwaukee. However, when he and Bill Quinn of that line were within one-tenth of a share of an understanding on exchange terms, the deal was scotched by objections from Rock Island director Henry Crown, who was interested in a Milwaukee-Northwestern merger. Crown suggested that the Rock Island seek a merger with the MP as an alternative, and he owned enough Rock Island stock to make his opinion stick.[7]

In Saint Louis, Jenks spoke briefly with Marbury and at some length with Harvey Johnson, executive vice-president of the MP. Neither Marbury nor Johnson had the slightest interest in merger with the Rock Island, but both were considerably interested by Downing Jenks. It was clear that the struggle within the Rock Island board over the Milwaukee merger favored by Jenks had not set well with him, and that he was not convinced his future at the Rock Island was entirely bright. Men like Jenks, single-minded as they are, ambitious and sure of their ground, do not always get on well with those of like singularity of purpose but differing opinion. Probably adding to difficulties with

[6]Charles T. Hill to Allan P. Kirby, July 8, 1960, copy of original letter, doc. 00112, 19(a), MP law department, Saint Louis.

[7]Interview with Downing Jenks, March 13, 1979, Saint Louis; for some back-

some at the Rock Island after the initial philosophical breach was Jenks's highly individualistic personal demeanor. He was a fastidious person who was genuinely comfortable in a conservative suit and hat and who disliked long hair on his employees. He brooked no moral and ethical compromise and subscribed to a code much like that of the Boy Scouts, of which he later became national president. In a way, he was a throwback to the nineteenth-century rail builder at the dawn of the Age of Aquarius. He was not interested in making any adjustment in personal temperament to the modern age, although he was one of its most flexible innovators in management technique.

Jenks had no idea whether he could get along with Marbury, but doubted it. The latter had a reputation as an unforgiving tyrant whom many persons feared. Little did Jenks guess that much of Marbury's unpopularity stemmed from the same base as his own, or that the sometimes crude, boisterous Marbury and the straitlaced, disciplined Jenks would get along well; they shared a sense of old-fashioned purposiveness, a feeling of destiny that had gone out of fashion years before. Yet Jenks felt driven away from the Rock Island and saw in the MP a more promising, though not less difficult, challenge.[8]

Marbury did not let the opportunity pass. "Would you like to come here and be president?" he asked Jenks shortly after the young executive was ushered into his office. Jenks allowed that it would be attractive but explained that if his Milwaukee merger went through he would have a much stronger railroad in the Rock Island. Why not talk again when that is decided? Marbury returned. Jenks did not hesitate. Fine. He would call Saint Louis the very day the Rock Island board meeting on the merger took place, November 14, and accept or reject the MP presidency. When that day came, Marbury's phone rang. "I am available," said the voice on the other end.[9]

Jenks was not one to look backward with regret, but he had

---

ground on the Rock Island, see William E. Hayes, *Iron Road to Empire: The History of 100 Years of the Progress and Achievements of the Rock Island Lines* (by the company, 1953).

[8] Interview with Jenks.
[9] Ibid.

taken a big step and was apprehensive. The meeting with Marbury was to be over lunch at the Saint Louis Racket Club early in December. Before it took place, but after arriving in Saint Louis, Jenks talked with Travis Fleischel, a Saint Louis friend whom he had known when the latter was a director of the Chicago & Eastern Illinois. Not knowing that Fleischel was now a director of MRFC, Jenks communicated his fears about Marbury and asked what sort of man he was. Fleischel laughed. Marbury was a great guy, he said, and had begun thinking about Jenks for this job partly at Fleischel's urging. Still, Jenks wavered some until after the lunch meeting, when he went to Marbury's house to meet the family. Here Jenks got a glimpse of Marbury's personal life and character, and found it good. Any man who had a wife and two daughters as delightful as Marbury's could not be as bad as rumor suggested.[10] Just how supportive Marbury could be of those he liked, especially of Jenks, the new presidential nominee was not to appreciate for some months.

At the directors' meeeting of January 16, 1961, Marbury resigned as chairman of the board in favor of Dearmont. Marbury remained head of the executive committee and director. Jenks became a director and president at a salary of $90,000 a year.[11] When he told the assembled directors that the railroad was in bad shape and needed massive capital improvements to operate properly, they applauded. None were shy about giving Jenks's talents needed space.[12]

The new president could hardly arrange the time in Saint Louis to attend his own election. In his first three months with the MP he traveled more than 30,000 miles while exploring the railroad, sometimes in a private car, sometimes in a Chevrolet rail car, and often on foot.[13] He remembered later: "In the condition I found the Missouri Pacific, you didn't need any industrial engineering outfit to tell you what to do." The northern part of the line was in fair condition, but the southern part, where ties

[10] Ibid.

[11] MP Railroad, directors' minutes, Jan. 16, 1961, pp. 3–4, MP archives.

[12] Interview with Jenks.

[13] MP Railroad, transcript of stockholders' meeting, May 9, 1961, p. 18, MP archives.

rotted in the high humidity and where the old International Great Northern had been unable for years to get maintenance money from the mother company, was awful. Yet from the southern section came most of the lucrative chemical traffic. The railroad seemed to Jenks to be in the business of preserving historic structures at its shop areas, running a hodge-podge of motive power, and insisting on procedures that were dated fifty years earlier. He reasoned that perhaps the older management had become accustomed to operating under the restraints of the court and did not think to innovate. Or they may be pursuing a "peace in our time policy" in order not to rock the boat before their retirement. Jenks noticed people "doing things here that I had never seen on any railroad and I'd been on a lot of them."[14] His conclusion was straightforward: "The company was a little like a dowager. It was already over a hundred years old then, and it acted like it. It was a little down at the heels."[15]

Jenks brought a team to the MP to help rehabilitate it. John H. Lloyd came from the Rock Island as vice-president of operations and Frank Conrad from the same company as vice-president of traffic. John German of the Great Northern became chief mechanical officer, while H. B. Christianson, formerly of the Public Service Company of Indiana, headed the newly created industrial engineering department.[16]

According to Jenks, working with the physical problems of the MP was "like these digs over on the other side of the river. You would go through one civilization and uncover another." He took down 155 buildings at the Sedalia shops alone and constantly used 500 gondolas just hauling the $35 million in scrap generated by his cleanup campaign. He made fast decisions, gave spot orders in the field, and pursued with vigor his goals: to abandon branch lines, get rid of passenger trains, rebuild all the shops, strengthen the track, and rebuild all the yards. Steam tools and even some steam engines were thrown away, including the engine kept at the Marshall shops for high-water use until

[14] Interview with Jenks.

[15] *St. Louis Post Dispatch*, Aug. 8, 1971, DBJ clippings, vol. 3, MP public relations office.

[16] *Modern Railroads*, April, 1962, in ibid., vol. 1.

Jenks asked how it was planned to protect the non-waterproof plain bearings most of the cars at that time had.[17] No maintenance expense was deferred, no useless structure was left standing, and no tradition was sacred to the president who became known on the line as "Mr. Clean." "All deferred work is to be made up this year," Jenks barked. "This means all depots painted, all buildings and shops fixed up."[18] "You've got to maintain your property, and you've got to keep it clean."[19]

By May, 1961, Jenks had walked through every diesel and car shop on the entire railroad, and many changes had been made. Jenks hoped to reduce the bad-order ratio (the percentage of cars out of service for repairs) to 3 percent, and to help with this took delivery on 1,100 new freight cars in 1961 at a cost of $12 million.[20] He took off passenger service between Omaha and Kansas City, although this meant doing away with the first Eagle streamliner ever run by the company.[21] Inventory control improved, thanks partly to the RAMAC computer system and Harold Hoffmeister's data processing team. Material and supply expenses were $4.1 million less than the year before. A new rail welding shop at North Little Rock produced continuous rail in 1,440-foot lengths that could be put in place rapidly. The fourteen divisions on the railroad system became four operating districts. "We'll still have superintendents," Jenks explained, "but they won't have big office forces. They'll spend more time out on the road and less on paperwork." The sales department was decentralized by creating eleven districts under managers called by wits "the 11 apostles." Specialists worked on piggyback and Less Than Carload traffic. Sixty-mile-per-hour "hotshot" freight trains ran on schedules wherever the track and signaling would permit.[22]

No one was more helpful in the early going than Lloyd, and

[17] Interview with Jenks.
[18] *Modern Railroads*, April, 1962, in DBJ clippings, vol. 1, MP public relations office. Jenks slowed capital expenditures slightly in 1961 "until I could find what the hell was going on," but they were $55 million in 1962.
[19] *Jefferson Republic*, May 11, 1961, in ibid.
[20] Ibid.
[21] *Falls City Journal*, May 29, 1961, in ibid.
[22] *Modern Railroads*, April, 1962, in ibid.

Jenks estimated that the two of them saved the company over $50,000 a day in 1961.[23] Lloyd's father knew Jenks's father, and the sons had been together on both the Great Northern and the Rock Island. Many people noticed the way Jenks and Lloyd seemed to complement each other. It was Lloyd who emphasized nuts and bolts and acted as a restraint on Jenks's wilder imaginings. Lloyd himself thought of Jenks as a builder and of himself as defender of the still useful status quo from the sweep of his partner's revolution. "He's an impetuous fellow," said Lloyd about Jenks. "I get madder than hell at him." Both men, however, were very often right, and there was a mutual respect that kept them listening to each other through the hot summer days of inspecting a railroad that did not look as either of them thought it should.[24]

Whatever their talent, the two would have been frustrated without the support they got from William Marbury. Although Marbury was once discovered by Lloyd inspecting the track behind a directors' special at 5 A.M., the MRFC chief made it a practice not to interfere in the day-to-day operation of the line. For example, when Jenks and Lloyd went to Marbury's office for the first time to discuss the capital improvements budget, Lloyd explained in detail a plan he had worked out with General Electric while still at the Rock Island. General Electric agreed to allow the Rock Island to pay for any new locomotives out of savings in operations. Lloyd felt this might help the cash-short MP. Marbury thought for a moment and then asked what was the best diesel available regardless of price or financial arrangements. The answer was quick—General Motors. Then, said Marbury, buy all General Motors. "We will get along better if you take care of the railroad and let me take care of the finance."[25] The two operating officers therefore ordered $9 million in new EMD diesels for that year.[26] Each year thereafter they went to Marbury's office before the capital improvements

[23] Interview with Jenks, March 13, 1979, Saint Louis.
[24] Interview with John Lloyd, July 12, 1979, Saint Louis.
[25] Ibid.
[26] *St. Louis Post Dispatch*, Sept. 11, 1961, DBJ clippings, vol. 1, MP public relations office.

budget was to go to the directors. Each year Marbury was non-commital at their private meeting. And each year at the directors' meeting, he not only supported the funding of their requests in full but insisted upon introducing the motion himself.[27]

Marbury was just as interested in improving people as in upgrading property. At the May, 1961, stockholders' meeting he pushed through a stock option proposal to insure a future for his managers despite the wrath of the B holders, who were not interested in the dilution that resulted from an extra stock issue for this purpose. "You have to do what is the American way," Marbury argued, "and that is to make them some money." He used the example of Downing Jenks, forty-five years old, a graduate of Yale, and already in his career the president of two railroads. "It is no small job to get people like that. When you get them, you want to keep them because their continuity of service to this property will be of great value to the stockholders."[28]

Jenks was a good speechmaker and lobbyist, and he had as many innovative ideas about national rail policy as he did about MP car distribution. He began early giving speeches about the consolidation of all freight carriers and said in a talk called "The Power of Positive Thinking in Transportation" that fights between good guys and bad guys in the same town were good only on television. Motor carriers, railroads, barge lines, and airlines had common problems, were all losing money, and had no business attacking each other, especially before congressional committees.[29] "The so-called 'railroad problem,'" he said, "has been the subject of more study but probably less action, than perhaps any other aspect of national industrial life."[30] He knew that a revitalized MP could yet fail in its promise if the long-range general environment for even the most efficient freight railroads was poor.

Jenks was more successful with the MP more quickly than anyone, including Marbury, imagined. Therefore, not much

[27] Interview with Lloyd.
[28] MP Railroad, transcript of stockholders' meeting, May 9, 1961, pp. 38–45, MP archives.
[29] *Traffic World*, Sept. 23, 1961, DBJ clippings, vol. 1, MP public relations.
[30] *Palestine Herald Press*, Dec. 27, 1961, ibid.

more than a year passed between the time Jenks first came to Saint Louis and the time Marbury, confident of his president's performance, began experiments to give MRFC complete control of the MP A stock. By July, 1962, MRFC had as much A stock as it could get at a reasonable price on the open market. Therefore, its officers placed a freeze on such buying, citing unfavorable economic conditions as a reason. To that point MRFC had been a major factor in the trading of the A, having purchased over 50 percent of all that stock purchased in the first five months of 1962.[31] That summer, on a rail inspection trip from Saint Louis to Colorado Springs, Marbury explained to the directors of the MP that MRFC would like to make a tender offer that would give it control of the A stock and therefore of the railroad's management. He asked that the board recommend to the stockholders that such an offer be accepted. There was discussion of this and less than universal support for the idea. The consensus was expressed by Herbert Gussman: "Assuming that a majority of Missouri Pacific are not familiar with Mississippi, you have a touchy project."[32]

Nothing Marbury said on that train ride or at the October 8 directors' meeting when the tender offer issue was again taken up could convince them. He told his fellow directors that MRFC was not a fly-by-night concern, but had 20,000 shares of stock in the hands of seasoned investors and had sent some of its best people, including comptroller Jack Maurer, to the MP. Also, the tender offer would provide instant diversification for the railroad: "The purpose is Mississippi River Fuel does not just want to have a railroad. We are making progress. The railroad industry is not a very profitable industry and return on capital investment is very poor. This complex of operations and unlimited opportunities appeals to Mississippi. We can protect it, we can work at it, and we can help it. In addition it opens up to the stockholders an opportunity to participate in the economic growth of America." It was bold rhetoric, but the board still refused to do more than send a carefully worded letter to the

[31] *St. Louis Post Dispatch*, July 10, 1962, MRC clippings, ibid.
[32] Robert Craft deposition, June 27, 1972 and Craft exhibit 3, space 0610102a, MP archives.

stockholders recommending that they give the MRFC tender offer serious consideration.[33]

The ambiguous action of the MP board probably insured that MRFC would not get the 80 percent of the A it wanted in order to consolidate the fuel company and the railroad for tax purposes. In confessing this to the press in November, Marbury insisted that even if MRFC succeeded in getting a bare majority of the A, the offer would not be a "flop."[34] MRFC already had 35 percent of the A and had invested $30 million, so there was no point now in withdrawing.[35] "We think we can make a great railroad of the Mo. Pac.," Marbury stated, "and if we do all the work, we think we should get the return."[36]

There was, however, another obstacle. Government agencies fell to arguing about which one would have jurisdiction over a pipeline company that controlled a railway. Would it be the ICC, the FPC, or the Securities and Exchange Commission (SEC)? There had never been a case like this one, although the reverse had once happened in California when the Southern Pacific invested in a pipeline.[37] Marbury must have found this familiar ground but could only press ahead, assuming something would be worked out among regulatory agencies. A *Wall Street Journal* reporter wrote about the quandary: "Maybe there's room for yet one more alphabetical agency, which perhaps would come to be known as the BBBB—the Bureau for Battered and Bewildered Businessmen."[38]

MRFC's tender offer was 1.2 million of its common shares in exchange for 900,000 MP A shares, or a ratio of 1.3 to 1. Only about a third of the shares requested were obtained. However, this gave MRFC 53 percent of the stock, and the fuel company decided for the moment to be satisfied with that, although it did not stop its open-market purchasing. It was not all that Marbury wanted, but it accomplished the not inconsiderable feat of put-

[33] Craft exhibit 4, ibid.

[34] *Wall Street Journal*, Nov. 12, 1962, MRC clippings, MP public relations office.

[35] *St. Louis Globe Democrat*, Aug. 25, 1962, ibid.

[36] *St. Louis Post Dispatch*, Oct. 19, 1962, ibid.

[37] *St. Louis Globe Democrat*, Aug. 28, 1962, ibid.

[38] *Wall Street Journal*, Sept. 25, 1962, ibid.

ting a pipeline company with assets of $150 million in control of a railroad company with assets of $1.1 billion. From that time no one snickered when William Marbury announced he intended to do this or that in the field of finance. With the taking of management control of the MP in November, 1962, Marbury truly arrived as a national business figure.[39]

The railroad MRFC now controlled was ready for big things. By 1963 it had a 75.1 percent ratio of operating expenses to revenues and a carry-through of 12.1 percent of revenue to pretax operating profit. In the first full year of Jenks's leadership, income went up 74 percent, the work force went down 17 percent, and the bad-order ratio dropped from the 8 percent of 1960 to 3 percent.[40]

Physical rehabilitation continued to be important to the railroad through the 1960s but was no longer the sole object of attention. Marbury was deeply involved in looking into the possibility of acquiring the Chicago & Eastern Illinois Railroad, where Jenks had had experience in the 1940s. Why the hurry? It was partly the national climate of merger and it was partly the hurry-up personality of Downing Jenks. He wanted to make railroad history and, considering the scope of what he aspired to do, could not waste many years.

[39] *St. Louis Post Dispatch*, Nov. 23, 1962, ibid.
[40] "Magnate of Mid-America," *Forbes*, June 15, 1963, MP public relations office.

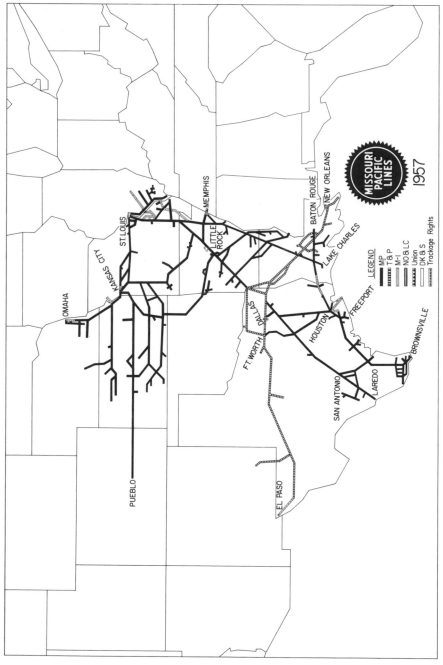

MISSOURI PACIFIC LINES

1957

LEGEND
MP
T & P
M-I
NO & LC
Union
DK & S
Trackage Rights

OMAHA
KANSAS CITY
ST. LOUIS
MEMPHIS
LITTLE ROCK
BATON ROUGE
NEW ORLEANS
LAKE CHARLES
FREEPORT
HOUSTON
DALLAS
FT. WORTH
SAN ANTONIO
LAREDO
BROWNSVILLE
PUEBLO
EL PASO

FILE B-6-504/(97ta)

CHAPTER V

# *Chicago*

---

**W**HEN the Missouri Pacific thought of merger, it thought
first of the Chicago & Eastern Illinois railroad, a line that formed
an 862-mile inverted trident with its base at Chicago and three
branches. The western branch connected with the MP at Saint
Louis, but not before a slow trip on one of Saint Louis's belt-
switching railroads from the Chicago & Eastern Illinois's Mitchell Yard in East Saint Louis to the MP's Dupo Yard. The middle
branch, also wholly in Illinois, met the MP at Thebes. It would
be possible using this line to direct traffic straight from Texas
and the Southwest to Chicago, bypassing delays in Saint Louis.
However, neither the MP nor the Cotton Belt, both of which
had Chicago & Eastern Illinois interchanges near Thebes, did
this as it would have meant short-hauling their own lines and
collecting less mileage on shipments. The third branch, the so-
called Evansville line through Indiana, was less important to the
MP, but of great interest to the Louisville & Nashville, with
which it connected. Also, the Illinois Central had a defensive interest in the entire Chicago & Eastern Illinois, which paralleled
many Illinois Central routes. All these companies were on the
scene in earnest in the late 1950s when the Chicago & Eastern
Illinois, overly dependent on coal traffic and unable to realize
economies of scale on its short line, began to fall behind on
maintenance and to search for help from a larger and stronger
partner.

The first idea at the MP was to buy the Chicago & Eastern
Illinois for cash. There was no question that it would be the
perfect end-to-end consolidation, giving all-important access to

Chicago and allowing the MP at last to go somewhere. However, the A-B stock situation at the MP was likely to complicate any stock exchange offer, and there was a question whether the Chicago & Eastern Illinois could survive in decent condition the long period of ICC hearings the expected opposition to a merger was likely to necessitate. Therefore, when first contacts occurred through the good offices of Travis Fleischel, who was on the board of both Chicago & Eastern Illinois and the MRFC, the talk was of buying enough Chicago & Eastern Illinois stock to give the MP control. There was a luncheon meeting in July, 1959, at the Missouri Pacific building in Saint Louis including Chicago & Eastern Illinois president David Matthews, Russell Dearmont, Travis Fleischel, and William Marbury. Marbury asked Matthews to inquire of the larger stockholders whether any would be willing to sell for $25 per share of common stock. The next day Matthews contacted owners of some 200,000 shares.[1]

The best prospect for getting Chicago & Eastern Illinois stock was Henry Hammack, who was represented by two directors on the railroad's board. When contacted, however, Hammack objected to a cash transaction because of its effect on his personal taxes. Also, attorneys for the Chicago & Eastern Illinois wondered if such a purchase would violate the Interstate Commerce Act by putting the MP suddenly in a control position without prior application to and hearings before the ICC. These reverses weakened the influence of Marbury, who wanted a cash purchase, and strengthened Dearmont, who favored formal merger negotiations and an exchange of stock. Matthews had a long meeting with Dearmont about a merger and then sent the company's general counsel P. C. Mullen to Saint Louis to work with MP attorneys on the details.[2]

The merger option was not smooth sailing either. Dearmont explained the long history of the reorganization to Mat-

[1] Testimony of David Matthews, March 29, 1962, pp. 2256–57, Bates 3017c, space 1150802b, MP archives; *Brief on Behalf of the Bureau of Inquiry and Compliance of the Interstate Commerce Commission*, Oct. 1, 1962, p. 8, Bates 3005, space 1150803b, ibid.

[2] Testimony of David Matthews, March 29, 1962, pp. 2257–60, Bates 3017c, space 1150802b, ibid.

Downing Jenks in the field during the Texas floods, 1966

Signing the receivership away, 1956.

The first meeting of the reorganization directors, 1956.

The first regular directors' meeting of the independent Missouri Pacific, 1957.

Senator Russell Dearmont, flanked by directors, speaking to one of the stormy stockholders' meetings of the late 1950s.

*Left:* John Lloyd in 1962. *Right:* Downing Jenks (*left*) and William Marbury shortly after Jenks's arrival at the Missouri Pacific.

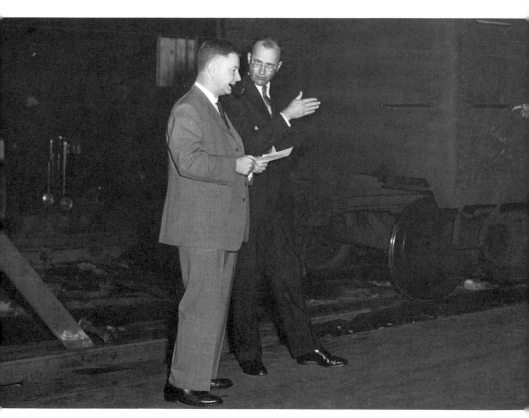

A strategy session on Jenks's initial system-wide tour.

Directors try their hands at fixing up the line, early 1960s.

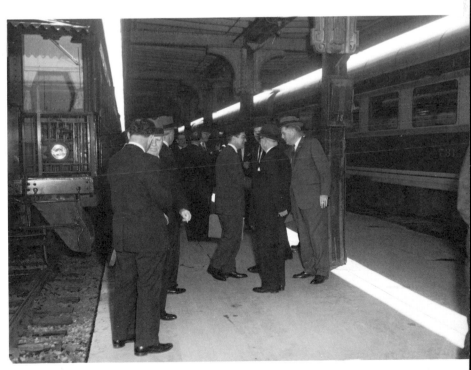

Directors' trip to the Rio Grande Valley to discuss revitalizing the profitable southern lines, 1962.

Jenks's communication link with Saint Louis during the Texas floods, 1966.

An example of "traditional" railroad upkeep on the Chicago & Eastern Illinois before the Missouri Pacific repairs.

Chicago & Eastern Illinois "nonstandard" office at the time of the Missouri Pacific takeover.

Stock transfer for the recapitalization, 1974. *Left to right:* C. J. Maurer, Thomas O'Leary, Lauk Walton, and Gilbert Strelinger.

Mark Hennelly (*left*) and Lauk Walton, whose respect for each other was the initial breech in the wall of enmity between the Missouri Pacific and Alleghany Corporation.

thews and said that before any new MP A shares could be issued for a merger he would have to confer with Allan Kirby at Alleghany. Such contacts were made, but the MP could not insure that Alleghany would support a merger.[3] In addition, there was a technical problem with the Chicago road's capital structure. The Chicago & Eastern Illinois's general income bonds, which bore contingent interest, contained a provision that they would become a fixed interest debt in case of merger. This meant that in a merger these bonds would be senior to many of the MP securities bearing contingent interest, a situation not greeted with enthusiasm among holders of this type of MP paper.[4] The Chicago & Eastern Illinois investors, on the other hand, would not give up the protection of this clause easily.

Despite the difficulties, negotiations continued on both merger and cash purchase. On Labor Day, 1959, Marbury, Dearmont, Fleischel, Matthews, and MP attorneys George Holmes and Gilbert Strelinger met at Marbury's Selma Hall mansion. Marbury thought that those stockholders who had agreed to $25 a share should be given that sum and then a tender offer should be made to the remaining stockholders for $21 a share. Matthews doubted that differing prices was a good idea. However, his counterproposals were likewise greeted with skepticism. All the parties could agree upon was to commission Wyer, Dick & Company to do a study of merger possibilities.[5] When finished, this study estimated that net income for the combined system would increase $11 million annually over that of the MP alone.[6] The prospects, in short, were worth the effort it might take to realize them.

During the spring and summer of 1960, while Marbury looked for a new president for the MP, there was hard bargaining with the Chicago & Eastern Illinois over a suitable exchange ratio for its stock. The talk to that point had been of 1 share of

[3] Ibid., p. 2261.

[4] ICC, F.D. 21755, *Brief for the Missouri Pacific Railroad Company*, Sept. 28, 1962, p. 8, MP law dept.

[5] Testimony of David Matthews, March 29, 1962, pp. 2261–62, Bates 3017, space 1150803b, MP archives.

[6] ICC, F.D. 21755, *Brief for the Missouri Pacific Railroad Company*, Sept. 28, 1962, pp. 3–4, MP law dept.

MP A for 2 shares of Chicago & Eastern Illinois common. But in late March, 1960, the MP offered a 1-to-3 exchange for the common and a 1-to-1.60 trade for Chicago & Eastern Illinois A stock. This was so offensive to the Chicago group that it refused even to recommend it to the board. In July the offer changed to 1 to 2.71 for common and .75 to 1 for the A. A special meeting of the Chicago & Eastern Illinois board considered this and accepted it. Matthews learned that the MP board would look at it on September 9.[7] There seemed every possibility that the merger would soon go before the ICC.

Matthews got a call from William Marbury on September 9, but it was not the kind he expected. Marbury told him that Dearmont was ill and that T. C. Davis, who could speak for the B holders, was in Europe. Therefore, any consideration of a merger must be indefinitely postponed.[8] Given the urgent nature of the negotiations so far, Matthews was taken aback. What had changed?

There were the obvious factors, which Marbury explained. Dearmont had been the one favoring merger, while Marbury wanted cash purchase. Now Marbury was temporary chairman of the board and Dearmont was in the hospital. It was only fair that Dearmont should be present to introduce the merger proposal to the board in any light he chose. Also, there would be trouble enough with the B holders without pushing anything along while Davis was absent. But in addition, the talks with Jenks were surely in the background. Jenks had experience with the Chicago & Eastern Illinois, and it is logical to imagine that Marbury wanted to delay things until Jenks was on the scene in Saint Louis.[9] To top the reasons for hesitation, the MP law department had doubts about the advisability of any type of merger.

Matthews learned more when Marbury visited him in Oc-

[7]Testimony of David Matthews, March 29, 1962, pp. 2264-69, Bates 3017, space 1150803b, MP archives. The offer is contained in R. Dearmont to David Matthews (copy), July 12, 1960, ex. H-78, Bates 3020, ibid.

[8]Matthews testimony, p. 2269, ibid. See also David Matthews to MP Board of Directors, Sept. 9, 1960, ex. H-80, Bates 3022, ibid.

[9]Interview with Downing Jenks, March 12, 1979, Saint Louis.

tober. The two talked in Matthews's office and on a ride to the airport. At that time Marbury told Matthews that the MP board would never approve the Dearmont merger plan and that he was preparing a plan of his own.[10] Marbury then returned to Saint Louis and went into a series of conferences with his attorneys.

The attorneys created a lengthy document, submitted November 4, titled "Legal Aspects Involved in the Contemplated Merger of the Chicago & Eastern Illinois Railroad Into the Missouri Pacific Railroad Company." This study concluded there was no way to merge and to avoid facing the MP's internal stock difficulties. The merger itself would require only a majority approval from all stockholders, but issuing additional shares, which would be required, meant, according to the MP's own charter, approval of a majority of both classes of stock voting separately. Opposition could be expected also from Chicago & Eastern Illinois dissidents and other railroads interested in keeping the MP out of Chicago. Last, the ICC preferred that mergers involve no increase in fixed charges. This one would, and the MP would have to argue it was prepared to assume these. "In view of the Missouri Pacific's already heavy debt structure," the attorneys pointed out, "this will not be altogether easy."[11]

The lawyers did suggest some ways of dealing with these difficulties. The MP could lease the Chicago & Eastern Illinois, or there could be a consolidation, where both companies were merged into a new corporation. The latter technique offered a legal procedure by which "the effective veto power of the relatively small issue of the B stock would be broken," and it was therefore discussed seriously. Consolidation was a more cumbersome process than merger, but it had the advantage of creating a larger system and a de facto recapitalization simultaneously.[12]

While this sort of thinking was proceeding, a final report

[10]Testimony of David Matthews, March 29, 1962, p. 2270, Bates 3017, space 1150803b, MP archives.

[11]"Legal Aspects Involved in the Contemplated Merger . . . ," Nov. 4, 1960, Bates 1511, ibid.

[12]"Memo Concerning the Possible Advantage of the Use of Corporate Consolidation in Effecting the Acquisition of Another Railroad by Missouri Pacific," n.d. [Nov., 1960], Bates 1571, ibid.

appeared from Wyer, Dick & Company concluding that the Chicago & Eastern Illinois was in worse shape than had been imagined. C. D. Peet commented that "obviously the C&EI would have little attraction for the Missouri Pacific except for its strategic location." The location was, however, attractive, and the report indicated that the MP could dispose of the eastern branch of the Chicago & Eastern Illinois, perhaps for the cash that would be needed in the merger.[13] On November 21, 1960, Marbury wrote on behalf of the MP board to David Matthews offering almost exactly what the Wyer, Dick report recommended: 1 to 1.6 for the A and 1 to 4 for the common.[14]

Marbury and Matthews met on November 22 and November 30 to discuss the details of this offer. Matthews was not satisfied with either meeting because he could not get a specific commitment from Marbury about how the MP would solve several outstanding difficulties of the merger.[15]

The November 22 meeting accomplished little but the delivery of the offer. However, Matthews followed it later with a letter on November 25 in which he reminded Marbury that the last word the Chicago & Eastern Illinois had was that the MP would use treasury cash to buy it. This offer was an exchange of stock. What about Alleghany, which had told Dearmont it would vote for no new A stock until the B issue was satisfactorily retired? Was this in the offing? If so, the Chicago & Eastern Illinois needed to know of it in order to revise its estimates of the MP's cash position and of the desirability of any merger's going forward. Also, the MP demanded that the provisions of the Chicago & Eastern Illinois bonds be changed so that they would not become fixed-interest obligations at merger. This problem could not be solved within the thirty-day period Marbury had given as a deadline for acting on the latest offer.[16] To insist on that timing was to invite rejection despite the fact that the Chicago & East-

[13] Memo from C.D.P., Nov. 10, 1960, Bates 3029, ibid.

[14] W. G. Marbury to D. Matthews, Nov. 21, 1960, ex. H-81, Bates 3023, ibid.

[15] Testimony of David Matthews, March 29, 1962, pp. 2270–75, Bates 3017, space 1150803b, MP archives.

[16] D. Matthews to W. G. Marbury, Nov. 25, 1960, ex. H-82, Bates 3024, ibid.

ern Illinois had a net loss of almost $700,000 for the first nine months of 1960 and was therefore in a hurry itself.[17]

The meeting of November 30 in Saint Louis was long but still did not answer Matthews's questions. Marbury did not want to be more specific. His idea was that the Chicago & Eastern Illinois board should approve his offer in principle and let developing circumstances determine the details. Matthews was willing to trust neither fate nor Marbury's demonstrated talents.[18] The Louisville & Nashville and perhaps the Southern Pacific were interested in his railroad as a merger partner and might offer more certain if not more lucrative deals. He reported to his board that "it appears to us that Missouri Pacific proposes to use a merger agreement with the C&EI as a '*guinea pig*' and as the vehicle for the solution of Missouri Pacific's vexing problem." The Chicago & Eastern Illinois's financial advisors strongly advised that no merger proposal from the MP be accepted without agreement to its terms in advance and in writing from Alleghany Corporation.[19]

Nothing clicked. Marbury would not extend his thirty-day time limit. He would not agree to an amendment accepting the Chicago & Eastern Illinois bonds as fixed obligations, though he said there would be no problem paying the interest on them. He rejected the idea that there should be guarantees to pay all fixed and contingent obligations on the securities of both railroads before paying dividends on MP A stock. He insisted that the MP have the right to call off the entire merger if the Chicago & Eastern Illinois went bankrupt. He would not change the 1-to-4 exchange ratio for common when Chicago & Eastern Illinois experts suggested that 1 to 2.3 would be fair. Why should the MP have things so much its own way? It needed access to Chicago, and if it did not close with the Chicago & Eastern Illinois, "the Missouri Pacific's last opportunity to secure such access on a rel-

[17] *St. Louis Post Dispatch*, Nov. 28, 1960, CEI clippings, MP public relations office.
[18] David Matthews to C&EI board of directors, Dec. 8, 1960, ex. H-88, Bates 3027, space 1150803b, MP archives.
[19] Ibid.

atively cheap basis will be lost."[20] There was reason to believe that a tough stance by Chicago & Eastern Illinois management would result in a better offer.

In this atmosphere there was no chance for the proposal, presented to both boards in December, 1960. Annoyed at the lack of specifics, the Chicago & Eastern Illinois board turned down the offer. A few days later the MP board voted to terminate all further negotiations with the Chicago & Eastern Illinois.[21] When asked to explain this at the May annual meeting, Dearmont said it was too complex to cover briefly. "We got further apart instead of closer together."[22] The drive to tap Chicago had reached a low ebb.

It appeared for a time that the MP was no longer a factor in the Chicago & Eastern Illinois saga. The Chicago road turned to negotiations with the Louisville & Nashville and the Chicago & Northwestern.[23] However, on June 26, 1961, Matthews warned the Louisville & Nashville that Saint Louis might look north again and strike quickly. Henry Hammack died in September, 1960, and his large block of Chicago & Eastern Illinois stock was up for sale to the highest bidder, not excluding William Marbury. If Marbury were to acquire that stock, he and the MP could exercise enough power to quash the Louisville & Nashville–Chicago & Eastern Illinois merger. Matthews advised the Louisville & Nashville to buy the stock as a protective measure.[24] It did not fancy spending the $1.4 million cash required and refused.[25]

There were rumors at this time that Downing Jenks and W. H. Kendall of the Louisville & Nashville were planning a joint purchase of the Hammack stock, with an understanding

[20] Ibid.

[21] ICC, F.D. 21755, *Brief for the Missouri Pacific Railroad Company*, Sept. 28, 1962, pp. 4–5, MP law dept.

[22] MP Railroad, transcript of stockholders' meeting, May 9, 1961, p. 23, MP archives.

[23] "Brief on Behalf of the Bureau of Inquiry and Compliance of the Interstate Commerce Commission," Oct. 1, 1962, p. 10, Bates 3005, space 1150803b, MP archives.

[24] Testimony of David Matthews, March 29, 1962, pp. 2281–83, Bates 3017c, ibid.

[25] ICC, F.D. 21755, *Brief for the Missouri Pacific Railroad Company*, Sept. 28, 1962, p. 5, MP law dept.

that the Louisville & Nashville would eventually get the eastern portion of the Chicago & Eastern Illinois. The first word in some time that Matthews had gotten direct from the MP, however, was a call from Jenks on August 3, 1961, informing him that the MP had purchased the Hammack stock outright and unilaterally.[26]

MP raised some of the cash for this move by selling its office building in Saint Louis and then leasing it back, but there was no tone of desperation in Jenks's explanation to Matthews.[27] He said that the MP wished the Chicago & Eastern Illinois to remain independent and wanted to keep the Hammack stock from going to the Chicago & Northwestern, the Louisville & Nashville, or the Southern. The MP would make recommendations for the two directors to which the Hammack stock was entitled but would not try to exercise control. Would the MP open the Thebes gateway? Jenks said no. Did not the purchase violate federal statutes because it was not cleared through the ICC? Jenks's view of what constituted control was different. Could not Matthews, Jenks, and Kendall have one more meeting to try to effect a compromise? Certainly.[28]

No compromise was reached at that meeting, which took place August 14. Instead, Kendall told Matthews that the Louisville & Nashville would not stand by waiting for merger hearings while the MP bought stock. The Louisville & Nashville subsequently purchased 150,000 shares of Chicago & Eastern Illinois stock, placed them in trust with the Bank of New York, and, on September 28, filed an application with the ICC to control the Chicago & Eastern Illinois through stock ownership.[29]

The intentions of the Louisville & Nashville were known to the MP directors at their September 13 meeting. Jenks said then that while sharing the Chicago & Eastern Illinois with the Louisville & Nashville would be fine, sole control of it by the

[26] Testimony of David Matthews, March 29, 1962, pp. 2287–88, Bates 3017c, space 1150803b, MP archives.

[27] Ibid., pp. 2283, 2286.

[28] Ibid., pp. 2290–92.

[29] *Brief for the Missouri Pacific Railroad Company*, Sept. 28, 1962, p. 7, MP law dept.

latter would be a disaster for the MP. The MP could take a defensive position by applying for control itself. As the MP attorneys put it later in their application to the ICC: "Mere negative opposition to an application by the L&N would neither improve the precarious financial condition of the C&EI, nor put the Missouri Pacific in the position to maintain a parity with the L&N." The directors authorized $1.5 million for the purchase of additional Chicago & Eastern Illinois stock immediately and added another $1 million to the fund in November.[30] A control application was filed on September 19. Then, as though things were not heady enough, the Illinois Central, fearing a mass invasion of its territory, filed an application for joint control of the Chicago & Eastern Illinois with the MP and the Louisville & Nashville.[31] This was amazing interest in the stock of a railroad that had not paid a dividend since 1957.

The MP was not at this juncture in as strong a position as it would have liked. The Louisville & Nashville acquired a larger block of Chicago & Eastern Illinois stock than the MP, 34 percent compared with the MP's 17 percent.[32] In addition, the MP was in a dangerous legal position because the leverage of its 20,000 shares of A stock might be interpreted as illegal control of the Chicago & Eastern Illinois. The company argued that the purchase of the Hammack stock was authorized by the executive committee and that a control application had been submitted at the next regular directors' meeting a month later. But why was a special meeting not called before the purchase? The company claimed that it had never attempted actually to control the Chicago & Eastern Illinois. But was technical control less a violation because no advantage was taken of it? The company placed all its

[30] MP Railroad, directors' minutes, Sept. 13, 1961, pp. 11–12, Nov. 29, 1961, p. 19, MP archives; "Application of Missouri Pacific Railroad Company . . . for an Order Authorizing it to Acquire Control . . . of the Chicago & Eastern Illinois Railroad Company. . . ." [Sept., 1961], p. 11, Bates 3001, space 1150803b, ibid.

[31] ICC, F.D. 21755, *Brief for the Missouri Pacific Railroad Company*, Sept. 28, 1962, p. 7, MP law dept.

[32] *St. Louis Post Dispatch*, Dec. 29, 1961, CEI clippings, MP public relations office. For a detailed breakdown of MP investments in the C&EI in the late months of 1961, see *Wall Street Journal*, Dec. 5, 1961, ibid.

Chicago & Eastern Illinois stock in trust with the Marine Midland Trust Company of New York in April, 1962.[33] But why was this done only in response to pressure and not at the time of the initial purchase? It was possible that the ICC would rule that the MP had illegally controlled the Chicago & Eastern Illinois, and if it did so, it could disallow the present application on those grounds.

The MP had advantages also in the fight for the Chicago & Eastern Illinois. Marbury and Jenks were modernizing the MP and making it a railroad capable both of financing the purchase and rehabilitation of the Chicago & Eastern Illinois and of operating it efficiently. The MP was a natural geographic partner for the Chicago line and had been joined with it in William Ripley's 1921 ICC plan for the consolidation of the U.S. rail system. While the MP had little interest in the eastern branch of the Chicago & Eastern Illinois, it could and would operate it. The Louisville & Nashville, by contrast, not only had no interest in the western branches, but would be hard pressed to finance their rehabilitation. The Illinois Central lines paralleled the Chicago & Eastern Illinois rather than joining it end to end, and it could therefore be asked if even joint control by that company would not result in slow dismantling of the Chicago & Eastern Illinois and a lessening of competition in the Illinois corridor. Despite possible technical errors in the means the MP used in going after the Chicago & Eastern Illinois, the ICC likely would be favorably influenced in its behalf by the overwhelming cost and operating advantages to shippers and to the public of their consolidation.

The Louisville & Nashville blinked first. It took a plunge by amending its application to ask for sole rather than joint control and then, late in January, 1962, withdrew it altogether. Concurrently, it filed a petition requesting that as a condition of granting control to either the MP or the Illinois Central, the commission require the successful applicant to sell the Chicago &

[33]ICC, F.D. 21755, *Brief for the Missouri Pacific Railroad Company*, Sept. 28, 1962, pp. 6–8, MP law dept.

Eastern Illinois eastern branch to the Louisville & Nashville "at a reasonable price."[34]

In the next months people at the MP primed for a battle. The attorneys prepared a case for ICC hearings, Marbury completed his tender offer to make internal control of the MP by MRFC final, and Russell Dearmont, after thirty years with the company, retired on his seventy-first birthday to leave the field to younger warriors.[35] Marbury and Jenks worked on strategy for what would be perhaps the most important acquisition their company would ever make. If it succeeded, it would prove that the MP was not powerless to expand even given its crippling internal stock problems. If it failed, it would be a blow to the officers' hopes of being one of the survivors of the 1960s drive toward large integrated systems.

The issues were complex and the Illinois Central opposition was stubborn. The MP did not get final ICC approval for its control of the Chicago & Eastern Illinois until 1965, and the Louisville & Nashville did not acquire the Evansville line until 1969. In the interim there were charges of illegal control and of possible conflict of interest arising out of the relation of MRFC to the MP railroad.

The MRFC issue was new and had to be dealt with quickly. It arose when the Chicago & Northwestern, which opposed MP control, argued that MRFC did not want the competition to its gas line represented by the coal hauled by the Chicago & Eastern Illinois from southern Illinois. The closest large consuming area to these fields was Saint Louis, and joining the MP and Chicago & Eastern Illinois would give the latter direct access to that city "if Mississippi River Fuel Corporation doesn't mind." The Chicago & Northwestern attorneys suggested, however, that MRFC did indeed mind and that industries in Saint Louis would not want to offend the pipeline company by patronizing coal fields in Illinois. In addition, there was the issue whether the fuel company now controlled two railroads and whether that re-

[34] Ibid., p. 7; *Journal of Commerce and Commercial*, Oct. 9, 1963, CEI clippings, MP public relations office.

[35] MP Railroad, directors' minutes, Jan. 31, 1962, pp. 14–17, MP archives.

quired it to apply to the ICC separately for permission to do so.[36] Marbury's prominent role in the management of the MP and his primary role in the Chicago & Eastern Illinois negotiations leading to the jettison of the merger plans and move for stock control prompted opposition attorneys to make much of the appropriateness of Mississippi's position.

The major MRFC witness before the ICC examiner was L. B. Tracht, who apppeared in May, 1962. Tracht emphasized that the fuel company was not a holding company designed to control railroads, but a genuine pipeline company with an independent operating history going back thirty years. Railroads were simply part of its attempt to diversify, which included also cement, chemicals, and oil supplies. He admitted that MRFC had sent an attorney to talk with ICC attorneys in 1960 about the Chicago & Eastern Illinois venture and that this attorney had asked specifically about prior cases involving control of two railroads by a nonrailroad company. He would not, however, say this implied that the MRFC now controlled or sought control of the Chicago & Eastern Illinois or for that matter even the MP itself. "In our business of course," he said, "we operate in a goldfish bowl, and we are subject to regulation by Federal Power and the Securities and Exchange Commission, and other regulatory bodies, and we are continually conscious of the fact in any kind of venture we go into what the extent is of regulatory requirements." The attorney's visit was for information only, Tracht stated. No, he did not know whether Marbury personally sought out Jenks for the MP presidency or played much of a part in the Chicago & Eastern Illinois negotiations.[37] Attorneys for the MP knew that criticizing the control application based on the role of MRFC was a legal long shot and were not interested in drawing more attention to the issue than necessary.

MRFC also submitted a formal brief. In it, the company denied that it controlled the MP but stated that even if it were found to control that railroad, that should not stop the MP appli-

---

[36] "Brief of Chicago and North Western Railway Company," Sept. 28, 1962, pp. 39–40, Bates 3004, space 1150803b, MP archives.

[37] L. B. Tracht testimony, May 8, 1962, pp. 2829–59, Bates 3018, ibid.

cation for control of the Chicago & Eastern Illinois. In fact, the MRFC tender offer, which would gain it 50 percent control of the MP, was still pending at the time of the examiner's hearings and it was not certain that it would be successful. On the conflict-of-interest issue, the brief argued that the fuel company did not sell coal in Chicago and that the Chicago & Eastern Illinois route (at least, as it presently existed) was too circuitous to allow its coal to be competitive in Saint Louis.[38] Even after the tender offer went through and there was no question that the MRFC controlled the MP railroad, the fuel company claimed that it employed the major part of its assets in and got most of its revenue from other businesses. Therefore, there was no reason for the ICC to regard it as a holding company with no direct business, or to suggest that it be classed and regulated as a common carrier.[39] This line of argument was eventually successful.

The MP was on shakier ground on the issue of illegal control, and the Illinois Central as well as the Chicago & Eastern Illinois management itself bored in hard on this matter. Matthews of the Chicago line said that the Hammack stock alone constituted control because, though it was not an absolute majority of the voting stock, it had a veto power over merger moves. "With these holdings in Missouri Pacific's hands I was in a position where I had to take my hat in my hand and go talk to them before I could talk merger with anybody."[40]

This could be interpreted as a form of de facto control, although there was room for MP attorneys to argue that it was not technical control and that the MP had not tried to exercise the veto power nor would have. In response to Chicago & Eastern Illinois charges that such control violated not only ICC regulations but the Clayton Anti-Trust Act, the MP attorneys countered that no trust violations could be involved since the two roads were not directly competitive.[41]

[38] "Brief in Support of Supplemental Application on Behalf of Mississippi River Fuel Corporation," Oct. 1, 1962, pp. 1–6, Bates 3003, ibid.
[39] "Exception of Mississippi River Fuel Corporation . . . and Brief in Support Thereof," Jan. 2, 1964, Bates 3007, ibid.
[40] Matthews testimony, March 31, 1962, pp. 2226–27, Bates 3017c, ibid.
[41] *Wall Street Journal*, Jan. 23, 1962, *Traffic World*, Feb. 10, 1962, in CEI clippings, MP public relations office.

But there was an aspect of the illegal control issue more serious than this. While the MP ostensibly held only about 10 percent of the total outstanding stock, despite its over 30 percent holding of the crucial class A shares, stock held by brokers friendly to the MP railroad was another matter. ICC examiners found that in 1962 and 1963, while the control hearings were going on, two brokerage firms—Eastman Dillon, Union Securities & Company and Dempsey-Tegeler & Company—accumulated by agreement with the MP almost $5 million worth of Chicago & Eastern Illinois convertible general mortgage income bonds. These were convertible into over 200,000 shares of common stock, which would give the MP, according to some calculations, over 50 percent ownership in the total outstanding Chicago & Eastern Illinois stock. To add to the atmosphere of suspicion, the firms bought about 60,000 shares of Chicago & Eastern Illinois common stock outright, though both they and the MP denied the stock was subject to any agreement to sell to the railroad on demand. This led to charges that the brokers were guilty of a short-swing insider transaction by profiting through speculation in securities of a company in which they had a large investment on their own account.[42]

Attorneys for the MP met this charge also with their usual vigor. They called the Illinois Central charges, which turned upon the MP's acquiring mathematical control through options with brokers, a "house of cards" constructed upon "semantic quicksand." The MP, through open-market purchases, had raised its holdings in Chicago & Eastern Illinois to over 19 percent of the stock outstanding during the first phase of the hearings, but it would not accept that the bonds held by it or by brokerage firms represented control. "It is apparent," went the MP argument, "that the Illinois Central's design is to beguile the ICC into treating the C&EI's general income bonds as voting stock simply because they are convertible." But there had been no conversion. Even if there were, the percentage of control would amount to 43.67, not 50, as represented. And that figure was accurate only if no other convertible bondholders converted. If all

---

[42] *Wall Street Journal,* Aug. 21, Sept 28, 1964, *St. Louis Post Dispatch,* Sept. 8, 1964, ibid.

of them did, the MP control, even if it converted all its bonds, would amount to only a little over 30 percent of the total stock. The attorneys said that the Illinois Central charge of mathematical control through brokers was "a carefully planned inaccuracy" designed to divert the commission from the real issue of efficiency of operation for the new Chicago & Eastern Illinois, an area where the MP position was strong and that of the Illinois Central weak.[43] Still, no argument would make the various charges of illegal control entirely go away.

However strong were the opponents of an MP takeover of the Chicago & Eastern Illinois on the matter of technical violations, they compensated with the weakness of their position on the all-important matter of what plan served shippers and the public interest best. The Chicago & Eastern Illinois did somewhat better financially during 1962 and 1963, and President Matthews tried for a time to contend that it could and should now remain independent of any partner. He was understandably concerned about the protection of the Chicago & Eastern Illinois security holders and doubtless wanted to find some way of gaining leverage on the MP to work out the best deal possible. He also felt that merger negotiations had been going well for the Chicago & Eastern Illinois both with the MP and the Louisville & Nashville "prior to the interference of the Missouri Pacific's dominant stockholder."[44] However, it was clear that prosperity for an independent Chicago & Eastern Illinois would be temporary. Likewise, the Illinois Central arguments against merger on operating and financial grounds were flimsy. Wayne Johnston, president of the Illinois Central, held that it would be willing to operate the Chicago & Eastern Illinois as a whole, while the MP would probably sell the eastern half to the Louisville & Nashville. The Illinois Central, however, was vulnerable to accusations that it would likely dismember the competitive Chicago & Eastern Illinois and was opposing MP control as a defensive move. Also, there were intimations that the Illinois Central was itself controlled by the Union Pacific and had studied merger

[43] *Traffic World*, Sept. 5, 1964, ibid.
[44] Matthews testimony, [1962], pp. 2, 14, 22–23, Bates 3017a, space 1150803b, MP archives.

with both the MP and the Louisville & Nashville.[45] The Illinois Central had a difficult time appearing to be defending the public interest, and Jenks's statement that it would be "more interested in drying up the C&EI than helping it" had a compelling logic.[46]

By contrast, the MP proposals for operating the Chicago & Eastern Illinois were tremendously attractive, both to shippers and to the ICC. MP witnesses noted that the Chicago line's unusual financial structure made it an unfit candidate for merger, and therefore it would have to be taken by a railroad that could afford to control it with cash purchases. That railroad should be a large, strong, and complementary system like the MP, which would give the bridge line a greater flexibility in car supply, an advantage in industrial development and traffic reciprocity, and less sensitivity to changes in local economic conditions. Mounting labor costs and competition from the highway system had made short-haul railroads with lots of interchanges impractical for the future. Under MP control, delays would be cut by using preblocking and through routes to avoid congested terminals and intermediate yards. This would allow full trains to run over maximum distances and would cut loss and damage incident to yard switching.[47] As one shipper put it, "The strong are going to have to take over the weak. . . . There are too many railroads; it is too difficult for shippers to even make rates with too many people."[48]

Central to the case was the matter of the efficiency of the Chicago & Eastern Illinois Thebes gateway in speeding traffic between the Southwest and Chicago via the MP. The MP hired University of Illinois professor William R. Hay to make a study of the operating savings, and his testimony was impressive. Cars for Chicago and points east could be preblocked at the MP electronic hump yard at Little Rock and transferred in trainload lots to the Chicago & Eastern Illinois at Thebes for movement to Chicago. There need be no breakup or yarding at Thebes and no

[45] *Traffic World*, March 9, 1962, CEI clippings, MP public relations office.
[46] *Wichita Eagle*, March 7, 1962, ibid.
[47] ICC, F.D. 21755, *Brief for the Missouri Pacific Railroad Company*, Sept. 28, 1962, pp. 48–52, MP law dept.
[48] *Traffic World*, March 31, 1962, CEI clippings, MP public relations office.

entry into Saint Louis at all. The route to Chicago via Thebes was thirty-five miles shorter than that via Saint Louis.[49] Even on cars coming into Saint Louis, a nine- to twelve-hour time savings could be effected by eliminating the Chicago line's East Saint Louis Mitchell Yard and routing the cars from the north directly across the river to the MP Twenty-third Street Yard in Saint Louis. The preferred Thebes routing would speed schedules dramatically. A car running from Los Angeles to Chicago would save twelve hours, while the El Paso–to–Chicago savings, where the whole route could be controlled by the MP, would be nearly twenty hours. Pooling of locomotive power between the Chicago & Eastern Illinois and the MP would make over a thousand locomotives available for distribution to points where needed over the entire system from Texas to Illinois.[50] So promising was this operating plan that the main problem the MP had in presenting it was offering adequate protections of existing gateways to insure that the new alliance did not too quickly destroy all the competition.

Given these advantages, it was no surprise that the MP application was considered favorably by the ICC examiner Hyman Blond despite last-minute intervention by the Wabash and a report from the commission's Bureau of Inquiry and Compliance concluding that the MP did acquire stock control of the Chicago & Eastern Illinois in technical violation of ICC rules.[51] Blond, in a report issued in September, 1963, concluded that control by the MP should be recommended to the full commission. There would be some adverse effect upon several railroads serving Chicago, but there was no evidence "that any existing Chicago carrier would play dead or otherwise fail to resist whatever inroads upon its traffic might be produced by acquisition of con-

[49] Ibid., March 7, 8, 1962.

[50] ICC, F.D. 21755, *Brief for the Missouri Pacific Railroad Company*, Sept. 28, 1962, pp. 51, 56, MP law dept.

[51] *Traffic World*, June 16, 23, 1962, Sept. 28, 1963, CEI clippings, MP public relations office; *Evansville Ind. Press*, Oct. 5, 1962, ibid. For a detailed explanation of the evidence for illegal control, see "Brief on Behalf of the Bureau of Inquiry and Compliance of the Interstate Commerce Commission," Oct. 1, 1962, Bates 3005, space 1150803b, MP archives.

trol." He recommended that the applications of the Louisville & Nashville and Illinois Central be denied.[52]

Reaction to examiner Blond's report was mixed. The MP was happy, as the report gave it all it wanted. The Louisville & Nashville was hopeful, though the report guaranteed it nothing. The Illinois Central was bloodied but unbowed, determined to fight to the last. The Chicago & Eastern Illinois was ambivalent, uncertain this was the best arrangement possible, but not sure it was not. The line's directors liked the operating advantages but were worried about the protection of their security holders. Chicago & Eastern Illinois earnings were up since the beginning of the negotiations, and it appeared that the road would have almost as much cash on hand as the MP was paying out to buy it.[53] The ICC Bureau of Inquiry and Compliance was upset with Blond for his leniency on the illegal control issue and filed exceptions to his report, indicating that he erred in finding that stock ownership that was enough to give veto power did not constitute control and in finding that the trust arrangement the MP created late in the game adequately insulated the company.[54] The Chicago & Northwestern was upset that Blond had barred admission of much evidence on the issue of a conflict of interest on the part of MRFC.[55] A substantial group of exceptions briefs were therefore filed early in 1964.

The MP, however, did not seem doubtful of the eventual result. William Marbury stated to the press in October, 1963, that he would not support any reopening of the record in the case and thought Blond had come to exactly the correct conclusions. "We've won the first game by a shutout," he added in characteristic fashion, "and we expect to sweep the series."[56]

[52] *Traffic World*, Sept. 28, 1963, MP public relations office.

[53] *Journal of Commerce and Commercial*, Oct. 7, 1963, ibid.

[54] "Exceptions of the Bureau of Inquiry and Compliance to the Recommended Report and Order by Hearing Examiner Hyman J. Blond," Jan. 6, 1964, Bates 3010, space 1150803b, MP archives.

[55] "Exceptions of Chicago and North Western Railway Company," Jan. 6, 1964, Bates 3011, ibid.

[56] *Journal of Commerce and Commercial*, Oct. 7, 1963, CEI clippings, MP public relations office.

Naturally, more than confident statements were needed, and the MP filed an additional extensive brief early in 1964 restating its position in the strongest possible terms. It noted that there was outright opposition to the takeover of the Chicago & Eastern Illinois by the MP from only two interests—the Illinois Central and the Chicago & Northwestern. The rest simply wanted some of the spinoff action. Even these two based their opposition on the dubious ground that "some innovation in the policies and decisions regarding unification of carriers in derogation of the public interest is involved." This, said MP attorneys, simply was not true. There were few cases in the history of the ICC that more nearly fulfilled congressional policy. It was an end-to-end merger; it joined the strong with the weak, and the generalized with the specialized. The claims that the MP should be barred because it acquired illegal stock control were not supported by the examiner and were "nothing more than suggestions and innuendoes drawn from some unrelated and fragmentary evidence designed to create an illusion of suspicion and intrigue." Nor was there any "Perry Mason routine" regarding the role of MRFC. When the negotiations started, the fuel company did not have control of the MP; and when it acquired such control, there was no attempt to hide it. Car studies pretending to show massive diversion to the new system were based on entirely illegitimate assumptions, including the one that held that railroads rather than shippers and government regulators determine where the traffic will go. The charge that there was a conflict between Chicago & Eastern Illinois coal and MRFC gas, the MP brief characterized as "not really lucid enough to be false; it is mere gibberish." In short, the MP attorneys dismissed the exceptions as either based upon inaccurate information or born of "a desire to confuse the mind and inflame the emotions of the reader."[57] They should not be taken seriously.

Hearings before the full ICC began in January, 1965, and a decision approving MP control of the Chicago & Eastern Illinois

[57] "Reply of Missouri Pacific Railroad Company to Exceptions to the Report Proposed by Examiner H. J. Blond," Feb. 2, 1964, pp. 2–4, 14, 22, 43, 47, 55, Bates 3008, space 1150803b, MP archives.

railroad came in March. The commission *did* find that the MP illegally controlled the Chicago & Eastern Illinois for eight months but ruled that the advantages to the public of MP control of the Chicago road outweighed the violation. Also, the approval contained the condition that the MP negotiate with the Louisville & Nashville and arrange within a year to sell it the Evansville branch of the Chicago & Eastern Illinois. The sixty-page decision, based on a study of 6,000 pages of hearing transcripts and 200 exhibits, concluded that "the need, in present-day railroading, for high-speed and heavy-duty facilities, for expeditious and direct long-line transport, for specialized equipment and tailor-made service, and for the other qualities demanded by a shipping pubic engaged in the keen competition which marks our national economy, makes it essential that Eastern [Chicago & Eastern Illinois] have access to revitalizing resources outside of itself, if it is to survive as a positive and contributing element of the national transportation system."[58]

The Illinois Central and the Monon Route (Chicago, Indianapolis & Louisville) objected strongly to the decision. Both applications for a rehearing were denied, but the Illinois Central carried its battle against MP control into the courts, claiming that the majority report from the ICC was "incredible" and that the views of the minority on the commission, who thought the rule violations on control were entitled to greater weight, should be heeded.[59] The Cotton Belt joined the cause and the case made its way through the courts, but it was a losing proposition. The commission's decision was upheld at all levels including the U.S. Supreme Court, which heard the case in the October term of 1966. The MP there argued successfully that the questions raised by the Illinois Central in this case were "collateral issues" that in no way compromised the conclusion that MP control was

[58] *Brief on Intervening Defendant Missouri Pacific Railroad Company in Support of the Commission's Order,* IC Railroad Co. et al vs. United States of America and ICC, et al., Civil Action No. 65 C 1393, U.S. District Court for the Northern District of Illinois Eastern Division, p. 6; *Traffic World,* March 13, 1965, and *Railway Age,* March 15, 1965, CEI clippings, MP public relations office.

[59] *Traffic World,* April 3, 14, 24, 1965, CEI clippings, MP public relations office.

overwhelmingly beneficial. "Appellant's opposition," wrote the MP attorneys, "while perhaps understandable, is far from commendable when viewed in the light of the public interest."[60]

Thus was the last legal barrier surmounted in what was without question one of the most successful consolidations of the 1960s. The MP increased its stockholdings in Chicago & Eastern Illinois to 40 percent in 1967 and placed four people on the fourteen-person board.[61] Work was begun in earnest on the physical rehabilitation of the new Chicago connection. Over the previous ten years 600,000 ties had been laid, while proper procedures would have required 900,000, and only about half the proper number of rails per year had been laid. Yard Center, a vital switching facility on the Chicago & Eastern Illinois, was found by MP people to be wholly inadequate and the repair shops "highly inefficient." To use the Thebes gateway properly, however, Jenks planned to run freights on accelerated schedules with heavy loads, running up to 137,000 pounds on four axles.[62] Therefore, the line was simply rebuilt at late-1960s prices. In speaking to the Chicago & Eastern Illinois board, Downing Jenks said that revenue per car was too low, the cost per car too high, and the switching needs too extensive. Much of the rail was forty-five years old, and "we'd spend the money picking up wrecks if we don't spend the money for maintenance." Cost of rehabilitation was set at $4.7 million for 1967, $5 million for 1968, and $5.6 million for 1969.[63]

This program resulted in net losses for the Chicago & Eastern Illinois for several years, but some of the slack in cash was taken up by the sale of the Evansville branch to the Louisville & Nashville in the spring of 1968 and by the discontinuance of all four of the Chicago road's passenger trains.[64] By the early 1970s it was clear from skyrocketing earnings on the Chicago & East-

[60] "Motion to Affirm of Appellee Missouri Pacific Railroad Company," in Bates 3012, space 1150803b, MP archives.

[61] *St. Louis Post Dispatch*, Feb. 16, March 10, 1967, CEI clippigs, MP public relations office.

[62] Draft report, May 5, 1967, CEI notebook, ibid.

[63] C&EI Railroad, transcript of stockholders' meeting, May 12, 1967, ibid.

[64] Jenks's comments, May 10, 1968, ibid.; *The Star* (Chicago Heights, Ill.), June 12, 1969, CEI clippings, ibid.; *St. Louis Post Dispatch*, March 13, 1968, ibid.

ern Illinois line that the MP's purchase and $15 million rehabili-
tation of the line was one of the wisest moves the MP ever made.

"In the early days, it was easy," Jenks later mused in thinking about the Chicago & Eastern Illinois deal. "The things that
needed to be done were so obvious."[65] MP management only
wished that every other enterprise it undertook during the
1960s had worked even half so well.

[65] Interview with Jenks, March 13, 1979, Saint Louis.

# CHAPTER VI

# *Alleghany and Others*

WILLIAM MARBURY was not one to base his future on the success or failure of a single plan. Therefore, it will not be surprising to learn that at the height of the negotiations and hearings over the Chicago & Eastern Illinois, the MP was developing other means of solving its stock problem through merger. For however desirable the Chicago line might be as a cash acquisition, that means of takeover did nothing to eliminate the veto power of the MP B stockholders. While that power existed, and while that class of stock was controlled by the powerful Alleghany Corporation, concerns entirely separate from the stock question could not and did not really exist for the MP. In all and through all appeared this class stockholding specter—the legacy of the reorganization.

An analysis of the MP made by Pierre Bretey of Hayden, Stone & Company in 1956 recognized both the power of the B interest and the unusual savvy of those who had invested in that stock. The B, he then wrote, was "a most unusual common stock. There is no other equity of which we are aware which possesses so much leverage." Bretey personally thought that it was "almost inconceivable" that the ICC should have approved such a "fag end" and small issue of stock in the first place but confessed that its holders were making the most of their opportunities. "The Burgundians of old, in fabled history," he concluded, "were stout-hearted men. Admittedly the Class 'B' stock is a vehicle only for the stout-hearted speculator of today."[1] Lauck

---

[1] Hayden, Stone report, March 8, 1956, Bretey exhibit 1, space 0616102a, MP archives.

Walton, who was one of Alleghany's principal attorneys through the 1960s, in retrospect agreed with this assessment: "No one had any business buying the B stock who was not a very sophisticated businessman indeed. It was not penny-ante speculators' stock. It was speculative, but only for big boys."[2]

None of the B holders were any more stout-hearted or any more committed than the managers of Alleghany Corporation. Alleghany had invested almost $80 million in the MP in the 1930s. It had been forced in 1939 to dispose of three-quarters of its preferred shares at a loss of $20 million and then see its remaining $59 million in securities decline to a value of $480,000 and be classed by the ICC as virtually valueless. After the long reorganization struggle resulting in the issuance of the B stock, Alleghany "for aesthetic reasons" increased its control of that class to 52 percent and then for definitely economic reasons tenaciously defended its foothold in the MP through the years.[3] Even when the prospects were dimmest, as in 1950 when Alleghany much reduced the book value of its MP common stock, it insisted that the "potential value" of its investment in the railroad was "substantial."[4]

The 1960s, when the railroad began to make money and had prospects of valuable mergers, was no time for Alleghany to soften its stand. On the contrary, the stout hearts in New York sensed final vindication and pledged, not only because of nostalgia about those who had fought the fight before them but out of economic common sense, never to sacrifice their MP interest for less than a figure far higher than what almost any B holder before 1960 would have dreamed possible. If such an offer were not forthcoming, Alleghany was satisfied to remain a stockholder in the MP, trusting that Jenks's success with the operation of the railroad would soon begin to yield large dividends, all of which, after the $5 a share was paid to the A stock, would accrue to the B. Also, the equity value of the railroad was increasing at a rapid

[2] Interview with M. Lauck Walton, March 12, 1980, New York City.

[3] Alleghany Corporation, *Annual Report 1963*, pp. 3–4. Interview with Clifford Ramsdell, March 11, 1980, New York City.

[4] C. L. Peckham to Alleghany Corporation, Nov. 15, 1950, doc. 800532, index Alleghany discovery documents, space 0610102a, MP archives; Minutes of Alleghany Executive Committee, Dec. 16, 1950, doc. 800534, ibid.

rate, and the B holders believed that was also theirs to claim. There were even thoughts that Alleghany might want not only to hold on to its present interest but buy a controlling interest in the A stock as well, thus unifying MP management under the aegis of Alleghany rather than MRFC. Marbury of MRFC was of course not interested in that and was outspoken on the worthlessness of the pretensions of the B holders. Allan Kirby and Cliff Ramsdell of Alleghany were equally capable of extreme and colorful rhetoric in their defense. The field was set for one of the most interesting stock fights of modern corporate history.

If Alleghany officers had been distracted from their devotion to the interest of the B stock by the internal struggles following the suicide of Robert Young in the late 1950s, the appearance in the MP management of William Marbury and MRFC called the soldiers there back to attention.

At the MP stockholders' meeting on May 9, 1961, there were objections from B holders to the issuance of new stock for the purpose of providing a stock option plan for Jenks and others in the management team. Marbury told the questioners that he had contacted Alleghany Corporation about this move and that it approved. The "sophisticated, seasoned men" there, Marbury said, realized that the B had no value at all unless the railroad operations were a success, and that this option plan would help insure that.[5] Actually, Marbury had not contacted Alleghany directly at all, but rather notified Empire Trust Company, which had voted Alleghany's MP stock ever since Robert Young's interest in the New York Central had forced the arrangement to prevent antitrust violations. So upset was Alleghany over Empire's acquiescence to Marbury's stock-option plan that it made an immediate attempt to escape the trust arrangement, which had been in force since 1957. The vote of Empire Trust for the stock-option plan, Alleghany officers said, did the B holders potential harm in that the option was for officers to buy A stock and would give them incentive to take action favoring the A stock at the expense of the B.[6] Alleghany said that it was safe for it to be re-

[5] MP Railroad, transcript of stockholders' meeting, May 9, 1961, pp. 39–41, microfilm, MP archives.

[6] *Des Moines Register*, Oct. 31, 1961, Alleghany clippings, MP public relations office.

leased from the trust agreement as it had a "very modest" percentage of the railroad's voting power and could not exercise
control. The MP, in arguing against freeing Alleghany from the
trust, held that the B stock was "highly leveraged" and did in
fact have great veto power.[7] In 1962 the ICC ruled that Alleghany must stick with the trust arrangement.[8] But the issue had
awakened the giant, and it was up and kicking.

The stock-option plan was a bone of contention, but at the
May, 1961, stockholders' meeting Marbury did not leave it at
that. He used the occasion also to expound his views of the status of the B stock in general in language well calculated to throw
down the gauntlet; it was a battle he was certain he could win.
When told that Alleghany could not vote its stock and questioned about what he meant when he said he had the approval of
Alleghany, Marbury said that he did not understand the legal
ramifications and was not interested in going back over the history of the reorganization to argue about the respective rights of
the classes of stock. He was looking to the future. He made no
secret, however, of his opinion that the B was a highly speculative stock that would be better eliminated if the MP were to
progress the way he wished it to.

> What its value will be and when it will be of value, I have no no-
> tion. I don't believe that it's the type of security that you offer
> these key people, even one of which can contribute this half of
> million through unusual executive ability and accomplishment. I
> think you leave the B to those sophisticated people and those
> people who can afford it to speculate very substantially. Now,
> that's my view. . . . But it's a class of stock that should never have
> been issued in my opinion, and it's traded at phenomenal prices
> created by people who have imaginary visions of its speculative
> worth. . . . It's like a bad eye or deaf ear. We go on with it. Maybe
> it will be worth something, but I can't see that far and I wish it
> weren't there.[9]

This was not the sort of statement likely to smooth relations with
Alleghany.

[7] *Traffic World*, Oct. 28, 1961, ibid.
[8] *Wall Street Journal*, March 9, 1962, ibid.
[9] MP Railroad, transcript of stockholders' meeting, May 9, 1961, pp. 44–45, MP
archives.

It was usually assumed by MP management during these years that the stock question would be solved by a merger in which the classes defined by the reorganization would disappear in a new stock issue. As has been seen, there was an early possibility of using a Chicago & Eastern Illinois merger for this purpose. More promising than that, however, was a possible merger of the MP with the Texas & Pacific Railroad, in which it had long had a dominant interest. Here, the recapitalization that could result from a merger would not be so likely to meet with external opposition, or to result in a delay in control that might cause loss of the potential partner, as was the case with the Chicago & Eastern Illinois. MP in essence already controlled the Texas & Pacific through historical connection and substantial stock ownership, and it had not formally integrated it into the system only because of the negative conclusions of the lengthy study resulting in the Suggs report of 1958. Those conclusions had met with some objection even in 1958 when Russell Dearmont, for example, questioned the operating figures used and emphasized the advantage that might come from a consolidation, which in his opinion would not in this case require a class vote.[10] When MRFC took control of the MP in 1962 and the merger movement throughout the nation heated up, there was more reason still to reconsider the device of merging with the friendly Texas & Pacific in such a way as to resolve the A-B stock question.

This kind of speculation led to a great deal of internal discussion, and to an unsigned and unaddressed memo that became the subject of much discussion in later litigation. Entitled "Proposed Stock Recapitalization to Facilitate Merger," dated September 23, 1963, and marked "Confidential," the document summarized some of the possibilities for the MP. First, the memo concluded that an ordinary merger could be blocked by the B shares, though they represented only 2 percent of the shares outstanding. On the other hand, the A stock, which represented 98 percent of the total stock, had only "limited incentive" to maximize earnings in any one year so long as earnings

---

[10] Deposition of Robert Craft, June 27, 1972, space 0610102a, ibid.

were adequate to pay the $5 dividend to which it was entitled. "In fact," the memo continued, "it would be only normal and human, in periods of peak earnings, to maximize those improvements which may be expensed . . . so that maximum dividends might be paid on the 'A' shares in leaner years." Knowing this, the B stockholders would be reluctant to authorize increased shares of any kind to facilitate a merger unless convinced that the A holders would pass along some of the possibly improved earnings in the form of dividends on the B.[11] There were real prospects that the A dividend would soon reach $5 (it did so in 1964), and therefore the issue was hardly academic.

The memo went on to suggest that a way around this impasse was to offer an exchange of both the A and B stock for a single class of shares in a new corporation formed by the MP to consolidate several of its subsidiaries, including the Texas & Pacific. The Chicago & Eastern Illinois, if it were acquired, could be included in such a consolidation as could the Muskogee Lines, a group of Oklahoma short lines that the MP had recently acquired for cash on favorable terms. Another method would be to create a new convertible preferred stock in exchange for the A and a common stock issued in part to the B. There would be enough of this common, however, to allow the A stockholders, after converting their preferred, to control it and thus keep the B people from preventing a merger.[12]

This thinking was not greatly different than the ideas passed around regularly since 1956. However, the last part of the memo suggested a policy that had been suspected by the B holders, but of which they had never had any hard evidence—namely, that there was some thought by the A holders of manipulating the market price of the B shares downward in order to effect a freeze-out or buy-out of their interest at a low figure. The memo stated that it would be wise for MP management to emphasize to all regulatory bodies the necessity for making high capital expenditures on the road, maintaining an adequate tax reserve, and in general finding ways to reinvest earnings that might otherwise be claimed as dividends by the B holders. Actually, this

[11] Confidential memo, Sept. 23, 1963, Craft exhibit 19, ibid.
[12] Ibid.

was not a difficult thing to do, as it was extremely hard to prove in a court of law that the judgment of any group ought to be substituted for that of a company board of directors regarding what were appropriate expenses and retained earnings and what it was appropriate to pay as dividends to any stock class. Also, methods of reporting earnings could be chosen in such a way as to most prominently illustrate that class A dividends were likely to increase while class B dividends were unlikely to exist in the foreseeable future. These policies, the memo suggested, would likely "reverse the present price relationship of the two classes" and bring the quoted market price for the B shares "more nearly in line with their per share earnings and dividend prospects." Once the market had been so "pre-conditioned," the MP could propose a merger with an exchange ratio between A and B to its liking, with every prospect that the ICC would approve.[13]

The contents of this memorandum were not known to Alleghany or the other B holders at the time of its composition. It became known only in the early 1970s when the discovery procedures in connection with a dividend suit against the MP allowed it to be copied from the company archives. Even then, MP officers who were examined denied knowledge of its authorship and in fact denied ever having seen it. Downing Jenks, for example, called the tone of the memo "impertinent and improper" and said in 1972 that if he had known who had written it he would have fired him. Jenks said he was especially offended by the suggestion in the memo that there was a regular method used by MP management to manipulate the market price of the B stock and thought that the entire document was "messed up."[14] The fact remains, however, that the memo was written in 1963, was marked "Confidential," and was in the files of the MP. It must be concluded that someone saw it and that the thinking in it must have reflected the views of some internal interest group. Certainly, all of it except the comments about stock price manipulation may be accepted as current thinking among top managers about how possibly to deal with the stock situation

[13] Ibid.
[14] Jenks deposition, June 22, 1972, pp. 202–206, ibid.

through merger. The evidence for that is simply what immediately occurred with regard to the Texas & Pacific.

Marbury and Jenks did not accept the conclusions of the 1958 Suggs study about the operating liabilities of merger with the Texas & Pacific. Jenks later said about the study that "it's absolutely wrong and we proved it wrong." He deduced that the reason the report came to negative conclusions was that some members of the study team were officers of the Texas & Pacific and were afraid that merger would cost them their jobs. "They did not realize at that time that it would take so long that everybody would be retired by the time the merger finally took place."[15] Marbury felt that the creation of a new company into which the MP, the Texas & Pacific, and possibly the Muskogee Lines could be merged was the only way the A-B stock problem could be solved. Direct negotiations with Alleghany concerning purchase of its B interest for cash, or even some kind of simple exchange for MRFC stock, would be difficult. Alleghany's tax situation was such that it was likely to need a large capital gain against which to offset the loss in relation to book value it would take on the sale of the B stock. Until it had such a gain, it was better off to retain the B stock and let the MP management team make it more valuable, while consistently agitating for dividends.

As early as 1961, there were rumors that negotiations were going on between Marbury and the Murchisons, temporarily in control of Alleghany, concerning dumping an old obligation in which they had no emotional interest in favor of the creation of a single class of common stock for the MP. Marbury said at the 1961 stockholders' meeting that he thought this would be a good idea "if it could be afforded." However, he did not believe it could be. Whether they had an emotional and historical commitment to the B or not, the Murchisons would sit on it, said Marbury, "because I'm not inclined to disbelieve that that's what I'd do, and they're smarter than I am, or at least as smart, probably smarter." Still, the MP would contact Alleghany and ask them "when they would like to be reasonable men."[16] Mean-

---

[15] Ibid., June 21, 1972, pp. 147–50.
[16] MP Railroad, transcript of stockholders' meeting, May 9, 1961, MP archives.

while, the railroad would attempt to get rid of the leverage of the B by other means.

Late in 1963 Marbury and Jenks pursued in earnest the idea of merging the Texas & Pacific with the MP by incorporating both into a new company, which would be called the Texas & Missouri Pacific Railroad Company and which actually was incorporated in Delaware.[17] The MP commissioned three studies by "outside experts," who were to recommend what might be a proper exchange ratio of the 10.5 million shares of common stock authorized for the new company for shares of MP A and B stock. Pierre Bretey of Hayden, Stone & Company did one of the studies; Isabel Benham and Charles Bergmann of R. W. Pressprich did a second; and William Wyer of Wyer, Dick & Company provided a third. All of the consultants came to Saint Louis for a thorough discussion of their findings with Marbury, Jenks, Lloyd, Suggs, and several attorneys. When Miss Benham and Mr. Bergmann arrived from New York about noon on November 25, the group had lunch, and the meeting, which lasted the rest of the day, began.[18] It was one of the most significant in its implications ever held in the history of the railroad.

Pierre Bretey passed out copies of his written conclusions and spoke first. "At the outset," he began, "one must characterize the Class B shares as a financial aberration." The reorganization of the MP itself, from which the present stock difficulties sprang, Bretey thought, "represented a violation of all accepted financial canons." However, the B in fact did have a veto power under the reorganization plan over any mergers the MP might wish to undertake, and it was Bretey's view that the B therefore had a substantial dollar value that would have to be considered in any exchange designed to eliminate it. "Unpalatable as this may seem to Missouri Pacific's management," he reported, "the price for . . . voluntary cooperation by Alleghany and likeminded shareholders in the elimination of the Class B, may well come high." Modern methods of evaluating stocks tended to

[17] *Dallas Morning News*, Dec. 5, 1963, Alleghany clippings, MP public relations office.

[18] Deposition of Isabel Benham, June 20, 1972, pp. 14–15, space 0610102a, MP archives.

emphasize earnings rather than dividends. There had been in the past few years not only large increases in the earnings of the MP but substantial reduction in the debt obligations coming prior to the B, all of which tended, in Bretey's view, to increase the value of that security. He therefore recommended an exchange ratio that recognized an 18-to-1 value difference between the B and A stock. He suggested that negotiations might start with an attempt to deal with the minority B stockholders at a more favorable rate: initial offers to Alleghany might legitimately be as low as 12 to 1. But the MP must be prepared to go higher eventually. Alleghany had a strategic position and was staffed by sophisticated people, who would not accept anything less. Bretey concluded:

> It is indeed ironic that the situation which arose as a mere figment of the imagination of Mr. Hart, Alleghany's attorney, has finally come to pass. This situation may not be a pleasant one for Missouri Pacific's management to contemplate. Yet, it was the prior condition by which Alleghany allowed the reorganized Missouri Pacific to come into being and it is far better to be adequately forewarned of the problem than to ignore it. Hence, our suggestion that Missouri Pacific's management recognize that painful though it might be to pay through the nose for Alleghany's minority interests, delays will doubtless compound the problem in the future and force an even more costly ultimate solution should Alleghany decide to hold its Missouri Pacific B stock indefinitely, in the face of what they would consider an inadequate offer by Missouri Pacific's management.[19]

Bretey had been a leading expert on stock values in Wall Street since 1919, and his opinion was entitled to respect. However, the MP officers and attorneys questioned him closely both on the proposed exchange ratio and on his suggestion that the minority holders of B stock be dealt with separately from Alleghany Corporation. It was clear to those present that William Marbury, at least, would not stand still for an offer on the order of 18 to 1, expert or no expert, and would not be at all interested in approaching the B holders directly with an offer to buy their

[19] Bretey memorandum to D. B. Jenks, J. T. Suggs, D. Peet, M. Hennelly, W. R. McDowell, G. P. Strolinger, n.d. [Nov., 1963], Craft exhibit 20, in ibid.

stock, as Bretey suggested, in preference to handling the matter through a merger.[20] Before he would sacrifice that much, he had several other ideas. The attorneys were certain it would be unwise to deal with some of the B holders on a different basis than others, although there was nothing strictly illegal about it at the time. It would have an obvious ring of unfairness and might jeopardize the whole of any deal that was made.[21]

Next came the report from Pressprich. Isabel Benham submitted an analysis of the legal factors involved in mergers generally. She emphasized that fairness to minority stockholders should be based on a statistical estimate of the contribution of their holdings to the earning power of a merged road over a long period, rather than simply on the current market price of the stock.[22] Charles Bergmann then gave an oral report to the meeting and Miss Benham passed out copies of worksheets, though written copies of the entire report were not distributed to everyone present. The conclusions, while perhaps not as shocking to those assembled as Bretey's, nonetheless again assigned the B great value in any merger. Bergmann and Benham presented a complicated plan for a Texas & Pacific merger, but one that when reduced to ratios set the B at about 1 to 7 in value to the A.[23]

Benham remembered later that it was "very hard for people to ask questions when they have such a volume of statistics presented to them," but she did recall that Marbury was vocal about the inaccuracy of this report, as he thought it overvalued the B stock. He himself had sold some of his MP B stock at $500, he said, and it was not worth even that. Benham and Bergmann were not bothered by this. Benham testified later that the study was done with no prior instructions from the MP (Bretey said the same thing). "We do mathematical calculations," Benham stated, "and the numbers fall where they do."[24]

William Wyer also gave an entirely oral report, but one that took a radically different tack from the others. Instead of basing

[20] Deposition of Downing Jenks, Sept. 20, 1972, pp. 244-45, ibid.
[21] Deposition of Pierre Bretey, June 20, 1972, pp. 21–22, ibid.
[22] Isabel Benham to C. D. Peet, Nov. 26, 1963, Davis exhibit 14, ibid.
[23] Deposition of Isabel Benham, June 20, 1972, pp. 14, 21, ibid.
[24] Ibid., pp. 17, 29.

the valuation on potential future earnings, as had both other consultants, Wyer thought the prime question was the likelihood of dividends on the B stock. He saw many more expenses in his crystal ball than did the others and emphasized the necessity of maintaining large contingency reserves against what otherwise might be net income available for dividends. Taking these factors into account, Wyer recommended that a fair value ratio between the MP A and B was 1 to 1.[25] Wyer, Dick & Company of Upper Montclair, New Jersey, was no less a force among experts than the other two. The firm had been involved in nearly every rail merger hearing since its establishment in the late 1930s.

Naturally, the MP officers present were especially eager to embrace the Wyer, Dick report. Downing Jenks summarized his reaction.

> This surprised us, because we had not been thinking along that line, but I'll admit that I was very much swayed by Mr. Wyer's arguments. He pointed out the terrific debt that the Railroad had. He pointed out the money that would have to be spent in upgrading our equipment, upgrading our track, rebuilding our yards, rebuilding our shops, the amount of money that would have to be spent for equipment, and having just been spending most of my time out on the property and being very mindful of the terrible job that we had ahead of us in the years, the coming years, and the amount of money it would take, his arguments that the cash requirements of the company were such that he did not think the "B" would ever get a dividend [made sense].

Jenks remembered later that the group of officers did not necessarily accept Wyer's premise that the value of a stock ought to be based on its dividend potential, but they were in agreement about the possible negative effect on earnings of high maintenance.[26] Therefore, the 1-to-1 ratio appealed to them as the one to go with in making up a proxy booklet for the proposed merger of the MP and Texas & Pacific into the new Texas & Missouri Pacific.

[25] Wyer, Dick & Co. to C. D. Peet, marked "Personal," Nov. 29, 1963, Craft exhibit 21, ibid.
[26] Deposition of Jenks, June 22, 1972, pp. 178–00, ibid.

There were serious questions immediately and later about the objectivity of the Wyer report, and about the extent to which MP officers were impartial in hearing the arguments of the consultants and in presenting their conclusions to the directors and stockholders later. Bretey said that it seemed to him Marbury wanted to hear that the B had relatively little value and would commission reports until he found one that confirmed this predilection. Bretey thought that Wyer's report was honest but that he was tied to the pessimistic atmosphere of the 1940s reorganization and did not have the idea that the Southwest would grow to the extent it did. Marbury and Suggs spoke most at the November meetings. Suggs's questions, according to Bretey's recollection, were mostly matters of clarification, while Marbury actively sought to knock down the testimony of Bretey and Bergmann, leaving Wyer almost entirely alone.[27] This atmosphere, combined with the wide difference between the other reports and Wyer's plus the immediate acceptance of the latter as the basis for the merger, led to suspicion. It could be recalled that William Wyer had worked for the MP railroad as its treasurer until 1938, and that the company had financed the original organization of Wyer's office as an independent consultant.[28] Perhaps these close ties were not entirely forgotten as Wyer considered the statistics upon which his 1-to-1 exchange recommendation was based.

Actually, it is unlikely that Marbury or other officers actively tried to influence the consultants' reports. All the consultants later testified that they had received no guidance whatever from the railroad, and Bretey said that he was unaware until the day of the meeting that other experts were even being used. Mark M. Hennelly, who was Marbury's chief legal advisor at the time and general solicitor of the MP railroad, is a man with unusually detailed recall. In a 1979 interview he remembered those times and said that in 1963 he was in almost daily contact with Marbury concerning the Texas & Pacific merger. Hennelly believed then and fifteen years later still believed that the MP was

[27] Deposition of Bretey, June 20, 1972, pp. 25–26, ibid.
[28] Transcript of Hearings, Nov. 14, 1938, pp. 333–38, ICC F.D. 9918, box 740, space 9340303a, Underground Storage, Hutchinson.

on strong legal ground in proposing that the merger could have been undertaken without a class vote. He granted, however, that perhaps none of the management, including Marbury, fully understood the dangers of the stock situation, and therefore in going with the merger probably did not choose the strongest possible vehicle. Hennelly said that Marbury was interested in a 1-to-1 ratio before the consultants were ever thought of, and saw it as a "floor" in a plan to be submitted to the ICC for their deliberation. In the earliest conversations, in fact, Marbury asked Hennelly if it would be legally possible to submit the merger plan to the commission with no recommended exchange ratio at all, leaving it entirely up to that body to determine one. When the consultants were called in everyone was surprised that Wyer recommended 1 to 1, but no one was surprised that, when he did, Marbury grasped at it. Others at the meeting were not so sure of their preferences. Hennelly preferred the Pressprich recommendation.[29] Jenks was perhaps doubtful about going with the Wyer plan: at least he later commented that the merger attempt might have been successful with a 5-to-1 or so ratio, but "we were just too tight."[30]

Certainly, however, even the officers present would confess that in the face of a will and personality such as that of William Marbury, the scholarly reports of consultants about what could or should be done in railroad finance were at best beside the point—a sort of formal prelude to the real action. Ultimately, it would be a contest of will and savvy between the leadership at MP and that at Alleghany. Both would have the reports of "experts" backing their point of view.

The men at Alleghany recognized these corporate truths well enough and knew the element of bluff and bravado present in it all. They also knew that even the most unlikely of Marbury's ideas had a way of translating themselves into reality, and that reaction to such a proposal as the 1-to-1 A-B exchange in the Texas & Pacific merger must be immediate and stated in the strongest possible language.

[29] Interview with M. M. Hennelly, July 10, 1979, Saint Louis.
[30] Interview with Jenks, March 13, 1979, Saint Louis.

It did not help the disposition of Allan Kirby that the announcement of the plan to merge the Texas & Pacific on these terms came to him, whether by accident or design, at a victory celebration commemorating his retaking control of Alleghany Corporation from the Murchison brothers.[31] It must have seemed to Kirby that the old B stock fight followed him like Banquo's ghost wherever he was and cropped up whenever things were going smoothly. Kirby characterized the 1-to-1 exchange ratio as "preposterous."[32] Most of the holders of B stock, including Alleghany, were thinking of about a 20-to-1 ratio, something like what Bretey had proposed, and many were not willing to accept even that. "Some members of the trade," wrote an Arkansas newspaper, "are wondering whether the management is really serious in its proposed merger terms."[33] Kirby did not doubt that they were serious, and he employed attorneys to work out a strategy of resistance. "We aren't irrevocably committed to any of our current investments," he told a *Wall Street Journal* reporter, "but while we hold them we are completely committed to their protection."[34]

Attorneys at the New York firm of Donovan, Leisure, Newton & Irvine, representing Alleghany, made a careful analysis of the intentions of MP management in order to advise Kirby on an appropriate action. John Tobin and Lauck Walton of the law firm were particularly active in advising on this section of Alleghany's business and met regularly with Clifford Ramsdell and John Burns of Alleghany over the next years. Walton and Tobin both felt that the Texas & Pacific merger proposal at 1 to 1 was a bluff. However, Wyer's report provided Marbury with a way to propose a low exchange ratio and to get the merger case before the ICC. There the stock case proper would be combined with the merger issue, and the public interest in the desirability of the merger would have to be taken into account along with the

[31] Interview with Clifford Ramsdell, March 11, 1980, New York City.

[32] *Wall Street Journal*, Dec. 9, 1963, Alleghany clippings, MP public relations office.

[33] *Arkansas Gazette*, Dec. 22, 1963, enclosed in Charles Ireland to Albert Barnes, Dec. 27, 1963, MP law dept.

[34] *Wall Street Journal*, Dec. 5, 1963, Alleghany clippings, MP public relations office.

legitimate interests of the B holders. Walton reasoned that the Wyer report was the result of pressure from MP officers and that the "outrageous" conclusions of that report were a ploy designed as a starting point in a struggle directed at the B holders.[35] Tobin guessed that if the case went to the ICC, given all the legal devices Alleghany could and would use, it would be there "until we were all grandfathers."[36] Therefore, the Alleghany strategy was to delay the submission of the merger proposal to the MP stockholders and try centering the battle in another arena.

The obvious way to do this was to file a lawsuit questioning the legal right of the MP to propose a merger to be effected without a class vote of its stockholders. Although the class-vote provision was clearly enough written into the MP charter, the technique of creating a third company into which to merge both the MP and the Texas & Pacific clouded the voting-rights issue, as did the bureaucratic procedures that would ordinarily be connected with a merger. The ICC, if it felt that a merger were in the public interest, had the power to override state law and charter requirements with regard to stock procedures. Tobin and Walton felt that a lawsuit could stop this line of procedure. Both thought that Marbury had made a mistake in accepting the Wyer report as the basis for the merger proposal. Doubtless, he never imagined that there would be a lawsuit in which questions of misleading the public would be raised. Rather, he predicted that the Wyer proposal was the initial salvo in what would be an "insiders'" struggle between sophisticated backers of Alleghany and MRFC, carried out largely before regulatory agencies. Marbury saw the Wyer report, thought Walton, as a "bargaining ploy and got carried away with his own rhetoric and public statements about it." In so doing, he handed Alleghany an advantage, since the arguments in a voting-rights lawsuit could begin with the strong premise that the Texas & Pacific exchange proposal was grossly unfair on the face of it.[37] This argument, in fact, was eventually to move the justices of the U.S. Supreme Court to some of the strongest negative language they had ever used with

[35] Interview with Lauck Walton, March 12, 1980, New York City.
[36] Interview with John Tobin, March 10, 1980, New York City.
[37] Ibid., and interview with Walton.

regard to a corporate maneuver, confirming Tobin and Walton's early hunches beyond their expectations.

The people at Alleghany were receptive to the idea that it was time to sue. The chance of influencing the MP board internally through T. C. Davis had come to an end when Davis broke with Kirby and backed the Murchisons during the Alleghany proxy fight.[38] But even had Davis remained a factor, the outrage of Alleghany management at the latest merger proposal combined with their sense that here was the most favorable ground upon which to make a stand would doubtless have led to the lawsuit anyway. Ramsdell vividly recalls the particular pain of the announcement of the merger coming on the day of the Kirby victory celebration, December 4, 1963: "It was the equivalent of a declaration of war on the first day back on the job."[39]

It was obvious that Alleghany had a fight on its hands that would not be a matter of a few months, but might well dominate the decade. If the MP was capable of what Alleghany people saw as the "unbelievable fantasy" of placing the B on equal footing with the A stock in the merger when the B had a market price seven times that of the A, Kirby had no choice but to tell the press the plan was "morally indefensible" and to consider a lawsuit.[40]

The day following the announcement of the MP merger plan, Alleghany put its defense in action. At a board meeting on December 5, the management told the directors it would litigate the class-vote issue and buy additional B stock in order to "protect its price."[41] This seemed especially wise after attorney John Tobin explained the Texas & Pacific merger proposal to the board and said there was the good possibility of Alleghany's winning the inevitable voting-rights suit.[42] Buying more B stock not

[38] Albert Barnes to Charles Ireland, Dec. 23, 1963, doc. 800302, 19(t), index to Alleghany Discovery Documents, space 0610102a, MP archives.

[39] Interview with Ramsdell, March 11, 1980, New York City.

[40] Arthur Weisenberger to Charles Ireland, Dec. 12, 1963, doc. 800312, 19(t), index to Alleghany Discovery Documents, space 0610102a, MP archives; *Journal of Commerce and Commercial*, Jan. 30, 1964, and *Wall Street Journal*, Dec. 5, 1963, Alleghany clippings, MP public relations office.

[41] Memo, W. H. Hernstadt to C. T. Ireland, Dec. 5, 1963, doc. 800290, 19(t), index to Alleghany Discovery Documents, space 0610102a, MP archives.

[42] Minutes of Alleghany Board of Directors, Dec. 5, 1963, doc. 800243, 19(q), ibid.

only would put Alleghany in a better position if a fair settlement were eventually made, but for the present would have the effect of pushing the price of B stock up to perhaps ten times that of A, further damaging "Marbury's case" for a 1-to-1 valuation. In the next few months Alleghany bought nearly 300 shares of MP B stock at almost $500 a share.[43] It also had Clifford Ramsdell write a history of the MP stock issue for Alleghany's 1963 annual report. This piece minced no words. It stated that the "new scheme" would subvert the victory Alleghany won in the 1956 reorganization and cut the B stock to a fraction of its worth. The report stated that the MP and MRFC were "involved in a conspiracy to defraud the Class B MP stockholders of more than $200,000,000 in the present asset value of the railroad system in a plan that violated the railroad's Articles of Association, the laws of the State of Missouri and the Constitutions of the United States and Missouri."[44] On December 9, 1963, Rose Slayton, a B holder from the Bronx, filed the first of several suits to be entered on behalf of all B holders, stating that the Texas & Pacific merger denied the B its voting rights and resulted "from illegal exercise by Mississippi River Fuel of its control of MP."[45]

The rhetoric from the other side did not cool down any either. William Marbury gave a talk at the Lawyers' Club in New York on December 12 which was largely devoted to his views on the B stock issue and his proposed solution to it through the Texas & Pacific merger. A representative of Alleghany was present and took interesting interlinear notes on his transcript of the address.

Marbury started out with an appraisal of the nature of the A and the B stock, stating that A always implied better than B and that that was the way those in charge of the reorganization intended it. The present proposal, he thought, was perfectly legal, since the charter made no provision for the merger of two companies into a third and since Missouri law in general would require only a two-thirds vote of all stock outstanding for such an

[43] Memo, W. H. Hernstadt to C. T. Ireland, Dec. 18, 1963, doc. 800244, ibid.; *Wall Street Journal*, March 26, 1964, Alleghany clippings, MP public relations office.

[44] Alleghany Corporation, *Annual Report, 1963*, pp. 3–6.

[45] *Wall Street Journal*, Dec. 11, 1963, Alleghany clippings, MP public relations office.

operation. True, there were those, like Mrs. Slayton, who were objecting in the courts, but Marbury seemed confident that his staff of lawyers, coordinated by J. T. Suggs, could deal with any court challenges. "If you are going to start a fight," Marbury said, "it is best to have it in your home territory where you know all the alleys and angles." Suggs was well connected in both Missouri and in Washington, where he was a friend of Sam Rayburn. (At this point in the talk, the Alleghany man began writing his notes. Here he jotted down "Implication—big political pull, stick with me.")[46]

Marbury went on to take the issues one by one and to dismiss them. He said he found it very unusual to have an inferior stock like the MP B selling at such high prices and suggested that Alleghany must be artificially buoying up the market. ("Implication—Dump the stock.") Rather than depend on the caprices of the market for a determination of fair value, the MP in its merger proposal suggested that the matter be decided by the neutral ICC based on a study of the property and not the speculative market value of any stock. The ICC had originally put a par value of $100 a share on both stocks. ("Implication—They will do it again.") The MP had good control of its railroad and could devote manpower now to solving the stock question, and it had $100 million in the kitty to finance such an effort. ("Implication—Because we are big spenders we will win.") The management of MRFC liked to "think big" and was sure it could effectuate the Texas & Pacific merger in the ICC. ("Implication—We have the ICC in the palm of our hand.")[47]

To close his talk, Marbury related the history of the MP's gaining control just that year of several small Oklahoma railroads known collectively as the Muskogee Lines. The three railroads constituting the 767-mile system—the Kansas, Oklahoma & Gulf; the Midland Valley; and the Oklahoma City–Ada–Atoka —had a strategic location in Oklahoma, Arkansas, Kansas, and Texas. The MP offered $18 million for them, which their management refused. Later, Dearmont offered $13 million, which

[46]Typescript of William Marbury's address to N.Y. Security Analysts, Lawyers' Club, with interlinear notes, Dec. 12, 1963, MP law dept.

[47]Ibid.

was again refused. At that point the MP began to route its trains around these lines rather than interchanging with them, which had the effect of drying up a good deal of their traffic. This resulted in the larger company's being able to buy the roads for $9.5 million. Immediately $7 million came back through the sale of the Oklahoma City–Ada–Atoka line to the Santa Fe, leaving a net cost of $2.5 million, with an expected annual revenue after taxes from these companies of $1 million. "All we did was run our trains around their lines and after they got hungry they were willing to sell out at a low price." The Alleghany observer may have pressed on his pencil a little harder at this point as he wrote his final observation: "Implication—He is a great wheeler-dealer. I can get rid of Alleghany the same way." [48]

Marbury's address represented the high point of confidence about being able to accomplish the merger and the stock deal simultaneously. Early in 1964 the plan began to run into considerable opposition, both from B holders and from holders of Texas & Pacific stock who felt that the merger "can only be promoted by the avarice of the Mississippi River Fuel Corp." [49] Marbury was the first major figure in MP management who had ever suggested that since the MP controlled the Texas & Pacific, that railroad should be operated as part of the system instead of as sovereign property. Texas cities were worried that their special prerogatives might be damaged by the merger and so joined the protest. The City of Palestine and Anderson County, Texas, filed suit at the federal district court in Tyler. [50]

Meanwhile, two more B holders, Jane Harris and Nathan Stutch of New York City, filed a voting-rights suit in the federal district court there, and early in February, 1964, Alleghany Corporation filed its own suit in the U.S. district court in Saint Louis. The Alleghany suit charged that MRFC would unjustly benefit from the "fraudulent and manipulative device" of proposing a merger without a class vote. [51]

[48] Ibid.
[49] *Traffic World*, April 11, 1964, Alleghany clippings, MP public relations office.
[50] *Palestine Herald Press*, Feb. 11, 1964; *St. Louis Post Dispatch*, April 15, 1964, ibid.
[51] *Wall Street Journal*, Feb. 3, 1964; *St. Louis Post Dispatch*, Feb. 5, 1964, ibid.

Reaction from Saint Louis was muted. J. T. Suggs said he had not been informed of the details of the Alleghany rights suit but thought it was "groundless and exaggerated."[52] Actually, there was a great deal to worry about, including a suit filed against MRFC by MP stockholders Robert Shea and John Bauer alleging that they and others had been unfairly deceived at the time of the MRFC tender offer of 1962.[53] It appeared that a Pandora's box had been opened full of outstanding legal issues, just as the MP was threatened on all sides by the strong national "urge to merge" of the 1960s and challenged on the operating side by the computer revolution. Certainly, it seemed the better part of valor to hold off on entering another ICC proceeding on a merger, especially one that promised to be as drawn out as the Texas & Pacific merger was likely to be. Therefore, in mid-March the MP agreed to postpone the vote on the merger, scheduled for the May stockholders' meeting, in voluntary deference to the court, which it was hoped would make a quick decision regarding the voting rights of the classes of MP stock.[54] The thrust had been parried, the device turned, and what promised to be another exuberant MP romp in the corporate fields, like the Chicago & Eastern Illinois or the Muskogee Lines proceedings, took on elements of a tedious and serious defensive action.

In fact, Alleghany gave serious thought to taking control of the A stock for itself. In December, 1963, Allan Kirby of Alleghany told a reporter at *Traffic World* that if the class B MP stock could be exchanged for the class A MP stock at a good ratio, Alleghany would trade. He hinted that Alleghany would benefit if the MP got control of the Chicago & Eastern Illinois and a link could be forged between the Chicago road and Alleghany's New York Central.[55] While Cliff Ramsdell later claimed Alleghany control of MP was not a serious threat, he did confess

[52] *Dallas Morning News*, Feb. 6, 1964, ibid.
[53] *St. Louis Post Dispatch*, March 20, 1964; *Wall Street Journal*, March 23, 1964, ibid.
[54] *Wall Street Journal*, March 17, 1964, ibid.
[55] *Traffic World*, Dec. 7, 1963, ibid.

that the MP was vulnerable and that "obviously somebody was giving it some thought."[56]

Enough thought was given the subject that a detailed memo was written from Ramsdell to Ireland on August 18, 1964, outlining a specific control procedure. Under this plan, Alleghany would offer to purchase from MRFC its one million shares of MP A stock for $80 a share in cash, equivalent securities, or a combination of cash and securities. Careful statistics were presented concerning the cost and returns to Alleghany if it pursued this strategy.[57] While nothing further was done along these lines at this point, the possibility of Alleghany's buying out MRFC's A stock was not forgotten.

The MP stockholders' meeting of May 12, 1964, bore more resemblance to the tempestuous sessions of the late 1950s than to the relatively calm gatherings for the election of directors than had been typical of the time since MRFC gained control. In fact, the practice of keeping a verbatim transcript of everything said at these meetings was abandoned in 1962 but was revived for one year in 1964, owing to the unusual controversy about the Texas & Pacific merger plan. Downing Jenks, after reporting to the stockholders on the year's capital improvements, the prospects for the Chicago & Eastern Illinois and Muskogee Lines cases, and strategies for dealing with the issue of diminishing the number of firemen working on trains, launched into an explanation of the Texas & Pacific merger and the stock questions it raised. We have been of the opinion, he said, that when the stockholders voted on the Texas & Pacific consolidation issue, they would vote in the aggregate, not as classes. Some B holders disagree with this and have filed suit in Saint Louis and New York. The vote on this matter has therefore been delayed.[58] That was the extent of Jenks's formal presentation, but he expected questions. The railroad was beginning to make money;

---

[56] Interview with Ramsdell, March 11, 1980, New York City.

[57] Memo marked "Confidential," Clifford Ramsdell to Charles Ireland, Aug. 18, 1964, MP law dept.

[58] MP Railroad, transcript of stockholders' meeting, May 12, 1964, pp. 4–14, microfilm, MP archives.

the dividend on the A stock was $4, headed for $5; there was a possibility of a B stock dividend for the first time since the reorganization; and Jenks knew that there was every likelihood that the B holders, for these reasons if for no others, would be restless and the stockholders' meetings long.[59]

There were questions, to be sure. Would the proposed consolidation eliminate the $5 dividend limit on the MP A stock? Yes. What were the prospects of a merger with the Atchison, Topeka & Santa Fe? Well, that was a long way off. "In fact, until we get a little further along with the T&P-MP consolidation, we are in a little difficult spot to talk terms of a trade with the Santa Fe." The Great Northern and the Northern Pacific had been trying to merge since 1907, and there was no telling how long these grand consolidation strategies might take to come to fruition.[60] These were the easier questions.

Robert Shea, one of the principals in the suit regarding the MRFC tender offer of 1962, started the specific questioning regarding the treatment of the B stockholders. He said he calculated that after the $4 dividend had been paid to the A stock, there should have been $17 million from the MP's 1963 income accruing to the B, or $435 a share. How, therefore, could the A and B be treated equally in the proposed Texas & Pacific consolidation? Jenks responded by explaining that there were many other purposes for which that $17 million must be used than paying dividends to the B stock, and that the consultants who had been brought in by the company had commented upon the large debt of the railroad and the necessity of spending huge amounts to maintain the property. The consultants felt that the B was unlikely to receive dividends for some time in the future and that the B and the A were, in view of these factors, worth approximately the same.[61]

Jenks did point out that there were three groups of consultants involved, and he specifically mentioned Pressprich and

[59] Jenks's perceptions are derived from interview with Downing Jenks, May 13, 1979, Saint Louis.

[60] MP Railroad, transcript of stockholders' meeting, May 12, 1964, pp. 15–16, microfilm, MP archives.

[61] Ibid., pp. 17–21.

Hayden Stone as well as Wyer, Dick.[62] It was later charged by attorneys for the B stockholders that the impression may have been left that all the consultants had come to similar conclusions.[63] There was certainly no attempt by Jenks to advertise at the stockholders' meeting the wide disagreement among the consultants, nor to emphasize suggested figures such as Bretey's 18 to 1. Neither did anyone ask him specifically to do so, and perhaps it is hardly surprising that he would not volunteer the information. One stockholder did suggest that Wyer and Pressprich at least had been among those analysts who during the 1940s debates had been of the opinion that the old common stock should have been wiped out. Why were firms not included with a background of more optimistic projections of the economic future?[64]

The final event of the 1964 stockholders' meeting was the reading by Robert Loeffler of a letter from Empire Trust Company, Alleghany's trustee, explaining its reasons for refusing to vote Alleghany's stock at this meeting. It was returning its proxies for 20,753 shares of B stock unsigned, the trust company's letter read, because it felt that the present slate of directors was treating the B interests unfairly, as evidenced by the Texas & Pacific merger proposal. If this merger were successful, it would unfairly divest the B stockholders of almost all their equity in the MP railroad, amounting to over $200 million, and transfer it to the A holders. This was, the letter charged, "particularly and primarily for the further purpose of unjustly enhancing the value of the investment made in Class A shares of MP by its controlling stockholder, Mississippi River Fuel Corporation."[65]

It was a gesture only, to be sure. The reply of the MP management, also read at the meeting, was correct in stating that there was no way any stock could be voted simply against a group of nominees unless the protesting parties were willing to

[62] Ibid., p. 21.
[63] Deposition of Downing Jenks, Sept. 20, 1972, pp. 234–36, space 0610102a, MP archives.
[64] MP Railroad, transcript of stockholders' meeting, May 12, 1964, p. 22, microfilm, ibid.
[65] Ibid., pp. 28–30.

make alternative nominations of their own. But, though Alleghany knew that its B stock holding constituted only 2.2 percent of the voting power and that it was pointless to go back to the days when T. C. Davis and others tried to concentrate B votes to elect one director to a fifteen-person board, it was felt that gestures of protest, at least, ought to be made. It served the purpose of making it clear to everyone present that there was opposition to the prevailing company policy and that that opposition intended to take positive action to change the drift of things.

Results of that positive action were not long in coming. In July, 1964, the district court in Saint Louis announced its decision on the voting-rights case. The court overruled the MP motion to dismiss the case and stated that the plan of consolidation was unlawful because it violated the right of the B stockholders to a class vote. "It matters not to whose advantage the plan accrues or whether the plan be fair or unfair," Judge James H. Meredith wrote. "The question is whether the two classes' relative rights, restrictions and limitations are to be altered and changed."[66] The MP attorneys by no means accepted the decision, and the company's formidable legal army, headed by Hennelly, quickly made plans to appeal to the circuit court and beyond if necessary. The decision was, however, a setback.

The court decision was followed by, and may have been the cause of, several internal reevaluations in Saint Louis. One was the so-called Weigel memorandum, later much celebrated by opposition attorneys. It was sent by G. K. Weigel to Downing Jenks and dated November 27, 1964. The memo was mainly a detailed criticism of the report by consultant William Wyer and suggested that many of Wyer's statistics on available net income of the company were erroneous.[67] What Weigel was really trying to do was to show that a larger dividend on the A stock was feasible, but understandably this memo, when it later came into the hands of attorneys for the B stockholders, was used to illustrate that different figures were used for different purposes by MP

[66] *St. Louis Globe Democrat*, July 14, 1964, Alleghany clippings, MP public relations office.
[67] G. K. Weigel to D. B. Jenks, marked "Confidential," Bates 725, 28(d), no. 10, index MoPac Discovery Documents, space 0610102c, MP archives.

management. Also, the memo was very specific in stating that the Wyer, Dick report had been based entirely upon the limited prospect for B dividends and that, therefore, despite increased earnings, "the payment of any Class B dividend prior to an ICC determination of a fair exchange for Class B stock would destroy the credibility of Wyer's argument." In his 1972 deposition, Jenks denied ever having seen the Weigel memorandum.[68]

Events following tend to confirm that if management saw the Weigel memo, its suggestions were not taken to heart. In December, 1964, a $5 annual dividend on both MP A and B stock was declared. While this was a dangerous move if Weigel were right about the basis of the Wyer, Dick report of 1963, there was some reason to view it as wise in the defensive context where the MP now found itself. The primary explanation of this move put forward by those who wished to see conspiracy in everything was that the $5 B dividend was a "sneaky attempt by management to show that the two classes are equal."[69] Alleghany Corporation, however, accepted its $5 dividend.[70]

The next event of crucial significance to the stock struggle was a while in coming. It was not until April of 1966 that the Eighth Circuit Court of Appeals in Saint Louis published its decision on the A-B voting-rights case. The decision was a tribute to the skill of the MP attorneys and a tremendous shock to the B holders, who felt here they had the strongest of all possible cases. The court reversed the decision of the lower court. It was not convinced that the MP articles of incorporation called for a class vote, or that class voting was required under state law in the particular situation envisioned in the Texas & Pacific merger. The court of appeals noted that rail mergers were desirable things for the nation, and that it was unwise for courts of law to look into the technicalities of them and thus usurp the legiti-

[68] Deposition of Jenks, June 22, 1972, pp. 218–22, space 0610102a, ibid. Attorneys at the hearing asked Jenks if he considered it a proper function of management to protect the credibility of Wyer's argument. Jenks replied that management opinion was not related to the Weigel memo, since it never reached Jenks's desk, or presumably anyone else's.

[69] Claude S. Rogers to Charles Ireland, Dec. 9, 1964, doc. 80087, index to Alleghany Discovery Documents, ibid.

[70] Charles Ireland to Theodore Sempunakis, Dec. 9, 1964, ibid.

mate jurisdiction of the ICC. In essence, the appeals court recommended that the original procedure envisioned by Marbury be pursued and that all arguments be heard and disposed of at hearings before the ICC, rather than in the courts.[71]

Understandably, the mood was very glum at the Alleghany offices in New York when word of the circuit court decision came. Clifford Ramsdell was "really flabbergasted" and recognized that the decision could be the beginning of the end for hopes held for so many years. He communicated the bad tidings to Allan Kirby and stayed waiting for some hopeful sign. Kirby was utterly dashed. As Ramsdell put it later: "Kirby didn't smile very often and certainly the gloom of his face [was severe]. . . . his reaction was 'my God after all the years and all the money put into this thing protecting ourselves, and they can take it away like that.'"[72] There was nothing for Alleghany to do in the face of the legal blow but hope for a reversal. An appeal was made immediately to the U.S. Supreme Court, but Alleghany attorneys were no longer confident whether the high court would even hear their case, much less be convinced by it.[73]

The turn of events centering on the circuit court decision resulted in a new approach by Alleghany. Early in May, Allan Kirby and Charles Ireland said to the press that Alleghany would rather negotiate a settlement with the MP than fight the company further in court. The Supreme Court appeal "should . . . provide the MP and Mississippi River Corp. with the incentive to negotiate the future of the railroad's capitalization in good faith—something which so far they have given no indication of even contemplating."[74] It was a backhanded peace offering, complete with face-saving insults, but a peace offering nonetheless. The two said that "we are prepared to struggle . . . in the 1960s and subsequent decades, if need be, to protect [our] rights from arrogant and rapacious assault." But it was evident

[71] *Wall Street Journal*, April 20, 1966, Alleghany clippings, MP public relations office.

[72] Interview with Ramsdell, March 11, 1980, New York City.

[73] *St. Louis Post Dispatch*, May 4, 1966, MRC clippings, MP public relations office.

[74] Ibid., May 5, 1966.

that the original cry from New York of "no compromise" and the original resolve to fight the court case to the end without negotiation had softened.

Mark Hennelly advised Marbury to take the opportunity that thus presented itself. Hennelly, one of the most outstanding criminal lawyers in the country before becoming one of its most respected corporate attorneys, had a finely honed sense of how much was enough in legal proceedings, and when things might be pushed too far. Here he sensed that Alleghany was probably at its low point, and that a deal resulting in MRFC's buying out the B interest at a ratio of maybe 1 to 5 or 6 to the value of the A would be quite possible. On the other hand, there was no guarantee of victory for the MP at the Supreme Court, and if that court decided against the railroad, Bretey's estimate of an 18-to-1 exchange might seem moderate. Hennelly told Marbury he should negotiate with Kirby. Marbury did not want to; he thought he was right and he wanted to prove it. The fight was built into his emotions. Call him anyway, Hennelly said. It is in our best interest. The next morning Hennelly got a call from Marbury. He had talked to Kirby, the entrepreneur said, and Kirby was not willing to negotiate. Fifteen years after the event, Hennelly was still not certain that Marbury ever made that call. The secret of the possible lost opportunity went with the MRFC chairman to his grave.[75] But it was certain Marbury had not forgotten the cold reception he and Russell Dearmont had gotten at the Alleghany offices in 1958, when the MP president and his new director had gone there to make an exchange offer of A for B at 10 to 1. The offer had been declined quickly, and Marbury was temperamentally unsuited to go begging a second time.[76]

The U.S. Supreme Court agreed in October, 1966, to hear the voting-rights case.[77] By January, 1967, it was evident from private and public comments of the justices that prospects for a victory by the MP and MRFC were bleak. In fact, seldom had the high court expressed itself more strongly during oral

[75] Interview with Mark Hennelly, July 10, 1979, Saint Louis.

[76] *St. Louis Post Dispatch*, May 5, 1966, MRC clippings, MP public relations office.

[77] *Wall Street Journal*, Oct. 11, 1966, Alleghany clippings, ibid.

hearings. Justice William O. Douglas, admittedly a liberal who generally favored the underdog, said that the Texas & Pacific merger plan and its A-B exchange ratio was "one of the most notorious pieces of predatory financing I've ever seen." Hugo Black expressed grave doubts whether any statute that would allow majority stockholders to take over the property owned by minority holders could withstand the constitutional requirement of due process of law. Black hinted that he might recommend a stockholder voting rule for the MP that would distribute voting power by value rather than by number of shares, thus giving the B holders probable voting control of the railroad. Justice Black asked an MP attorney whether he could see anything fair about a situation in which holders of a small part of the value of a company could overrule the larger value. The attorney answered that the ICC should make the ultimate judgment on the fairness of the package. "There are some things," Black snapped back, "that are so unfair that one might not be willing to trust even the ICC to decide them."[78]

The final court decision came in February and was 8–0 in favor of Alleghany's position. The court stated in its written opinion that exchanging four shares of stock in the new Texas & Missouri Pacific company for one share of B was like "exchanging four rabbits for one horse." If such a thing were allowed, the B stock, which the court determined had the equity in the railroad, would be relegated to ordinary shares and engulfed by the class A.[79]

This decision had an effect more startling than had the surprise of the circuit court decision of 1966. In a matter of days the market price of MP B stock shot up 50 percent, from $1,100 a share to over $1,700. After the Eighth Circuit Court decision, it had dropped to $490, but had slowly recovered with each piece of news from Washington.[80] Marbury announced from his winter residence in Palm Beach, Florida, that the MP would abandon

[78] *St. Louis Post Dispatch*, Jan. 20, 1967, *St. Louis Globe Democrat*, Jan. 21, 1967, ibid.

[79] *Wall Street Journal*, Feb. 28, 1967, ibid.

[80] *Washington Post*, March 5, 1967, ibid.

its attempt to merge the Texas & Pacific along the lines of the Wyer report.[81]

Despite the tremendous blow to its plans represented by the legal setback of the voting-rights case, the MP was not free simply to turn away from the question of the B stock and Alleghany's control of it. There were several attempts during the time of the voting-rights litigation to effect mergers between the MP and potentially powerful allies, as well as to block possibly dangerous maneuvers among roads seeking strong positions in the MP trade territory. These experiences made it more certain than ever that the class B veto, now confirmed by the courts, was a substantial power and one that could be used to hamstring the railroad in the future if the B stock could not be eliminated through negotiation. It was now clear that the price for the B would be high. But the financial future was promising, and the realistic alternatives to arms-length bargaining with Alleghany were now few. As John Burns of Alleghany put it, the railroad had always known, and recognized especially in the late 1960s, that it had to "get rid of this bastardized capital structure and become not a Pinocchio but a real live boy."[82]

[81] *St. Louis Post Dispatch*, April 7, 1967, ibid.
[82] Interview with Burns, March 10, 1980, New York City.

# CHAPTER VII

# *The Best Defense*

O<small>N</small> June 6, 1963, as early thoughts about specific proposals for the Texas & Pacific merger plan were floating around the MP corporate offices in Saint Louis, Marbury and Jenks each received a copy of a detailed memo from Mark Hennelly. It did not concern the legal intricacies of the ambitious "inside" merger with the Texas & Pacific and recapitalization that the company was about to undertake or the complications which had developed with the Chicago & Eastern Illinois cash-control plan then just underway, but rather introduced an entirely separate, and equally stupendous, line of policy. The memo outlined alternative means for the MP and MRFC to gain control of a railroad referred to simply as "Railroad X." To those in the counsel of Marbury it was no secret that this mystery railroad was none other than the Atchison, Topeka & Santa Fe.[1]

Next to the Union Pacific and the Southern Pacific, the Santa Fe was the most profitable railroad in the country. It operated 13,000 miles of line covering twelve southwestern states. It had assets of $3.1 billion, as contrasted with the $1.2 billion of the MP and the $149 million of MRFC, which intended to control the entire package.[2] The move by the former pipeline company to seize control of a railroad corporation thirty times its size demonstrated graphically that Marbury did not intend to sit quietly by while awaiting reaction by the B stockholders to his Texas & Pacific merger proposal. There would be other projects

<hr>

[1] Mark Hennelly to D. B. Jenks, William Marbury, and J. T. Suggs, June 6, 1963, Bates 3130, space 1150005b, MP archives.

[2] *Wall Street Journal*, Oct. 11, 1966, MRC clippings, MP public relations office.

awaiting only a turn of circumstance to become that one idea out
of every fifty Marbury had to become pure gold.

The Santa Fe plan originated in a series of discussions between Marbury, Jenks, and Robert Craft (who was head of the
MP finance committee) at Marbury's Florida home. Despite the
later tendency of the press to characterize the romantic Santa Fe
negotiations as part of "Marbury's Dream," there is evidence
that in these early discussions Marbury was uncertain about the
wisdom of undertaking such a project, especially given the con-
tinuing uncertainty of the stock situation and the tremendous
demands from elsewhere on the cash generated by the MP and
MRFC. The idea was originally presented by Jenks. Robert
Craft, a banker conservative about finance, agreed it was worth
a try. John Lloyd was also strongly in favor of it. He and Jenks
thought the Santa Fe was an excellent "fit" with the MP geo-
graphically and that it had income potential much higher than
was being realized by its current management. Also, the Santa
Fe was taking a keen interest in the moribund Rock Island.
Rather than allow it take over the southern part of the Rock Island and enter the MP territory as a competitor, the MP leadership thought it would be good defensive strategy to ally the line
with the MP instead. A Santa Fe merger would also provide another opportunity to solve the B stock question through an exchange offer, perhaps at a rate higher than in the Texas & Pacific
plan. Using cash to seek control would be a justifiable means of
tying up large amounts of treasury cash that might otherwise be
demanded by the B holders as dividends. (Naturally, there
were, in the later dividend suits, vigorous denials that this last
possibility was ever considered.)[3] These arguments, taken together, were convincing to Marbury, and, once convinced, he
seized upon the idea with his customary enthusiasm.

So grandiose was the idea of little MRFC's controlling the
historic Santa Fe that a number of journalists as well as a good
portion of rail management concluded, when the idea became
generally known, that it was a bluff aimed primarily at heading

[3] Deposition of Downing Jenks, Sept. 20, 1979, pp. 253–58, space 0610102a, MP
archives; interview with John Lloyd, July 10, 1979, Saint Louis.

off Santa Fe interest in the Rock Island. MRFC, for all its miracles to date, could not possibly raise the estimated $300 million it would cost to achieve cash control of the Santa Fe line, and the MP stock situation precluded merger deals. Those close to Marbury knew otherwise. Both Thomas O'Leary and Mark Hennelly in interviews fifteen years after the fact felt *very* certain that Marbury was completely serious. O'Leary, formerly an officer of First National City Bank of New York, was working for Craft at the time and knew that Marbury established a line of credit in New York for his Santa Fe bid. O'Leary put it succinctly: "It was a cheap vote. You could buy a vote for $9."[4] Hennelly's opinion of Marbury's aims came from more striking circumstances. The "Railroad X" memo he wrote in 1963 led eventually by steps to a telephone call from Marbury at five-thirty one Saturday morning in 1966, as the chief was doing his early morning financial ruminating. Marbury had some questions about legal aspects of investing in the Santa Fe and about how much stock he could buy without getting into trouble with the ICC for illegal control. Could Hennelly go down to the office, look some things up, and be ready to answer these questions when Marbury called back at ten o'clock? Hennelly went downtown, answered the questions, and the next Monday morning Marbury agreed to MP's buying what was eventually to amount to $33 million worth of Santa Fe preferred stock. Marbury explained to Hennelly then that he intended to achieve control of the Santa Fe and discussed exactly how it would be done. He would take a substantial position in the preferred stock, giving him veto power similar to that exercised by the B stockholders in the MP, and then wage a proxy fight. He felt that the Santa Fe management was old and traditionalist, and would not fight back as hard as necessary to save the independent status of the railroad. When that was accomplished, Marbury told his chief attorney, he was going to look for an eastern railroad and form the first true transcontinental.[5] Experiences like this convinced Hennelly that his boss was quite serious in all he proposed.

[4] Interview with Thomas O'Leary, July 9, 1979, Saint Louis.
[5] Interview with Mark Hennelly, July 10, 1979, Saint Louis.

The 1963 memo suggested four means of approaching the Santa Fe. First, the MP could enter discussions with Santa Fe with a view of allowing both railroads to be part of a merger with a third (like the Rock Island). This would have the advantage that no new stock would have to be issued and would therefore, according to the legal theory current in Saint Louis before the voting-rights case was resolved, avoid the necessity of a class vote and trouble with the MP B stockholders. The second possibility was for MRFC with ICC approval to buy stock in the Santa Fe or to exchange stock of the MP which MRFC would buy on the open market. Then, with control of both the MP and the Santa Fe, MRFC could merge them. Third, the Santa Fe could be acquired by a brokerage house for cash, with the MP taking an option to buy and guaranteeing the firm against loss. This was similar to a technique being used in the Chicago & Eastern Illinois case, and it was not yet evident how little the ICC would think of it. Fourth, the MP could apply at the outset for authorization to control the Santa Fe and lay out a plan whereby it would acquire its own stock through tenders by MRFC and others. This would work only if the ICC were willing to set aside portions of the Clayton Anti-Trust Act that prevented a holding company like MRFC from making stock deals with companies it controlled. Also, this strategy could result in the B stockholders' blocking the merger, a dilution of MRFC's control over the MP, or both.[6]

Hennelly thought the first alternative would be easiest and safest, and might "also have advantages not readily apparent."[7] These advantages were doubtless that the MP could be recapitalized this way. Method two had the disadvantage of temporary dilution of MRFC's control, or large drains of cash, but was closest to the means eventually used. Method three would produce price fluctuations. The fourth looked good and was the method recommended by several MP attorneys. The big "if" there was whether the ICC would go along with the unusual

[6] Mark Hennelly to D. B. Jenks, William Marbury, and J. T. Suggs, June 6, 1963, Bates 3130, space 1150005b, MP archives.
[7] Ibid.

technique, which it shortly refused to do.[8] There was a fifth means, suggested by Marbury. This would have offered a 1-to-4 exchange of 400,000 shares of MP A stock for 1.6 million of the stock of the Santa Fe. It was a method of control, but Hennelly thought it was fraught with legal difficulties and would probably be unattractive to the seller.[9] The only uncontroversial thing to do was to buy stock for cash, hoping that the money would be well spent as an investment even if control were never acquired. That is what Marbury eventually did so decisively after his early-morning call to Hennelly in 1966. But he got that certainty not from simple intuition, but from sifting the lessons of two years of high strategy directed at the national merger scene.

In June, 1963, exploratory merger talks began with President Ernest Marsh of the Santa Fe, presumably touching upon aspects of several of the plans in Hennelly's memo. Marsh and Jenks announced to the press that consideration was being given to letting other lines in on the merger, although no names were given.[10] Early in 1964 traffic studies were made by the MP concerning precisely how the MP and the Santa Fe could be operated as a single unit and at what savings. The study concluded that merger would increase the length of haul on 18,100 cars and increase the MP gross freight revenue by over $4 million, the Texas & Pacific by $1.2 million, and the Kansas, Oklahoma & Gulf by $80,000. Savings in operating expenses were estimated at $3.5 million a year.[11] C. D. Peet reported to Jenks that the contributions to combined net income of the respective roads over several years was about 77 percent Santa Fe and 23 percent MP. However, if only the latest figures were used, this came out about 70 percent and 30 percent, and the MP might demand one-third of the combined equity, or 12 million of 36 million shares. There could be an exchange of both classes of MP stock for Santa Fe stock at a ratio of about 1 to 6, but the value of the

[8] Interview with Hennelly.

[9] Mark Hennelly to D. B. Jenks, William Marbury, and J. T. Suggs, June 6, 1963, Bates 3130, space 1150005b, MP archives.

[10] *Houston Post*, June 16, 1963, Santa Fe clippings; *St. Louis Post Dispatch*, June 6, 1963, both in MP public relations office.

[11] C. L. Butler to C. D. Peet, Jan. 23, 1964, Bates 4355, space 1150005c, MP archives.

deal to the A stockholders would be uncertain until it could be known what it would cost to eliminate the B as a separate class.[12] The question of the B stock worried the Santa Fe also, which had to consider as well whether it wanted the MP for a merger partner at all. Talks between the MP and the Santa Fe were broken off in November, 1964. Marbury typically lost none of his panache. "We're just not going to sit around and wait to see what they want to do," he told a reporter from his Saint Louis office. "The Missouri Pacific has other activities and ideas of its own in mind which we are starting to work on."[13]

When the MP negotiations broke down, the Santa Fe began talks, ultimately unsuccessful, with the Saint Louis–San Francisco.[14] Meanwhile, both the Santa Fe and the MP spent large amounts of time on what became the rail consolidation question of the decade: what to do with the ailing Chicago, Rock Island & Pacific.

The Rock Island looked for a merger partner from the late 1950s on. Things heated up in 1963 when the Union Pacific made a serious effort to merge with the Rock Island and managed to get the approval of the Rock Island stockholders for a proposal joining the granger road with the Union Pacific. As was often the case with lengthy merger negotiations, however, the Rock Island management changed its mind before the ink was dry on the agreement and turned its attention to other suitors as the ICC hearings approached. Of these there were many, some interested in entering the case to defend territory from competitors who might use the Rock Island trackage to gain operating advantages. By the mid-1960s alliances were formed. On one side was the Union Pacific, which wanted the Rock Island in order to get direct entry into Chicago. The Union Pacific was joined in its proposal by the Southern Pacific, which in return for its support would get the right to buy track giving it access to Kansas City. On the other side, opposing the Union Pacific deal and offering it a purchase package of its own, was the Chicago & Northwestern. It wanted to block further intrusion into the mid-

[12] C.D.P. to D. Jenks, Jan. 31, 1964, Bates 4356, ibid.
[13] *Wall Street Journal*, Nov. 20, 1964, in Bates 4371, ibid.
[14] Ibid.

western trade territory by western roads and to add the Rock Island to its system. Related to the Northwestern proposal was one from the Santa Fe asking that if the Chicago & Northwestern were granted the Rock Island, the Santa Fe be allowed to take its southern portion and to have trackage rights over the Rock Island into Saint Louis.[15]

A dozen railroads intervened in the case after the ICC decided to allow the Union Pacific merger proposal, with its Southern Pacific rider, to go forward. The Milwaukee did not want the Union Pacific in Chicago, as it fed that road traffic through Omaha. The Santa Fe did not want the Southern Pacific in Memphis or Kansas City. The Frisco supported the Southern Pacific, as it did not want to lose its Santa Fe interchange if the Northwestern proposal were favored. The Rio Grande did not want to be encircled further by the Union Pacific and demanded the right to buy the Rock Island lines from Denver to Omaha and Kansas City in case the Union Pacific proposal was approved. The Chicago, Burlington & Quincy did not want the Southern Pacific to control the Rock Island's southern lines, which competed with its own. The Kansas City Southern feared the Southern Pacific's getting into its territory. The Missouri, Kansas & Texas did not want to be isolated by any of the plans and asked that it be included in any merger.[16] To grant the Rock Island to the Union Pacific/Southern Pacific, wrote attorneys for the Northwestern, would be a classic case of the rich getting richer, while competition among smaller roads would be virtually eliminated.[17] "We are convinced," said Ben Heineman of the Chicago & Northwestern, "that the Union Pacific–Rock Island merger would be a loaded gun aimed at the heartland of America."[18] Said another rail executive, "This is the most ill-

[15] Dan Cordtz, "The Fight for the Rock Island," *Fortune* (June, 1966), pp. 141–42; Mark Hennelly and Leon Leighton, *Brief of Protestant Missouri Pacific Railroad Company Volume I*, Jan. 27, 1969 (F.D. 22688 and others), pp. 1–5.

[16] Richard Saunders, *The Railroad Mergers and the Coming of Conrail* (Westport, Conn.: Greenwood, 1978), p. 225. Saunders's book is an excellent overview of the merger situation of the 1960s.

[17] C&NW Railroad, "The Proposed Rock Island Merger," MP public relations office.

[18] *Omaha World-Herald*, Jan. 19, 1965, U.P./R.I. clippings, ibid.

conceived railroad merger suggested since the invention of the steam locomotive."[19]

Ill conceived or not, the Rock Island merger was certainly one of the most complicated and controversial ever conceived, and its failure was the central event responsible for the demise of a seemingly certain thoroughgoing consolidation of western railroads along simplified lines, suggested since the 1920s. Before 1968, ICC examiners heard 275 days of testimony covering over 48,000 pages of transcript. There were 1,200 exhibits amounting to 100,000 pages and 500 lawyers working on the case at one time. The railroads entering the case spent over $40 million on it.[20] Most involved recognized that the Rock Island was a test case and that the precedents set in resolving the issues that arose there among intervening railroads would be of vast importance for the future of them all.

The MP was not against consolidation as such. "Only through consolidation into a handful of big systems," Marbury told the *Wall Street Journal*, "can the railroad industry catch up to the times. The scope of railroad operations today is geared to the early part of the 20th century rather than to the mass production transportation needs of the economy today."[21] However, in the specific case of the Rock Island, several of the possibilities for consolidation were so threatening to the MP financially that it had to take the role of spoiler. Leon Leighton, an attorney of vast experience in cross-examining witnesses, was employed by the MP to represent it in the Rock Island proceedings. Leighton proposed in 1967, much to the chagrin of other parties to the merger, to cross-examine every one of the 400 shipper witnesses whose statements had been filed in the case.[22] Officers of the MP held meetings all along its line to encourage chambers of commerce in cities that depended on the railroad to write to the ICC opposing the Rock Island plans. They emphasized to their audiences that, especially until the MP solved its own stock situation and knew something about the prospects for a major consolida-

[19] *Denver Post*, Nov. 30, 1965, ibid.
[20] *Wall Street Journal*, Feb. 29, 1968, ibid.
[21] Ibid.
[22] *Traffic World*, Jan 7, 1967, ibid.

tion of its own, the partition of the Rock Island among powerful roads from outside the area could be a "deadly serious situation."[23] Downing Jenks made a public call for a summit meeting among the rail powers to resolve privately the midwestern merger situation "before thousands of man-hours and millions of dollars are wasted in fruitless efforts to work out the assorted plans."[24] Several roads, including the Union Pacific, expressed interest in such a meeting, but none volunteered in the meantime to drop the quest for the Rock Island.[25]

The pressure of the Rock Island case led to all sorts of private negotiations and some truly revolutionary proposals that were never to see the light of day. In 1966, for example, Ben Heinemann offered to sell the Chicago & Northwestern to the Union Pacific as a way out of the impasse, and when that was turned down, he proposed that the Chicago & Northwestern buy the Union Pacific.[26] There were those who said that the entire interest of the MP in the Santa Fe was a defensive move to try to divert the Santa Fe from the Rock Island. While that was probably not the case, the MP interest in the Illinois Central in the mid-1960s was surely directly related to its defense against the Rock Island's suitors.

Late in June, 1965, William Marbury and Robert Craft began secret negotiations with W. A. Johnston of the Illinois Central and Robert Lovett of the Union Pacific concerning a possible merger of the Illinois Central with MRFC.[27] The Illinois Central was familiar with the MP people, as there had been a series of merger negotiations between the roads in the spring of 1961, which had broken down as the Chicago & Eastern Illinois case went forward.[28] This time it was Marbury's thinking that the fuel

[23] *North Little Rock Times*, Dec. 2, 1965, ibid. At several of the meetings all the railroads in the Rock Island case were represented and there were debates among the interests. At one along the MP line in Arkansas, a representative of the C&NW showed a film called "The Great Train Robbery—1960s" in which the UP/SP combination was portrayed as a modern version of the James gang. *Arkansas Gazette*, Jan. 19, 1966, ibid.

[24] *Wall Street Journal*, Jan. 13, 1966, ibid.

[25] *Omaha World Herald*, Jan. 14, 1966, ibid.

[26] Saunders, *The Railroad Mergers*, p. 230.

[27] Memo, R. H. Craft, July 21, 1965, file 1, space 1150803c, MP archives.

[28] *Wall Street Journal*, May 22, 1961, p. 28, c.1; July 18, 1962, p. 24, c.2, both in MP public relations office.

company might change its structure slightly and become more specifically a rail holding company, with the Illinois Central its first prize in the new dress. In May, 1965, the name of Marbury's pipeline company was changed from Mississippi River Fuel Company to Mississippi River Corporation (MRC).[29]

Robert Craft met with Robert Lovett of the Union Pacific on August 5, 1965. Lovett was visibly upset with the management of the Illinois Central and frustrated that the Union Pacific, which had a large stock interest in the Illinois Central, could not take a more direct role in it due to possible charges of conflict of interest. Craft told him that this would be a benefit of merger of the Illinois Central and the MP: MP management could be installed. Lovett, however, said that there were major obstacles, among them the large MP debt and the B stock situation. Craft explained that the proposal was for MRC, not the MP railroad, to buy Union Pacific's stock in the Illinois Central and then merge both the Illinois Central and MRC into a new company called Mid-America Corporation. According to the legal theory that cropped up so often in these years, this creation of a third company would avoid problems with the B stockholders' class vote altogether. Craft also explained that the debt could actually be an advantage, given its special nature. Lovett understood this but thought a heavy debt of any kind was not a good idea under present world conditions. Craft reported to Marbury that Lovett seemed interested but did not want to make a move until the Rock Island hearings ended. Lovett did think the Union Pacific would like to get rid of its Illinois Central stock because it was frustrating to have control without being able to exercise it. He also said it would be well to sell it to another railroad, possibly one that was opposing the Union Pacific control of the Rock Island, in exchange for withdrawal of that opposition. The discussion between Craft and Lovett ended without a deal concerning the Illinois Central.[30]

The Illinois Central plan, however, was not the most am-

---

[29] Ibid., May 28, 1965, MRC clippings. Pipeline operations thereafter were controlled by a subsidiary called Mississippi River Transmission.

[30] Memo from R. H. Craft, Aug. 5, 1965, dividend file, space 1150803c, MP archives.

bitious thing that MP officers had to talk about with Union Pacific officers. Lovett and Craft at their August meeting "philosophized" about the possibility of a merger involving the MP, the Illinois Central, and the Union Pacific combined into one supersystem. The problem there was that neither the Union Pacific nor the MP had direct access to the East or West Coast, but this could be solved by bringing in other roads.[31] Dreaming, maybe. But the times were right for such thoughts. Jenks and Marbury had made a formal offer to merge the MP with the Union Pacific.[32] Perhaps it was only the Rock Island snafu that prevented such a proposal from going to the ICC in the 1960s rather than waiting until 1980.

Paralleling these moves was the unfolding of Marbury's strategy toward the Santa Fe. The Frisco–Santa Fe talks terminated in August, 1965, and for some months the MP was too busy with aspects of the Rock Island case, including the possibility of a merger of the Denver & Rio Grande Western, MP, and Western Pacific as a defense against a merged Union Pacific and Rock Island, to return in earnest to the Santa Fe question.[33] In February, 1966, however, the financial press reported large dealings in Santa Fe stock by an unknown buyer. At one midwestern exchange a bloc of 851,000 shares of Santa Fe preferred was sold, the largest transaction ever effected at that location. Both Alleghany Corporation and the New York Central Railroad denied being the purchaser, and it was some days before it was learned that William Marbury had made his move.[34]

Between January 1, 1966, and the end of February the MP, using treasury cash, purchased $22 million worth of Santa Fe preferred stock. This amounted to 2 million shares or about 16 percent of the preferred outstanding and 6.3 percent of the total shares outstanding (the eventual total investment would be $33 million).[35] Marbury typically denied that he was seeking control and said, as he had at the time of MRC's early purchases of MP

[31] Ibid.
[32] Interview with Jenks, March 13, 1979, Saint Louis.
[33] *Pueblo Chieftain*, Nov. 25, 1965, MP public relations office.
[34] *St. Louis Post Dispatch*, Feb. 18, 22, 26, 1966, Santa Fe clippings, ibid.
[35] Ibid., Feb. 24, 1966.

stock, that the Santa Fe was just a good investment for excess cash. Few, however, doubted his intentions this time, as the MP had become overnight the largest single holder of Santa Fe stock by a considerable margin. Alleghany president Charles Ireland noted that Marbury was pursuing his traditional strategy by exercising a "penchant for preferred stocks," and doubtless would try to turn this foothold into control as soon as possible.[36]

That was also the opinion of the ICC's Bureau of Inquiry and Compliance, which watched closely the Santa Fe buying for any signs of illegal control. On February 4, Marbury had a letter from Thaddeus Forbes, the ICC deputy director of finance, inquiring about his intention in buying Santa Fe stock. R. H. McRoberts of the law firm employed by the MP in Saint Louis to work on the voting-rights case advised Marbury that he did not have to communicate with the ICC as long as he did not buy a controlling interest in the Santa Fe, but that it would be wise to reply frankly to the letter. Marbury did so, stating that neither MRC nor the MP was trying to obtain control of the Santa Fe and would not do so without filing an appropriate control application with the commission.[37] This reply was apparently not convincing because on the morning of March 3, David Laird, a special agent for the ICC Bureau of Inquiry and Compliance, arrived without notice in Jenks's office in Saint Louis and asked to see the MP files on the Santa Fe deal. He was sent to the office of MP attorney G. P. Strelinger and shown all the records the railroad had, which consisted of press releases and some brokers' receipts. Laird seemed satisfied and told Strelinger that it did not look to him as if the MP were about to control the Santa Fe. The lawyer readily concurred.[38]

On the day Laird was in Saint Louis, Mark Hennelly and Downing Jenks were in Washington explaining the Santa Fe situation directly to Thaddeus Forbes of the ICC. Jenks and Hennelly said that they wanted to be perfectly open about the whole thing. Their motivation for the buying, they said, was that the

[36] *Wall Street Journal*, Feb. 24, 1966, ibid.

[37] R. H. McRoberts to W. Marbury and W. G. Marbury to Thaddeus Forbes, both Feb. 10, 1966, Bates 3141, space 1150005b, MP archives.

[38] Memo, G. P. Strelinger to W. G. Marbury, March 3, 1966, Bates 3145, ibid.

MP did not want to be left out in the cold if the trend toward merger continued. Also, the Santa Fe preferred stock was considered a good investment no matter what the future held. The two reported that Forbes gave "tacit, though not unreserved acquiescence" to this. The official said that the letters to Marbury were prompted by inquiries of various persons asking the ICC what was going on with the MP and the Santa Fe, and that it was an embarrassment to the bureau not to be able to respond. He indicated that nothing so far suggested illegal control but warned that in determining control, ability to influence management might be a more important factor than percentage of stock owned. Alleghany controlled the New York Central, he noted, though it owned only 9 percent of the stock, because the ownership was diverse. Forbes also explained in great detail what it meant to be in negative control through a veto power. Hennelly and Jenks assured him that this situation would not arise with the Santa Fe.[39]

However meek the MP might appear before government bodies, the Santa Fe move was a serious play in corporate diplomacy. The MP had news of its victory in the voting-rights case in the Eighth Circuit Court of Appeals and was confident for the time being. Jenks said in a speech in April that the rail situation was "ridiculous" and that he expected that the current twenty-eight western railroads would shortly be consolidated into about six major systems.[40] In April also, the MP executive committee discussed the Santa Fe at length. There was some concern over whether MRC would be brought into the case if there were an application for control or merger, and whether the MP's debt structure would be an obstacle. Nevertheless, the board authorized Marbury to continue buying Santa Fe stock. The executive committee had authority from the regular board to go so far as to authorize filing of a control application without calling together all the directors. Marbury told them that it was the time for quick decision. He said that "the very highest priority had to be given to the survival of the Missouri Pacific in the railroad indus-

[39] J.T.S. memo, March 4, 1966, Bates 3146, ibid.
[40] *St. Louis Post Dispatch*, April 20, 1966, DBJ clippings, vol. 2, MP public relations office.

Part of the control system for the 1958-vintage analog computer controlling the bowl retarders at North Little Rock.

Another view of the pioneering Little Rock computer.

Harold Hoffmeister with the IBM RAMAC computer at Saint Louis, 1962.

Almost routine: the Missouri Pacific computer room, Saint Louis, 1966.

An older style dispatcher's console.

Computerized dispatching in the 1980s.

A modern, computerized yard tower.

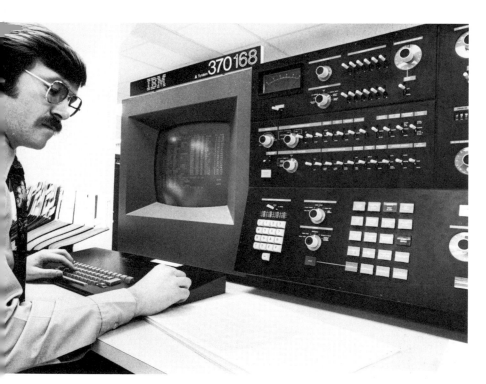

Running the TCS (Transportation Control System) software.

A TCS training session in the early 1980s.

A recruiting table on a college campus in the early 1970s. Behind the table is Paul Morey, director of personnel planning, while the man second from the right is Wade Clutton, a key member of the original computer team at the Missouri Pacific.

The *Colorado Eagle* on the Pueblo line, in what proved the final days of the Missouri Pacific passenger train.

Typical equipment for piggyback loading.

Laying continuous weld rail.

Transporting and unloading long sections of rail present some special problems.

A target for "Mr. Clean"—a historic but inefficient station at Shelbyville on the Chicago & Eastern Illinois, as Jenks found it in the 1960s.

The "new style" yard building—yard office, tower, and intermodal terminal at Shreveport.

try as it is presently evolving," and he pointed to the ICC decisions on the Penn Central and Burlington Northern mergers as
indications of a trend.[41]

Early in May, Downing Jenks went to Chicago to speak with
E. S. Marsh and J. C. Gibson of the Santa Fe about either merging the Santa Fe with MRC or coming to some sort of agreement
about a control situation.[42] Buying stock on the open market
with no security as to the eventual result was indeed a dangerous thing to do. Thomas O'Leary later reflected that perhaps
in making as large an investment as he did Marbury "bit off
more than he could chew." He dynamited the price of the stock
from 8 to 12 in a short time and was himself buying at 12, an
unprecedented price for the security, and a price too high if it
were being held simply as an investment for resale.[43] Jenks
pointed out to the Santa Fe people that the appeals court had
just decided in MP's favor in the Alleghany case, which made it
unlikely that the B stock would prove a barrier to merger. He
also said that the MP was worried about the Santa Fe position in
the Rock Island case.[44] Could not something be worked out to
prevent a costly battle on that field?

Marsh's response was negative in the extreme. Why should
the Santa Fe want to merge with MRC, he said, when MRC's
stock holding was entirely in the A stock, which was limited to a
$5 dividend? He was not worried about MP's position in the
Santa Fe preferred, though he was upset that it did not vote the
stock at the Santa Fe annual meeting. As to the Rock Island,
Marsh simply said that the Santa Fe had a contract with the
Northwestern to buy the southern half of the road if the Chicago
& Northwestern application were successful. He was aware that
the MP would prefer that the Rock Island remain independent,
or go as a whole to the Chicago & Northwestern, but he saw no
reason to change the policy of the Santa Fe because of opinions

[41] Drafts of Minutes, April 29, 1966, Bates 5489 and 280–81, spaces 1150005c and
1151003b, MP archives.

[42] D. B. Jenks to M. M. Hennelly, May 6, 1966, Bates 3147, space 1150005b, ibid.

[43] Interview with O'Leary, July 9, 1979, Saint Louis.

[44] Transcripts of Minutes, April 29 and May 10, Bates 5489, 280 81, spaces
115005c and 115003b, MP archives.

expressed in Saint Louis.[45] The talks broke off abruptly. Late that month MRC announced to the press that it would shortly file an application with the ICC to control the Santa Fe railroad through stock ownership, and asking that this control case be joined for decision with the already mammoth Rock Island docket.[46]

It was a piece of awesome audacity. Financial writers were aghast just at the scope of it, since achieving 50 percent voting control in the Santa Fe would require an investment at current market prices of $340 million![47] The *Wall Street Journal* entitled its article on the application of MRC and the MP to control the Santa Fe "Tail Has Dog Bite a Lion." It objectively reported, however, that William Marbury had every confidence he could accomplish the task. A Santa Fe–MP merger, he said, would be a combination of strengths and that was what the nation truly needed. "You can't do the job that needs to be done for the country," he told the *Journal* reporter, "by thinking in terms of the weak. Overconcern for the weak is a curse of our times." What about all your other problems, his interviewer inquired? What about the Chicago & Eastern Illinois, not yet final, or the voting-rights case, still in the courts? One cannot allow circumstance to dictate, Marbury replied, but circumstance rather should be controlled. "Nobody was dealing us a hand," Marbury concluded, "so we decided to get our own deck to play with."[48]

The press was not alone in its skepticism. Other railroads quickly and negatively responded to the MP application, particularly those that were involved in the Rock Island hearings and did not want to see them further complicated by a new issue. The Santa Fe itself submitted three petitions. One asked the ICC to dismiss the MP application to control the Santa Fe on the grounds that it forced the commission to formulate a broad plan for the consolidation of the nation's railroads, a job Congress had relieved it of in 1940. A second petition asked the right to inter-

[45] D. B. Jenks to M. M. Hennelly, May 6, 1966, Bates 3147, space 1150005b, ibid.
[46] *St. Louis Post Dispatch*, May 27, 1966, Santa Fe clippings, MP public relations office.
[47] *St. Louis Post Dispatch*, May 31, 1966, ibid.
[48] *Wall Street Journal*, Oct. 11, 1966, MRC clippings, ibid.

vene if the ICC did not dismiss the case, and a third petition objected to the consolidation of the matter with the Rock Island docket, stating that to do so would cause unjustifiable delay.[49] Wrote the Santa Fe attorneys: "We submit that the Commission should not permit its administrative processes to be abused by assuming jurisdiction of this application, thereby imposing upon itself and all others concerned the heavy burdens of a major finance docket proceeding when it is manifest that the application is misdirected in purpose and lacking in substance."[50] The Union Pacific, Southern Pacific, and Rock Island filed a joint petition with a similar thrust. It said that the MP-MRC application was "too premature and tenuous" to be consolidated with the Rock Island hearings, and there was no evidence that the MP was financially capable of achieving control even if granted permission to try.[51] The Chicago & Northwestern likewise opposed the application, stating that it introduced into the Rock Island question a completely independent issue.[52] Most of the railroads involved in the Rock Island docket would probably have gone almost as far in their criticism as did the Union Pacific–Southern Pacific–Rock Island brief, which characterized the MP application as "premature, inappropriate and unfair." The MP stock buying, the brief charged, was "little more than a self-serving declaration by the applicants of an ultimate objective."[53]

The MP team of attorneys did not snooze through all this. They composed a lengthy and vigorous brief in defense of the application for control. We are not trying to force the ICC to make up a plan for nationwide consolidation, they wrote, but we do feel that the 1940 amendments to the Interstate Commerce Act were intended to help the industry proceed on its own toward a consolidation plan. The Rock Island proposal "when viewed in proper perspective" could be seen as the first move

[49] *Wall Street Journal*, June 13, 1966, Santa Fe clippings, ibid.

[50] "Motion to Dismiss . . . ," June 10, 1966, Bates 3217, space 1150005b, MP archives.

[51] *Traffic World*, June 25, 1966, Santa Fe clippings, MP public relations office.

[52] "Answer of Chicago and Northwestern Railway Company . . . ," June 14, 1966, Bates 3125, space 1150005b, MP archives.

[53] "Answer and Objections . . . to Petition of Mississippi River Corporation . . . ," n.d., Bates 3126, ibid.

toward just such an industry restructuring, and the MP–Santa Fe proposal was merely another. The brief went on to say that the MP was perfectly capable of controlling the Santa Fe through cash purchases of its stock. As of July, when the brief was written, it owned 2.9 million shares, or 8 percent of the total Santa Fe shares outstanding, and the MP alone had invested $30 milion. The MP intended to continue its purchases until it reached the 10 percent limit imposed by rules of illegal control, and it had arranged financing to carry its strategem to that point and beyond. "It is obvious that the Applicants mean business," wrote the attorneys. "They are not here asking this Commission to treat with an insubstantial, frivolous ploy."[54]

In addition to the legal briefs, the MP carried out a large public relations effort, especially among the doubting members of the financial press. On July 8, for example, Marbury gave what one member of the audience called "an inspiring pitch" to the New York Society of Security Analysts.[55] Both Marbury and Jenks spoke extemporaneously at the meeting, but the proceedings were taped and available in case anyone present missed some of the details.

Marbury introduced himself and MRC as "the greatest bulls in the rail market." He said that in the last five years "Mississippi River Corporation has bought three railroads and it's trying to buy a fourth, so I come here as a man who believes in the industry that you spend your time analyzing." After explaining something about the history of the MRC, Marbury launched into a series of comments about the Santa Fe issue. He told those gathered what he often told his associates, that his primary motivation for buying into the Santa Fe was that he believed in the future of the "heartland of America" and the railroads that served it. "We are certainly new and reasonably novice in the railroad business," Marbury said,

> but we found that the railroad business doesn't differ a great deal from other businesses—that three essentials of the railroad busi-

[54] R. H. McRoberts, "Reply to Motion to Dismiss," July 1, 1966, Bates 3128, ibid.
[55] *Wall Street Journal*, July 11, 1966, Santa Fe clippings, MP public relations office.

ness are true the same as in any other business. You've got to have management. . . . You've got to have money. . . . And you need some time. We've got all these. We've got the management. We've got the money and we'll be given the time. Now, when you get away from that, then you have to talk about geography, you have to talk about the development of the country in the area in which you're in, and though we can't boast of California at this state, we do have Texas and Texas is quite a big place and the Mississippi Valley is quite a place.[56]

Marbury professed to be surprised that the Santa Fe was not responding enthusiastically to MRC's overtures. "I think it's very flattering to be singled out by the people that have made the largest rail investments in this country in the past five years as a candidate for further investment." While both the MP and the Santa Fe were great systems by themselves, he said, the combination would be greater still "and wouldn't you like to own some of that." Marbury said he certainly would. He showed the group a map, pointing out the railroad system that would be formed by the MP, the Santa Fe, and the Chicago & Eastern Illinois—from New Orleans, Baton Rouge, Memphis, Saint Louis, and points west to the coast. "That's a real railroad. And I'd love to have it." So, he thought, would the Santa Fe stockholders, who would support MRC's bid.[57]

True, national policy was that the strong should support the weak rather than the strong joining the strong, but MP had done its share of supporting the weak in taking over the Chicago & Eastern Illinois and the Muskogee Lines. Now it should have something it did not have to rebuild. "Now, if the ICC or if America is going to have a dynamic railroad system in the last third of the 20th century, we must get out of the first third of the 20th century and begin to progress into the last third." Consolidation of rail systems was already underway in the East, but it had been done piecemeal and great errors had been made. It was clear to all that consolidation was coming to the West.

[56] Transcript of remarks before New York Society of Security Analysts, July 8, 1966, pp. 3, 9, MP law dept.
[57] Ibid., p. 14.

And we also know this, that once you trigger this, through breaking up the Rock Island, and putting the UP in Chicago and the SP in Kansas City and a few of those other little for you only deals, you've triggered off a chain of events that must have a lot of consequences. So we thought we'd get ours in real quick. Now, we acted unilaterally. Now, the reason we acted unilaterally is because that bilaterally, it takes more than one person. We only had one guy to act with, so we acted unilaterally. . . . We're sincere about it. We've got $30 million in it and we're prepared to put a lot more, and if you hear any of this business, "Where are they going to get the money," just leave that to us. We'll get it. We've got it lined up.

Marbury wanted the analysts to recognize and communicate that the MP was not conducting a raid on the Santa Fe, and that the interests of Santa Fe stockholders were not hurt by the investment. The MP was not opposed to acting bilaterally and would talk with Santa Fe management at any time. The only reason for the unilateral action was that the Santa Fe had refused to treat and "there was only one of us that wanted to act."[58]

Jenks admitted Marbury's was "a hard act to follow" but did add detail about the Santa Fe prospect from an operating point of view. The MP was doing very well and making money. "Now, if there is no change—if everything stays as is, we're content and comfortable and secure." However, management did not think the status quo would be preserved for very long. There would be a few great systems, and the MP fit best with the Santa Fe. This would give the Santa Fe access to the booming Gulf industrial areas served by the MP and the MP the advantage of the Santa Fe's fine layout. "It will combine the Missouri Pacific's traffic gathering ability with the Santa Fe long haul." It would utilize the car fleet more efficiently than on present smaller systems, make better use of shops, and eliminate many duplications in accounting, traffic, and marketing departments. Jenks, like Marbury, made it clear that the MP-MRC combination was financially capable of the Santa Fe control. It had invested $33 million that year, but its cash reserves were down only $6 mil-

[58] Ibid., pp. 15–18.

lion from what they were at the same time the year before. The ICC would see the logic of the strong system that would be formed by joining the MP and Santa Fe, Jenks thought. "We're going to want railroads that are depression proof and will provide good, competitive service, that are wealthy enough to stand the cyclical effects of business."[59] This was the basic story MP officers tried to get across all over the country.

Privately, there were some slight differences in the strategy from that advertised to the public. There was a question whether the MP could simply buy the Santa Fe for cash, or wanted to. Marbury said at one public meeting that "it might take $300 million to swing the deal, but we could do it." Really, he wished he did not have to and hoped that the initial moves would motivate the Santa Fe to take some action to merge with or take over the MP or MRC. Marbury could not understand why the Santa Fe should be willing to pay $100 million for the southern part of the Rock Island when for twice that figure it could acquire MRC and pick up the entire MP in the bargain.[60] He thought the financial logic was inevitable, while Jenks and Lloyd thought the operating logic of the joined system was equally inevitable. That it was not happening as planned, they could only attribute to a peculiar stubbornness on the part of Santa Fe management.

In October, 1966, the ICC ruled that the MP application for control of the Santa Fe was legitimate and should not be dismissed, although the question of whether it should be combined with the Rock Island case was left open for the moment.[61] In Saint Louis, further traffic studies were made, there were detailed calculations of exactly how control through stock ownership would be achieved, and attorneys spent what time they could, given their tremendous case load, preparing models for specific testimony to be given at the hearings on the Santa Fe. The calculations on stock were discouraging. The MP would have to acquire 40 to 50 percent of the total outstanding stock of the Santa Fe in order to control it, and even at that it would take

[59] Ibid., pp. 23–26.
[60] *Forbes*, Aug. 1, 1966, MRC clippings, MP public relations office.
[61] *Wall Street Journal*, Oct. 5, 1966, Santa Fe clippings, ibid.

four annual elections to achieve a majority of nine on the board of directors. With 30 percent of the stock, the MP could elect five of the sixteen directors within four years but could never get any more, whatever technique was used.[62] The case, however, was closely related to other things in which the MP was involved, and it was hoped that circumstances would change before it came time for the hearings.

In the meantime, there was plenty to do in the Rock Island hearings. Understandably, the Union Pacific, which at least had a deal approved by the Rock Island stockholders, was upset at the number of railroads that had intervened in the case, and it questioned whether they had the public interest in mind. The Rock Island was also annoyed, as it sank into increasing poverty, and so were members of the ICC. The case had come to be characterized as a "huge corporate orgy" that kept two steno-typists busy for years taking down testimony daily and then air-mailing it to the members of the ICC in Washington for their bedtime reading.[63] Commissioner William H. Tucker once threatened to call the whole thing off on the grounds that it had degenerated into an "endless parade of unrealistic claims, counterclaims and recriminations," and that it was impossible for the ICC to render a decision that would satisfy anyone. Jervis Langdon of the Rock Island told his stockholders in 1967 that "a distressingly large part of the record so far has little to do with the merits or demerits of the merger but reflects the maneuvers of those who believe they stand to gain by delay and inaction."[64]

The MP may well have been one of those to which Langdon had reference. When MP witnesses testified in the Rock Island case in the summer of 1967, it was obvious that they felt their railroad had a great deal to lose no matter which of the proposals before the commission might be approved and that it was working desperately to guarantee its own salvation before any decision was made. However, in the interest of the "statesmanship

[62] Outlines of testimony (1967–68), Bates 4359, 4361, 4364, and Cleon Burt to William McDowell, Nov. 25, 1966, Bates 3154, space 1150005b, MP archives.

[63] *Arkansas Gazette*, May 20, 1967; *Denver Post*, June 18, 1967, UP/RI clippings, MP public relations office.

[64] *Forbes*, May 6, 1967, DBJ clippings, vol. 2, ibid.

from the railroad industry" that Commissioner Tucker called for, the MP changed its original position somewhat. In the 1967 testimony, rather than opposing all the possible plans, the MP people said they would support an order giving the Chicago & Northwestern the entire Rock Island without any participation by the Santa Fe. This would cost the MP an estimated $1.3 million a year in diverted revenue, but, Downing Jenks said, "these losses could be absorbed if the public interest requires it." What could not be tolerated were the losses that would result if Union Pacific, Southern Pacific, or Santa Fe acquired a piece of the Rock Island pie. The MP argued that if the Santa Fe got a part, it would gain $9.3 million a year, or about 10 percent of its 1966 net income, while the MP would lose in the same transaction $4.4 million a year, or 16.3 percent of its 1966 net income. This kind of loss would mean the MP would have to cut back on the capital expenditures program that had been such a success in the 1960s, thus creating a snowballing effect, which in a few years would cost the line business and make further maintenance reductions necessary.[65] Jenks was all too familiar with this pattern from observation of other railroads and did not want to oversee such a decline on the road he had brought up by the bootstraps.

Cross-examination of the MP witnesses by attorneys for other railroads centered upon the MP stock problems (especially the recent unfavorable Supreme Court decision), and the extent to which the MP's own actions in other areas contradicted its arguments in the Rock Island case. The MP, for example, argued that it was not in the public interest " for the strongest, the second strongest, and the fourth strongest railroad in the nation, Union Pacific, Southern Pacific, and Santa Fe, to aggrandize themselves at the expense of their weaker competitors." Yet was it not precisely Marbury's stated philosophy that it was time for the strong to join the strong? Was not the move to control the fourth strongest railroad in the nation (Santa Fe) "an attempt by the Missouri Pacific to aggrandize itself?" If the Rock Island plan

---

[65] Testimony of D. B. Jenks, Aug. 5, 1967, box 3, space 011002c, MP archives. The MP archives contain the complete exhibits and complete hearing transcripts of the Rock Island case, amounting altogether to about forty large boxes of material.

made the rich richer and the poor poorer, as the MP witnesses said, would not those enriched include the ailing Rock Island, and would that not be a public benefit? Was not the MP willingness to allow the Northwestern to take the entire Rock Island merely a selfish attempt to insure a weak system rather than a strong one as a competitor? Did not the MP arguments that there already existed a single-line service where the Union Pacific–Rock Island combination proposed to provide it apply also to the imagined MP–Santa Fe service? If the Santa Fe got the southern part of the Rock Island and the MP acquired the Santa Fe, would the MP be willing, in the public interest as it now argued it, to give up that southern Rock Island route?[66]

These were difficult questions, but the MP tried to meet them and others straight on. Leon Leighton in his redirects of MP witnesses brought out that in any situation that would do as much damage to other railroads as this one was likely to do to theirs, they would expect to have to pay compensation or give route guarantees, which in fact was eventually done in the Chicago & Eastern Illinois matter.[67] Leighton and Hennelly, however, stuck to their basic point in a brief written as the case dragged on into 1969. The Rock Island should be transferred intact to the Northwestern rather than turned over to its stronger suitors because any benefit to be derived from unions with these latter would be more than overcome by the disaster it would bring to numerous other railroads in the Midwest. However long the hearings took, it was a basic right of all the railroads so affected to have a fair and exhaustively complete hearing of their grievances.[68] If delay was part of the MP purpose here, its tactics succeeded beyond imagining. The Rock Island case was not finally disposed of for more than a decade.

Stalemate in the Rock Island case and defeat in the voting-

[66] ICC, F.D. 22688 et al., Stenographers' minutes, Feb. 1, 1968, pp. 43085–87, 43089, 43102, 43110, 43125, 43135, 43180, box 13, space 0530104a, MP archives. The hearings alone amount to over 300 volumes and are contained in 16 boxes.

[67] Ibid., p. 43194.

[68] Mark M. Hennelly and Leon Leighton, *Brief of Protestant Missouri Pacific Railroad Company Volume I* (F.D. 22688 et al.), Jan. 27, 1969, *passim*, MP law dept. This brief is an excellent summary, both of the MP's position and of the history of its involvement in the case.

rights matter left the Santa Fe control issue. The voting-rights outcome had a negative effect upon the hopes for Santa Fe control, as it appeared more and more likely that the B stockholders would have to be bought out at a sum perhaps approaching $100 million. This, plus the $300 million it would cost to buy control of the Santa Fe (which was showing no signs of voluntary movement toward merger), would put a crimp in even Marbury's financial style. Also, it was obvious that while the Santa Fe was important, the MP's internal stock question was critical. For a time it had looked as though the stock question would be solved through the Texas & Pacific merger, and at that time also the Rock Island merger and the Santa Fe's part in it looked especially threatening to the MP. By 1967, however, the Santa Fe–Rock Island threat cooled down, mired in the endless bureaucracy of the hearings, while the class issue among the stockholders got a big boost from the Supreme Court. There were still prospects for doing something with the Santa Fe. There exist in the MP files notes by Jenks outlining a possible system including the MP, Santa Fe, Frisco, and Western Pacific.[69] But the priorities had definitely undergone a change.

In November, 1967, the MP came out in opposition to the creation of Santa Fe Industries, a diversified holding company that would dilute the leverage of the MP's preferred stock holdings. The move by the Santa Fe was an admission of sorts that it was vulnerable to being controlled from the outside and needed to change its stock structure to protect itself. Marbury hoped that it might mean also that Santa Fe was positioning itself to discuss merger with MRC. In this, however, he was disappointed, and when asked about it could only say, "They don't talk to us at all."[70]

As he was speaking, accountants in Saint Louis were calculating how the MP's 3 million shares of Santa Fe might be sold. They advised that at the current market price it would produce a loss for the MP of $8.9 million.[71] In January, 1968, the

---

[69] The notes are in Bates 4361, space 1150005c, MP archives.

[70] *Wall Street Journal*, Nov. 2, 1967, Santa Fe clippings, MP public relations office.

[71] Memo, T. M. to Mark, Nov. 2, 1967, Bates 3157, space 1150005b, MP archives.

MP asked the ICC for a delay in the Santa Fe control hearings to allow attorneys more time for preparation.[72] In May the MP agreed to swap its Santa Fe preferred stock for 6.25 percent subordinated convertible debentures of Santa Fe Industries.[73] In June the new Santa Fe president, John Reed, said in a speech in Saint Louis that he would resist all efforts by MRC and the MP railroad to control his company.[74] In July the ICC dismissed the Santa Fe control case at the request of the MP.[75] In December the MP began exploratory merger talks with the Southern.[76]

Thus, in a rapid and quiet series of events, the great bid for the Santa Fe ended. Marbury and Jenks were above all pragmatists, and they concluded that the application for control no longer served any purpose other than impeding other "present prospects and constructive action," and maybe incidentally a part of "Marbury's dream."[77]

The time for the dream was temporarily over, both because the need for it receded and because overwhelming technical considerations took its place in the forefront. The Rock Island quandary, combined with the failure of the Penn Central merger to live up to expectations, were the shoals on which the "urge to merge" of the 1960s was wrecked. Nothing could have been luckier for the MP. The hiatus in the national planning of consolidation designs gave it time and finances to devote fully to the solution of the internal problems that had plagued it since the capitalization of 1956 was announced. Management knew that these must be dealt with immediately because it also knew that the time for the dream would soon come again. When the western systems once more began to maneuver for position in forming five or six great systems, the MP wanted to be ready.

[72] *Wall Street Journal*, Jan. 26, 1968, Santa Fe clippings, MP public relations office.

[73] Ibid., May 17, 24, 1968.

[74] *St. Louis Post Dispatch*, June 12, 1968, ibid.

[75] To Neil Garsen, n.d., Bates 3164, space 1150005b, MP archives. The case was dismissed on July 8.

[76] *Wall Street Journal*, Dec. 24, 1968, DBJ clippings, vol. 3, MP public relations office.

[77] Ibid., July 3, 1968, Santa Fe clippings. The MP subsequently disposed of its holdings in Santa Fe Industries.

CHAPTER VIII

# The Recapitalization

As the merger movement slowed and as the Missouri Pacific people recovered from the voting-rights case and began reexamining the old stock question in a new light, the railroad itself continued to be a stable and prosperous instrument. In the 1960s it went from a near laughingstock teetering on the edge of renewed bankruptcy to one of the most profitable and efficiently operated rail companies in the United States. And there was strong evidence that this was by no means the peak. For freight railroads in general and for the MP and its booming Gulf Coast industries, it was likely that the 1970s would be even more kind than the 1960s had been.

Alleghany Corporation thought so also. But the railroad was more frustration than boon until there was a specific means for the investment company to utilize it. If the MP were taken up as part of a western rail merger movement, Alleghany wanted to insure that the B stock would be adequately compensated. In March, 1967, for example, there were memos floating about the Alleghany offices concerning possible financial structures for a merger of the MP with a railroad "I" (probably the Illinois Central) as well as with the Santa Fe, or even with both of those railroads simultaneously.[1] A merger between Alleghany and MRC remained a possibility, as did an Alleghany stock takeover of the MP.

The most likely solution, however, appeared to be a pur-

[1] Memos, Clifford Ramsdell to Charles Ireland, March 6 and 23, 1967, doc. 800526–30, index to Alleghany discovery documents, space 0610102a, MP archives.

chase of the B stock interests, including that of Alleghany, by the MP for stock and cash, followed by a tender offer from MRC for Alleghany's former block of stock. This would remove Alleghany from the picture entirely and set the stage for a complete re-capitalization of the MP with MRC yet in control. Alleghany was ready for negotiations leading to such a result but was content to wait, Supreme Court decision in hand, until the offer was right. The MP did not want to be exploited on any deal that was made, but, unlike Alleghany, it could not afford to wait too long.

There was some activity relating to a possible recapitaliza-tion in the summer of 1967. Albert W. Ambs, a vice-president of First National City Bank in New York, drew up a plan for re-capitalization and sent it to Thomas O'Leary and Robert Craft at the MP. He suggested that the railroad negotiate with Alleghany Corporation and buy its B stock at whatever price it would take. Then an exchange offer should be made to the A holders for a subordinated income debenture, and the B stock should be split 100 to 1.[2]

O'Leary did not think this plan would work, as, among other faults, it would create $108 million of additional debt. If Ambs was right in assuming that Alleghany would sell its B stock at a reasonable price in arm's-length negotiations, O'Leary wrote to Craft, then the battle was won. It would be simpler to create a single class of common stock and provide acceptable A and B ex-change ratios for the new common, thus effecting a recapitaliza-tion without a debt increase.[3]

There was activity from the Alleghany camp as well that summer. The officers of that corporation stepped up their efforts to achieve public recognition of the true value of the B stock from Alleghany's point of view in anticipation that it might soon be sold. Alleghany's leadership was particularly upset that the MP, on advice from the SEC, had stopped reporting earnings per share on either the A or the B stock in its annual reports. Alleghany felt that this unfairly damaged the interests of the

[2] Memo, A. W. Ambs to E. B. Whit, July 7, 1967, Bates 738, 28(d), index MoPac discovery documents, ibid.

[3] Memo, T. H. O'Leary to R. H. Craft, July 23, 1967, Bates 739, 28(d), ibid.

B, which would have had a high eps.[4] Also that summer, MP recapitalization plans developed by John Vaiani and Clifford Ramsdell were under discussion in New York. One proposal followed Ambs's closely. Another suggested using B stock other than Alleghany's in exchange for MRC's A stock, thus effecting the Alleghany takeover of MP that was always in the wings. But all envisioned a deal that would give the B a much more substantial return than had ever been considered by the MP—something on the order of a 50-to-1 value ratio with the A.[5]

This kind of study and counterstudy might have gone on for a long time. The minority B holders, however, were elated by the victory in the voting-rights case and determined to pursue other matters at issue in the courts. Suits were filed late in 1967 by two individual B holders, Betty Levin (in New York) and Robert LeVasseur (in Saint Louis). Both suits alleged that the B stock was being systematically and unfairly denied adequate dividends while MRC prospered from the MP's success. Both suits suggested that this was due to a "conspiracy" among the officers of the MP and MRC. The Levin complaint cited the "predatory" Texas & Pacific merger plan as evidence of this, as well as the fact that Marbury and other officers had "publicly denigrated" the class B stock on numerous occasions. The suit asked that the court compel the railroad to pay reasonable dividends and that it issue an injunction to restrain the MRC and the MP boards of directors from "illegal oppressive and arbitrary use of power" in denying the B stock higher dividends.[6]

There is no denying that the Levin case, into which Le-Vasseur's was eventually merged, was of overreaching importance to the modern history of the MP railroad. But it was im-

[4] Robert Whitter Dudley to Charles Ireland and to Hugh Owens, March 27, 1967, doc. 00158, 19(i), index to Alleghany discovery documents, ibid.; Clifford Ramsdell to Wm. Kester, May 2, 1967, doc. 00156, ibid.; Charles Ireland to editor *Forbes*, Feb. 15, 1967, doc. 800032, 19(k), ibid.

[5] Letters, John Vaiani to Fred Kirby, Clifford Ramsdell, and Charles Ireland, April 10–June 6, 1967, doc. 800281, 19(v), ibid.; E. Y. Beaugeard to Fred Kirby, Nov. 15, 1967, doc. 800553, ibid.

[6] Missouri Pacific, Class B Dividends, Outline of Case, Dec. 29, 1967, in General No. 1, space 0610102b, MP archives.

portant for reasons other than those that might immediately come to mind. It was important more because Alleghany joined it in 1968 and made it a class action than because Levin and LeVasseur filed it. And it was important more because the discovery provided for in the case resulted in mutual trust between attorneys for Alleghany and MP than because the MP was forced to any settlement out of fear of losing it. There was, in fact, very little chance that the railroad would lose a dividend suit. Marbury was confident enough to tell the *Wall Street Journal* in January, 1968, that no court could "compel directors of any company to pay more than they think prudent."[7] It was not the threat, but rather the accidental opportunity for interaction the case provided, that eventually broke down the twenty-year deadlock over the stock question, provided for private recapitalization negotiations, and insured that the Levin case never came to a final hearing on its original charges.

Alleghany attorneys at Donovan, Leisure, Newton & Irvine in New York were as aware as Hennelly in Saint Louis that a dividend case was virtually unwinnable and would never have filed such a case on Alleghany's behalf alone. However, being the majority holder of the B stock, Alleghany was legally bound to represent the class, not to mention the public relations consequences of perhaps having to play the "big bad guy," as Cliff Ramsdell put it, and veto a settlement worked out by the MP, the courts, and the minority B holders. "This was not the form which we would have preferred to make a stand on," Ramsdell of Alleghany later said, "but we had to intervene as a plaintiff in that suit in order to control it."[8]

Lauck Walton and John Tobin at Donovan, Leisure did feel, however, that there were better and worse strategies to be pursued in the case and worked on the better ones. For example, they worked hard early to insure that the suit became a class action and that LeVasseur was allowed to intervene in the Levin case in New York. The proceedings therefore were held on Alle-

---

[7] Interview with Mark Hennelly, July 10, 1979, Saint Louis; interview with Lauck Walton, March 12, 1980, New York City; *Wall Street Journal*, Jan. 8, 1968, Alleghany clippings, MP public relations office.

[8] Interview with Ramsdell, March 11, 1980, New York City.

ghany's rather than Marbury's turf. After the jurisdiction was decided, the Alleghany attorneys introduced an amendment to the complaint detailing the conspiracy to freeze out the B holders and in effect to confiscate the B stock by merger. Thus, they were able to introduce evidence on the outstanding issues between the A and B stock that went far beyond the strict dividend payment issue without endangering the jurisdiction they found most favorable.[9] It was the first clever move by that team on behalf of Alleghany, but it was not the last. As John Tobin put it, "Any loser can be a winner."[10]

Through the year 1968, the shape of the lawsuit was debated while both sides prepared for battle. MRC had to pay attention as well to the Shea lawsuit, which resulted in a reward of $1.2 million to the plaintiffs, who argued that MRC had deceived them at the time of the 1962 tender offer for MP A stock.[11] In May, Alleghany was offered a place on the MP board of directors as a "good will gesture." Fred Kirby, Allan Kirby's son, was to be the appointee, but the company's attorney, John Tobin, advised him against accepting. A representation of one could do no good at this late date, Tobin told him, and accepting might place him in an awkward position personally.[12] It was difficult to keep the stockholders and analysts satisfied that the railroad was profitable, while at the same time pleading a kind of technical poverty to the B holders. MP officers, however, argued that the sadder picture was the true one, and that any "off the cuff" remarks suggesting outrageous prosperity should not be taken as seriously as the sworn statements given before the courts and regulatory bodies.[13] The company called on two of its standbys in such emergencies: A. W. Ambs and William Wyer.

[9] Interview with Walton, March 12, 1980, New York City. On the venue question, see also *Wall Street Journal*, April 16, 1968, and *St. Louis Post Dispatch*, Aug. 7, 1968, Alleghany clippings, MP public relations office.

[10] Interview with Tobin, March 10, 1980, New York City.

[11] *St. Louis Post Dispatch*, May 5, 1968, Alleghany clippings, MP public relations office.

[12] Ibid., May 14, 1968, MRC clippings; interview with Tobin, March 10, 1980, New York City.

[13] *Wall Street Journal*, April 10, 1968, DBJ clippings, vol. 3, MP public relations office.

Both produced studies showing that cash requirements of the railroad were unusually large and that none could be spared in the near future to increase the dividend on the B stock beyond the current $5 a share.[14]

MP people were not pleased that attorneys representing Alleghany would soon be able to rifle the railroad's files in Saint Louis, and that they all might be called upon to explain embarrassing memos to the court and to the press. Also, certain activities of Alleghany were perplexing and might suggest strategies quite independent of the Levin suit. In October, 1968, Alleghany acquired a small Pennsylvania trucking company called Jones Motor Company. This move had the technical tax advantage of freeing Alleghany and its huge Investors Diversified Services (IDS) subsidiary from regulation as investment companies and placing them under the ICC. It could also be the first step toward making Alleghany a giant transportation holding company, including trucking and (who knew?) maybe railroads.[15] Downing Jenks was disturbed at that prospect, since it paralleled so closely his own vision of the kind of company that would be required for the transportation future. Therefore, in July, 1969, Jenks went to New York to confer in detail with Alleghany officials concerning their plans and his own.

Fred Kirby, who had become president of Alleghany during the illness of his father, met with Jenks for three hours on July 24. Jenks brought Kirby up to date on the MP's current operating figures and his own vision of the western merger situation. The crux of the financial presentation was that although the figures looked promising, there were lots of nonrepeatable anomalies involved. In 1967 there had been a windfall award in the Transcontinental Divisions case, compensating the MP for past discrimination against it by other roads. That year also, there had been a "big mistake" in paying abnormally high dividends from the subsidiaries to the parent company because of Marbury's desire to collect cash for the Santa Fe venture. This kind

[14] A. W. Ambs to W. G. Marbury, Nov. 15, 1968, Craft exhibit 4, space 0610102a, MP archives; Wyer, Dick & Co. study, May 12, 1969, Levin file (Wyer), space 1150803c, ibid.

[15] *Forbes*, May 15, 1969, DBJ clippings, vol. 3, MP public relations office.

of "freak year" should not be taken as normal nor be the basis for Alleghany expectations about the kind of dividends it would be receiving in the future. Jenks said he had been advised that the MP would probably win the dividend suit, but not without a great deal of expense to both parties. And at the end of it, there would still be no solution to the capitalization problem. If some "amicable arrangements" were not made in private between the railroad and the investment firm, the merger movement would eventually return and the MP would be slowly "eaten away" by other railroads, leaving little in earnings for either the A or the B stockholders.[16]

Jenks was not short on ideas about how "amicable arrangements" could be effected. He admitted that the Texas & Pacific merger attempt of 1963 "was dreamed up *solely* for the purpose of forcing a recapitalization of Mop," and he now hoped that more above-board negotiations could accomplish a similar result. One possibility would be for Alleghany to take over MRC and therefore itself become a holding company in control of both the MP A and B stock. This was not unlike plans that had been bandied about since 1964. More unusual, but ingenious enough, was Jenks's suggestion that Alleghany help the MP put together through merger the kind of system he himself envisioned. One way would be for Alleghany to buy working control of the Santa Fe and then force that company to merge with the MP. A second choice would be a similar move toward the Southern, or even better toward both the Santa Fe and the Southern at the same time, creating a true transcontinental. The third choice would be for Alleghany to force merger of the MP and the Seaboard Coast Line. According to Kirby's notes, Jenks waxed very eloquent when speaking about these possibilities: "He emphasized that he feels that we in Alleghany are in a unique position, both strategically and financially to play a leadership role in a western railroad merger scene. He even resorted to flattery two or three times in an effort to be convincing on this point."[17]

[16] Memo marked "Confidential," F. M. Kirby to Clifford Ramsdell, John Burns, and John Tobin, July 24, 1969, MP law dept.

[17] Ibid.

Kirby listened politely but was not interested particularly in these possibilities. He was, however, interested in heading off the Levin lawsuit and in coming to some negotiated agreement with MP to relieve Alleghany of its B stock and allow the company to move into other areas. There seemed a new willingness to begin such negotiations. Kirby wrote of the meeting:

> He [Jenks] emphasized that he has not got a financial, accounting or legal mind but does know how to run a railroad since he has been in it all his life. He has not been able to come up with any suggestions, nor has anyone connected with him been able to come up with any suggestions which they deem a promising base from which to negotiate for the reconcilement of our differences. I told him we were in somewhat the same posture and asked him if he was in the frame of mind to be willing to stretch in order to reach an agreement which would, hopefully, remove us as an obstruction to their merger possibilities and avoid the prolonged dividend litigation which otherwise seems inevitable. He replied he was willing to stretch but did not know from just what position he would be invited to stretch. . . . He indicated that he feels that it is in the best interests of both Mop and Alleghany to make strenuous efforts to reach agreement, because, if we continue to fight over an extended period of time, he is afraid that we shall find that eventually we are fighting over a relatively empty shell.

On that note the Kirby-Jenks conference ended, but serious recapitalization negotiations began.[18]

After so many years of struggle, it was not to be expected that negotiations would move quickly or smoothly at first. Alleghany did not wish to take the first offer that came along, no matter how favorable, and Marbury, who turned over the presidency of MRC to Jenks for a time during an illness, was recovered by the spring of 1970 and back making confident statements.[19]

Some of the early offers had possibilities. The Southern Railway, which was involved in merger talks with the MP, approached Alleghany with an offer for the B stock. Alleghany

[18] Ibid.
[19] *St. Louis Globe Democrat*, May 29, 1970, DBJ clippings, vol. 3, MP public relations office.

turned it down.[20] In 1969 there were discussions between the
Frisco and Alleghany regarding a merger with the MP and a recapitalization, as well as proposals from the Alaska Power and
Telephone Company to pool its rail portfolio with that of Alleghany.[21] None of these plans was seriously considered. The B
stock was going up in value on the market thanks to speculation
about a recapitalization, and Alleghany officers were interested
only in plans that would yield about a 50-to-1 ratio between A
and B values in any recapitalization.[22]

*Forbes* magazine in September, 1970, wrote that the negotiations reminded an observer of the pushmi-pullyu fictitious
beast in *The Story of Dr. Doolittle*. There was a drawing of this
animal with the article, and it had two heads facing in opposite
directions and two sets of front legs trying to gallop off east and
west at the same time. The caption said "Going My Way?"[23] MP
attorneys wrote a letter of protest to *Forbes*, saying that "articles
dramatizing conflict are detrimental to any resolution of the
problem" and hoping the magazine would refrain from further
commentary on the negotiations.[24] But the image of the strange
animal stuck, and it was not an inaccurate symbol at the time.

The earliest negotiations involving attorneys for both sides
were begun in December, 1970, between the Alleghany attorneys who were pressing the Levin case and Thomas E. Dewey
of Dewey, Ballantine, Bushby, Palmer & Wood of New York representing the MP. Dewey, having been governor of New York
and nearly president of the United States, had the prestige necessary to coordinate such delicate negotiations. He was familiar
with the MP, having represented MRC for several years, and
had Robert Craft and Thomas O'Leary at the meetings to aid
him. However, the meetings that took place at the Dewey, Bal-

[20] Interview with Ramsdell, March 11, 1980, New York City.

[21] Memo, John Burns to Clifford Ramsdell, Sept. 26, 1969, no document no., 19(k),
Arthur Garrett to F. M. Kirby, Feb. 11, 1970, doc. 00204, 19(p), both space 0610102a,
MP archives.

[22] Anonymous memo, n.d. [1971], doc. 800285, 19(v), ibid.

[23] *Forbes*, Sept. 1, 1970, DBJ clippings, vol. 3, MP public relations office.

[24] Cleon Burt to Thomas E. Dewey, Sept 10, 1970, Levin file, space 1150803c, MP
archives.

lantine offices did not move things much closer to resolution. Clifford Ramsdell felt that Dewey "parroted Marbury" on the B stock, and Ramsdell was put off when Dewey once stated about it, "You don't really have anything here."[25]

The Dewey meetings were abruptly broken off when Thomas Dewey died early in 1971. However, it did seem that negotiators had established a contact which would be permanent. The parties were fairly far apart at first, Alleghany insisting on about $3,500 a share for the B and the MP beginning its offers at about $1,200.[26] Everyone involved, however, thought that the technical problems of coming to a settlement were not so much a barrier as the emotional heat that had built up over the years and the extremes possible in the personalities of both Allan Kirby and William Marbury. In May, 1971, Alleghany revealed the existence of the talks in its annual report, and both sides talked to the press about them. It was decided that in order to prevent "emotions and pocket-book interests" from clouding the discussions, both sides would appoint outside experts (Eastman Dillon, United Securities for the MP and Kuhn Loeb & Company for Alleghany) to continue talking about the issues introduced in the Dewey discussions.[27]

These discussions also were broken off just before William Marbury himself died on July 11, 1971, at age fifty-nine.[28] This placed overall MP policy at a transition point and exacerbated the hard issues that were truly in the way of a settlement. One of these was that, although MP profitability was high, it was not as high as it soon would be, and there were not quite enough pieces of the corporate pie to satisfy everyone's expectations. As Joseph King, chief negotiator for Eastman Dillon put it, there was not enough net income to satisfy Alleghany's "idea of value." An agreement that would have satisfied Alleghany would have had to have been unfair to the MP and MRC.[29] The other side

[25] *Wall Street Journal*, March 29, 1971, in Recapitalization Notebooks, 1972, MP public relations office; interview with Ramsdell, March 11, 1980, New York City.

[26] Interview with Thomas O'Leary, July 9, 1979, Saint Louis.

[27] *St. Louis Globe Democrat*, May 12, 1971, MRC clippings, MP public relations office.

[28] *Wall Street Journal*, July 15, 1971, DBJ clippings, vol. 3, ibid.

[29] Ibid., May 12, 1971, MRC clippings.

had similar feelings, complaining that the impasse came because the Eastman Dillon people insisted that the A stock was worth par and more, thus making the total cost of a settlement worth more than earnings justified. John Burns of Alleghany thought that only further increases in earnings could break the logjam by allowing the negotiations to "tailor the cloth to fit the size of the individual who was going to wear the suit." Besides, Alleghany was in no hurry: "The key from Alleghany's point of view was not to give too much at all, because there was really no incentive to give. If we just sat there compound interest and time would make you come out whole."[30] At the moment of Marbury's death, therefore, it could not have been more uncertain whether his dreams for the MP would ever become reality.

Because there was an impasse in the secret, private negotiations, the dividend suit went forward at full speed. In the fall of 1971, depositions began to be taken in the Levin suit, and attorneys from the various firms involved arrived at the offices of their opposition to go through boxes of files and keep copying machines warm creating exhibits. Literally everyone in the upper echelons of MP management was cross-examined by Alleghany attorneys. So important was their testimony to the prospects of recapitalization, not to mention to the outcome of the lawsuit, that the MP legal staff prepared an extensive set of instructions outlining the company's policy, its major defenses, and traps to be aware of.[31]

The depositions taken in 1971 and 1972, combined with the documents copied from the files of the MP, MRC, and Alleghany Corporation, formed a rich source of recent company history. The MP witnesses were asked embarrassing questions often but were confident that the opposition had no real legal ammunition in the Levin case, and so answered calmly, and often with a touch of humor. Even T. C. Davis, who had gone from crony of Robert Young and Alleghany ally to defendant in a lawsuit brought by Alleghany, was effective in justifying the dividend policy of the railroad and in insisting that there was no

[30] Interview with Burns, March 10, 1980, New York City.
[31] "Guidelines for MoPac Officers and Directors in Depositions Taken by Plaintiffs," Oct. 31, 1971, p. 56, space 0610102a, MP archives.

"conspiracy" with MRC. Davis said that the Texas & Pacific merger would have been good for the MP and that it was not simply a device to "freeze out" the B holders. "Colonel Davis," asked an attorney, "would you have voted for the merger of a company with Missouri Pacific Railroad, if that merger had resulted in a net loss, economic loss to the Missouri Pacific Railroad?" Davis answered in typical fashion, "Hell, no. And you can keep the 'hell' in there, too, will you?"[32] Extensive exhibits on the heavy MP debt structure were effectively backed by the testimony of Robert Craft and Isabel Benham.[33] When asked about the manipulation of B stock prices, Craft was as outspoken as Davis: "I think this is a perfectly stupid statement. I don't know what—how it could be possible for us to attempt to . . . influence the quoted prices of the 'B' shares." Certain irregularities did not, in Craft's opinion, suggest fraud. "We are not clairvoyant," he stated. "We calculate earnings in accordance with the rules. We live by the rules."[34]

Downing Jenks was questioned more extensively than anyone else, as, in the absence of Marbury, he was the most powerful of the MP "insiders." He was indeed on the hot seat, faced with copies of a number of internal memos which at least suggested that the charges of the Levin case were true. He said later, however, and the transcripts indicate, that he rather enjoyed the opportunity to confound attorneys trying to corner him on his own turf—i.e., on the question of what it takes to operate a railroad. He noted that the MP was spending less per mile on maintenance than the Pennsylvania, which was supposed to be in trouble, and less than any other major railroads but the Rock Island and the Frisco. "If we were gold plating it, we were sure putting a pretty thin coat on."[35] He kidded about Marbury's statements concerning the B stockholders and claimed he had not read one *Forbes* article in 1963 where Marbury was quoted, though Jenks's picture was on the cover of the maga-

[32] Davis deposition, Nov. 18, 1971, p. 56, space 0610102a, MP archives.

[33] Both testified in June, 1972. See "Debt Analysis," March 16, 1972, Reorganization Notebook, 1972, MP public relations office.

[34] Craft deposition, June 29, 1972, pp. 236, 215, space 0610102a, MP archives.

[35] Interview with Jenks, March 13, 1979, Saint Louis.

zine. He said it was a "poor likeness" and that every friend of his who ever had his picture on the cover of *Forbes* had shortly met with disaster. He was on the road when the magazine came out, and when he got back it was such "ancient history" that he did not even bother to discuss it with Marbury.[36] This seemed unlikely to Lauck Walton and other examining attorneys, and public statements of Marbury and Jenks remained a feature of all the briefs submitted by Alleghany attorneys.[37] Still, the evidence was circumstantial, and the questioning did not yield a confession. On the proper amount of investment in the railroad, Jenks was on stronger ground. "What was good enough for 1964," he said, "would not be near good enough now with the chemical business we're handling, the faster train speeds we're operating and the additional traffic that we are handling."[38]

It appeared the dividend case might actually run its course and that Judge Edward Weinfeld of the U.S. District Court of the Southern District of New York would render a verdict that did not go very far toward solving the underlying difficulty. However, it was recognized by attorneys on both sides that Weinfeld was one of the country's most distinguished jurists, and that there existed an opportunity in this case for him to place a powerful imprimatur upon a private agreement for the quashing of the Levin case, the purchase of the B interests, and the recapitalization of the MP railroad. The attorneys themselves were gaining the kind of respect for each other through the Levin proceedings that might make possible negotiations instigated not by the elder and warring principals of the two sides, nor by "outside experts," but by the two sets of attorneys. Marbury was dead, the elder Kirby was incapacitated by a stroke, and in their places were younger men like Jenks and O'Leary at the MP and Burns and Fred Kirby at Alleghany who were less

[36] Deposition of Jenks, Sept. 20, 1972, pp. 282–92, space 0610102a, MP archives.

[37] The briefs and all other procedural documents in the recapitalization case are contained in "Missouri Pacific Railroad Company, Recapitalization. Mississippi River Corporation, Related Tender Offer, 1972–74," MP public relations office. These are 757 pages of photocopied documents bound in a large black volume, hereinafter cited as Recapitalization Book.

[38] Jenks deposition, June 21, 1972, p. 79, space 0610102a, MP archives.

committed to positions taken in the distant past than their pre-
decessors had been and more aware of the emergencies presented by the future.

Mark Hennelly was at first "very antagonistic" toward Lauck
Walton as the latter came to Saint Louis to sort through the MP
files—antagonistic almost "to the point of counter productivity,"
according to Hennelly's own memory of it. But slowly he gained
respect for Walton and Walton for him. They began talking
about the possibility of a negotiated settlement, and this talk
soon extended to John Tobin of Donovan, Leisure and Downing
Jenks of the MP.[39] Therefore, as the depositions in the Levin
case were being taken and the lawyers were "fussing around"
with pretrial preparations, the formal arms-length negotiations
that had been broken off between Eastman Dillon and Kuhn
Loeb in May, 1971, began again at various locations in New York
among the attorneys and officers of the companies themselves.[40]

Lauck Walton felt that the negotiations that took place in-
termittently in 1971 and 1972 at attorneys' offices and over lunch
at New York's Players' Club were a "wearing down" process, in
which the new wave people tried to convince those committed
to the holy wars to soften their position. It was never completely
successful. At Alleghany, Clifford Ramsdell voted against the
final settlement and Fred Kirby abstained.[41] However, people
like John Burns at Alleghany and Thomas O'Leary at the MP
were convinced by the pushing of the theme, with variations,
that the A stock was "stuck" or "stymied," and that the B veto
power was keeping it from either getting further dividends or
appreciating in price on the market.[42] O'Leary saw MRC's investment in the MP in the first place as an "if come" proposition, and he did not want to see that company end up holding a
hybrid security. If the B stock problem could not be solved,
MRC would end up with $60 million "locked into a very static,
almost defenseless entity." It would hold a security in the A
whose potential had been fully realized and whose value would

[39] Interview with Hennelly, July 10, 1979, Saint Louis.
[40] Interview with Ramsdell, March 11, 1980, New York City.
[41] Ibid.
[42] Interview with M. Lauck Walton, March 12, 1980, New York City.

be eaten up by inflation. And how would MRC divest itself of this? Who would want to buy "a civil war with Alleghany?"[43]

Hennelly and Walton had come very close on a price for the B before the negotiations ever started, about $2,500 a share. It was not possible reasonably to go much below this because the B had actually sold for that on the market at one time, and, although two dozen different recapitalization plans were studied during the year of private negotiations, this is about the figure that was at last arrived at.[44] The MP by July, 1972, came up to an offer with a value of $2,000, and Alleghany came down to $2,800. A "final" offer of $2,400 in cash from the MP was rejected, but some hope was held out for a combination stock-cash offer with a value exceeding $2,400.[45] Even then, there was a last-minute delay when an offer of sixteen shares of the common stock of a recapitalized MP and $800 cash for each share of the B stock was rejected by Alleghany. The cash offer was raised to $850 and the deal went through.[46] Downing Jenks was hunting in Montana when a rented plane dropped him the news that the negotiators in New York had at last cracked the most difficult and longstanding MP puzzle of all.[47]

The agreement cost the MP and MRC $97 million, not counting legal fees, an outlay for which O'Leary had been preparing the company's finances since 1971. The terms were approved by Judge Weinfeld in May, 1973, and the Levin suit thus brought to a close. By the agreement, which John Tobin called the most carefully worked out he had ever had experience with, each share of A stock was converted into a share of preferred stock in the recapitalized company, with an option to convert to common. Each share of B received sixteen shares of new common and $850 in cash. Mississippi was required to make a cash tender offer to all class B holders for at least 400,000 shares (or

[43] Interview with O'Leary, July 9, 1979, Saint Louis.

[44] Interview with Walton, March 12, 1980, New York City; interview with Hennelly, July 10, 1979, Saint Louis; *St. Louis Post Dispatch*, Jan. 28, 1973, Reorganization Notebook, 1973, MP public relations office.

[45] *St. Louis Post Dispatch*, Jan. 23, 1973, Reorganization Notebook, MP public relations office.

[46] Interview with Hennelly, July 10, 1979, Saint Louis.

[47] Interview with Jenks, March 13, 1979, Saint Louis.

63 percent) of the new common stock at $100 per share, and Alleghany must tender all its new common shares (399,888), thus giving MRC control of the new company.[48]

Then was shown the wisdom of Marbury's keeping MRC's money in New York. O'Leary went to the president of First National City Bank to arrange a loan. "How much do you need?" the president asked. "Maybe $100 million," O'Leary replied. "You can get it all here," said the banker. O'Leary arranged a $40-million loan at First National City to take care of MRC's tender offer and a $30-million loan at Chemical Bank of New York to cover the railroad's one-time cash payment.[49] Finally, the independence of the MP came down to a specific price.

Even with these hurdles crossed, the complete recapitalization was not automatic. Although attorneys from both sides had taken care to see that the minority B stockholders were treated in exactly the same way as was Alleghany, there were objections from several of them, who tried to stop consummation of the recapitalization and then carried on suits in the courts for years to try to overturn provisions of it. Some quite unusual methods of stock valuation were presented as evidence.[50]

Some of these dissidents voted no at the June 15, 1973, MP stockholders' meeting that confirmed the recapitalization; some objected before the SEC and the ICC; and some pursued court cases.[51] None was successful. In December, 1973, the ICC approved the recapitalization settlement and the U.S. Supreme court declined to review the plan that had been approved by both the district court and the U.S. Court of Appeals.[52] Division 3 of the ICC rejected the argument that the dividend case had

[48] Interview with Tobin, March 10, 1980, New York City; *Betty Levin, Alleghany Corporation and Robert LeVasseur, Plaintiffs* against *Mississippi River Corporation, Missouri Pacific Railroad Company, Robert H. Craft, T. C. Davis and Thomas F. Milbank, Defendants,* 67 Civil 5095, opinion pp. D–4,D–5, May 8, 1973, in Recapitalization Notebooks, 1973, MP public relations office.

[49] Interview with O'Leary, July 9, 1979, Saint Louis.

[50] Consult, for example, various briefs filed by Edward and Barbara Garfield and their attorneys Greenbaum, Wolff & Ernst in Jan., 1973. These are contained in Recapitalization Book, MP public relations office.

[51] MP Railroad, transcript of stockholders' meeting, June 15, 1973, in Recapitalization Notebooks, 1973, MP public relations office.

[52] *New York Times,* Dec. 15, 1973; press release, Dec. 17, 1973, ibid.

been illegally changed to a recapitalization and that therefore the recapitalization had a "congenital defect." It was also unimpressed by claims that the B holders deserved book value for their stock and that the 1956 capitalization could not be changed over the dissent of a single B holder. The ICC board decided that the proxy statement on the recapitalization was clear and anything but the "masterpiece of deception" the dissidents claimed it was.[53]

In June, 1974, Judge Weinfeld reduced the fees for the Levin and LeVasseur attorneys to $1,750,000—still substantial, but, the judge said, no more than adequate for over 11,000 hours of work covering ten years on a purely contingent basis. The time invested by Donovan, Leisure attorneys on behalf of Alleghany had been over 14,000 hours.[54] Jenks might have heard faint "Amens" from several quarters when he noted in defense of the settlement that it would free a good number of talented people for tasks other than the seemingly endless one of fighting the battle of the A and B stock.[55] When one stockholder at the meeting to approve the settlement continued for a long while to pursue the question of technical errors in the settlement and suggested that in future dealings these be corrected, Jenks wearily responded, "Next time we recapitalize."[56]

At 10:00 A.M. on January 21, 1974, in Saint Louis MP officials made the final exchanges of money and stock to effect the recapitalization.[57] Alleghany Corporation, which received a package valued at $50 million, was particularly elated that its "40-Year War" with the MP had come to such a conclusion after it had appeared on so many occasions that the Van Sweringens' original investment in the railroad would turn out to be worthless. Fred Kirby said, "For as long as I have had any authority around here, I have wanted most to get the company out of the

[53] The ICC proceedings before Division 3 can be followed in Recapitalization Book, Dec. 6, 1973, MP public relations office.

[54] Weinfeld opinion, June 26, 1974, 67 Civ. 5095, ibid.

[55] Jenks affidavit, Jan. 22, 1973, ibid.

[56] MP Railroad, transcript of stockholders' meeting, June 15, 1973, in Recapitalization Notebooks, 1973, MP public relations office.

[57] Closing Memorandum, Jan. 21, 1974, Recapitalization Book, MP public relations office.

atmosphere of constant controversy and into the constructive activity for which we're in business, which is asset management."[58] Alleghany sent out a press release containing a brief chronology of the struggle over the B stock since 1929 and pointing out that by the agreement MRC would at last have undisputed control of the MP Railroad and the class B stockholders as a whole would have $95 million for "their once-despised 'token speculation.'"[59] Kirby's only regret was that neither his father, Allan P. Kirby, nor Robert R. Young had lived to see "how well justified was their seemingly endless struggle against powerful opposition and great odds."[60]

The only people happier than those at Alleghany were those at MP and MRC. The recapitalization doubled earnings per share for MRC and freed it and the railroad corporation at last to make the internal readjustments that had long been thought desirable, as well as to compete for merger partners on equal or superior footing with any other railroad in the country. It was no wooden puppet anymore, tied to any interests but its own, but a real live boy at last. In fact, John Burns's Pinocchio image turned out to be a little underdrawn. The 1970s proved that the MP was not a boy at all, but a burly giant that had been waiting in the wings to prove just how extraordinary its assets could be when unfettered. By 1980, those at Alleghany would have cause to believe that it was the MP, not themselves, who ultimately got the long end of the stick from the recapitalization negotiations. Both companies, however, made much of going their separate ways, and there is no question among financial analysts that the recapitalization of the MP was both one of the most interesting and most significant corporate readjustments of the mid-twentieth century.

[58] *Forbes*, March 1, 1974, DBJ clippings, vol. 3, ibid.
[59] "Alleghany Corporation and the Missouri Pacific: The 40-Year War," in Recapitalization Notebooks, MP public relations office.
[60] Press release from F. M. Kirby, Jan. 21, 1974, ibid.

# CHAPTER IX

# Railroading: The MoPac Style

WHILE the managers of the Missouri Pacific were spending a tremendous amount of their time in the 1960s working out the financial reorganization of the company and finding for it suitable merger partners, they were at heart rail operating people. The goal in all the strategic maneuver was to free the MP railroad to compensate its owners through the handling of profitable traffic in efficient equipment over a sound roadbed. None were more relieved than Jenks and Lloyd to put the recapitalization behind them and to spend more time again out on their railroad. Since they had not neglected doing this during the time of the financial and legal crises, they had a property that responded better than any other to the kind of railroading its managers loved.

Nothing is more fundamental to any railroad than its traffic. The MP in the 1960s was well situated to take advantage of the growth in the region it served. It had the good fortune to have both deep-water and river ports and to connect the industrial Midwest with the Gulf chemical industry. However, its Gulf lines needed repair, its service to the new industries required revamping, and both the rate structure on individual types of commodities and the MP's means of estimating the profitability of its specific traffic mix, carload by carload, would be influenced greatly by electronic data processing capabilities. Through the 1960s and 1970s, the Traffic Department and its sales force worked very closely with the Operating Department to promote industrial development along the MP and to make certain that the profitable commodities were hauled as quickly and economically as possible. That at base was what railroading in any era was all about, but in the inflation-ridden 1960s and 1970s, when problems could not be easily solved by adding more cars, more motive power, more yards, more signals, or more double main line unless it could be certain that existing facilities were utilized to the maximum, traffic decisions and their accompanying operating strategies became more important than ever.

One of the keys to being competitive in attracting profitable traffic is innovation in service. Here the MP applied new technology imaginatively, while creating new strategies for handling the traffic cards it already held.

Paul Neff was in the 1950s interested in the idea of piggyback shipping (the loading of truck trailers onto rail cars), which eventually meshed with containerization (intermodal interchanges of freight in standard containers), and he saw to it that the MP was one of the first railroads to get into that business. It may, in fact, have entered the field too early, as the business then consisted of loading with gantry cranes that were not standardized and were often unavailable on connecting lines. Between 1955 and 1965, however, piggyback volume quintupled, so the MP's head start became advantageous.[1]

Jenks pushed the piggyback method hard when he arrived, and in 1962 the railroad offered all five rate plans and could claim that 2 percent of its total traffic was piggyback. In 1965, MP instituted several new high-speed freight trains, including the Texas Piggyback Special, which left Saint Louis each morning and arrived at Dallas, Fort Worth, and Houston the next morning. It ran almost as fast as the Texas Eagle passenger train and delivered trailers a whole day earlier than any previous Saint Louis–Texas service.[2] In 1969, when MP piggyback volume was up 10 percent compared with a national average gain of 2 percent, the company started the Eagle Piggyback Fleet, a set of five expedited trains linking Chicago, Saint Louis, and Texas cities. The railroad handled 4,475 container loads that year, triple the figure of a year before, and estimated that container traffic could eventually equal piggyback when the company built

[1] Interview with Joseph Austin, July 23, 1981, Saint Louis.
[2] Davis exhibit 8, Feb. 19, 1965, space 0610102a, MP archives.

adequate container-handling facilities at its Gulf terminals.[3] In 1970 the increase in piggyback slowed to 1.3 percent a year, with 157,431 trailers hauled, while containerization was up 3.1 percent, with 4,613 loads. The company instituted a concept called Containerpak, which was a systematic description for shippers of the various types of container service available.[4] By 1972 the fast upward trend reestablished itself. In that year piggyback traffic was up 28.8 percent on the system as a whole and 35.9 percent on the Chicago & Eastern Illinois, while container loadings rose by 40 percent. This last statistic was especially helped by so-called mini-bridge shipments from the West Coast to the Gulf Coast and back.[5] The trend through the rest of the 1970s was a leveling off in the rate of increase in piggyback proper, and spectacular growth in containerization, up 56 percent in 1977 alone.[6] In 1969 Jenks noted in several speeches that container-laden unit trains running from deep-water to river ports along the MP could turn cities like Saint Louis into genuine port cities for the import-export trade and could revolutionize international marketing.[7]

Closely related to the development of piggybacking and containerization was the continued promotion of intermodal traffic. Jenks spoke regularly of a time when the western railroads would be consolidated into five or six large systems, when they all would have applied late twentieth-century technology to their business, and when outmoded regulations would be changed. It should then be possible to have a "unified transportation system," where the MP would operate "as a total transportation and distribution company," including trucking, freight forwarding, air freight, and even ocean shipping.[8] A budding intermodal transportation industry had developed in the late nineteenth century but was cut off by antitrust legislation. Jenks told a meeting of the Association of American Railroads at Wash-

[3] MP Railroad, *Annual Report*, pp. 2–3, MP public relations office.
[4] Ibid., *1970*, p. 4.
[5] Ibid., *1972*, p. 4.
[6] Ibid., *1973, 1975, 1977*.
[7] *Longview Morning Journal* (Longview, Tex.), July 11, 1965, DBJ clippings, vol. 2, MP public relations office; *Traffic World*, Feb. 1, 1969, ibid., vol. 3
[8] MP Railroad, *Annual Report, 1968*, pp. 25–26.

ington that "back in 1900 the Great Northern could take a shipment from Buffalo, N.Y. to Yokohama, Japan. They'd use their own ships on the Great Lakes, then their railroad, and finally their own ships again on the Pacific. That's the business we should be in, the transportation business."[9]

The MP president repeatedly expressed through the 1960s the thought that there was no excuse for the "vicious infighting" that went on among common carriers, when it was in all their interests to share the $44 billion freight transportation market in the United States. Joining their operations into several completely integrated companies would give the freight business a better standing before Congress and end the sad situation in which truckers argued before committees against the interests of railroads, railroads criticized barge lines, and the legislators passed overlapping and piecemeal bills that pleased no one.[10] Jenks pointed out that the railroads' "abysmally low" rate of return on investment of 3 percent was caused partly by a set of regulations designed at a time when rail had a near monopoly on the transportation business. These regulations made it impossible for modern railroads to generate the capital needed for improvements. "The railroad industry pays its own way, while fighting for traffic against competitors who receive hundreds of millions of tax dollars in the form of subsidies. At the same time, a mass of antiquated regulations restricts the railroads' abilities to offer more attractive prices and additional services."[11] Jenks told an audience in 1962 that perhaps his intermodal transport idea seemed "too much like a dream, but you will have to admit that what we are doing now looks too often like a nightmare."[12]

The MP took specific steps in the direction of intermodal traffic handling. It lobbied to change the rules limiting the MP's use of its subsidiary truck line. It owned over 2,000 tractors and trailers but was limited by the ICC to soliciting business along routes that paralleled the rail line of the parent company. The railroad felt that freeing its truck line to compete with other

[9] *Forbes*, Dec. 1, 1968, DBJ clippings, vol. 1, ibid.
[10] Ibid.
[11] MP Railroad, *Annual Report, 1969*, p. 1.
[12] *Packing & Shipping*, Dec., 1962, DBJ clippings, vol. 1, MP public relations office.

motor carriers would be the first step toward horizontal integration of the freight-carrying business.[13] An ICC order of June, 1975, did permit the MP truck lines to utilize motor billing and rates competitive with other motor carriers instead of as a substitution for rail service.[14] In 1966 the company asked permission from the ICC to operate a barge line to any port served by the railroad. This included operating on the Arkansas and Verdigris rivers, which were being improved at taxpayer expense. The MP, along with the Frisco and the Kansas City Southern, argued that railroads paid taxes and should be as free as other citizens to use and profit from the facilities government provided. Barge line owners successfully stopped this move by claiming that introducing large rail corporations to the barge business would be the ruin of small contractors.[15] In 1968 a new MP officer was appointed, with the title Traffic Manager—Containerization, who devoted full time to negotiating interchange agreements with steamship companies and other container owners. A Far East office in Tokyo and a Canadian office in Toronto supplemented the railroad's traditional Mexican direct foreign contacts. The MP became a participating line in a Land Bridge tariff instituted in 1968, and in the same year Missouri Pacific Intermodal Transport Company was incorporated in Missouri and filed a tariff with the Federal Maritime Commission to serve as a nonvessel ocean operator.[16] That same year the railroad began application to the Civil Aeronautics Board to form Missouri Pacific Airfreight, Inc., a process that lasted until 1972 before full clearance was obtained. The air freight company handled forwarding through commercial air carriers from any MP station. By 1973 it was serving 153 U.S. airport cities from ten on-line terminals.[17] In 1970 the intermodal idea was highlighted in a promotional campaign entitled "MP Hauls All" that emphasized the rairoad's sixteen different transportation and distribution services.[18]

[13] *St. Louis Globe Democrat*, ibid., vol. 2.

[14] MP Railroad, *Annual Report, 1975*, p. 9.

[15] *St. Louis Post Dispatch*, Jan. 17, 1966; *Wall Street Journal*, Jan. 17, 1966; *St. Louis Globe Democrat*, Jan. 18, 1966, DBJ clippings, vol. 3, MP public relations office.

[16] MP Railroad, *Annual Report, 1968*, p. 3.

[17] Ibid., *1968*, p. 5; *1969*, p. 3; *1972*, p. 2; *1973*, p. 7.

[18] Ibid., *1970*, p. 6.

Many additional service innovations were first designed for specific customers or were a part of the MP's attention to industrial development. In the late 1950s and early 1960s when finished automobiles began moving by rail again, the MP went after that business. It agreed to build auto loading and unloading sites at strategic points on the line and worked with U.S. auto makers to establish auto assembly plants in Mexico and to insure the offsetting export traffic from Mexico which would allow increased U.S. investment there without negative effects on the U.S. balance of payments. Innovations were made also in the hauling of grain, a major part of the railroad's traffic mix. The MP was one of the leaders in the use of covered hopper cars for grain. These reduced claim damage, and more grain per car could be hauled than in 40-foot boxcars. The MP was in a good position to participate in international trade since it had connections with the terminals of major international grain trading companies, both on the Mississippi and on the Gulf. Mexico became a prominent trading partner, especially after it discovered oil to trade for U.S. grain. Coal had always been important to the MP, and after the early 1970s OPEC embargo it increased rapidly in importance. The relatively high-sulphur coal from the Illinois fields needed to be mixed with western coal in order to meet environmental restrictions, but the company was able to participate in these hauls from its western terminus at Pueblo, Colorado. Chemicals, of course, were uniquely important to the MP, and arrangements were made to expedite chemical trains despite legal restrictions on the handling of hazardous materials. The chemical cars were blocked in such a way that they could be flat switched and then routed around the hump yards direct to the customer.[19] The MP was the first railroad to develop a computer-generated hazardous materials emergency response system. All crewmen on chemical trains were provided after 1977 with detailed instructions for each car by its position in the train and the proper measures to take in case of accident.[20] In 1977 the MP had two solid trains of chemicals per day with 75 to 100 cars per train running between Houston and Saint Louis

[19] Interview with Austin, July 23, 1981.
[20] MP Railroad, *Annual Report, 1976*, p. 4.

with no setouts or other work en route. The Intracoastal Waterway was a major competitor to this service, but the water fleets owned by many chemical companies were old and the railroad hoped those companies would decide to change methods of transportation rather than buy new vehicles.[21] Attention to service in these specific areas was important to the income statement. In 1976, for example, revenue ton miles on the MP were up a modest 6.8 percent, but revenues rose strongly in eleven of the road's twelve top commodity areas. Revenues were up 19.2 percent in chemicals that year, 35.2 percent in autos, and 32.2 percent in coal.[22]

Not only were the types of cars changed, but so were the way they were loaded into trains and delivered to the customer. In both grain and coal shipments the unit train was a significant service innovation. It allowed large shippers to receive an entire trainload of a product that was run over the railroad on a high-priority schedule without the usual switching delays experienced by mixed freight trains. Such movements were more economical for the railroad as they involved known tonnages at known locations and allowed scientific assignment of motive power. Unit trains provided rapid turnaround with minimum times when cars sat empty on sidings. It was an advantage both to shippers and the railroad to have turnaround times of three to four days instead of the month often involved previously in single-car shipments. Also, as shall be seen, computerized car scheduling and car tracing made a large difference in guaranteeing a specific level of service. Partly as a consequence, industrial development along the line soared. Between 1965 and 1970, 1,483 new plants or expanded plants were located on the MP, built at an investment of $2.57 billion. In the next five years 1,100 firms invested $862 million in new on-line plants.[23]

Attention was paid to the needs of the small shipper as well as the large one. Amid skepticism from other carriers, Jenks early in his MP career made it a sales policy to go after Less

[21] *Barrons*, Jan. 31, 1977, p. 12.
[22] MP Railroad, *Annual Report, 1977*, p. 7.
[23] Interview with Austin, July 23, 1981; MP Railroad, *Annual Report, 1970*, p. 7; ibid., *1975*, p. 5.

Than Truckload and Less Than Carload shipments. These were profitable because of the imaginative application of new technologies to freight handling in automatic freight houses. The first such facility on any railroad was the Miller Street freighthouse, installed at Saint Louis in 1963. This installation used electronic machinery developed by General Electric and was so efficient that several freight forwarders moved their operations there. Two continuous chains recessed in channels below floor level served as tow lines for 1,200 carts equipped with electronic seeing-eye sensors to automatically shuttle them to trucks or rail cars at 120 feet a minute. The $500,000 warehouse used an automatic package-classificiation system to sort 600 cars or 200,000 pounds of freight an hour for loading into rail cars.[24] Later, the MP expanded this to other locations with the supreme confidence born of experience.[25]

In 1972 with the aid of computers the railroad started the Scatback Small Shipments service to customers. Its advertising logo was a football player carrying a package, and it emphasized more frequent schedules, faster transmit time, and a good monitoring program for Less Than Carload and Truckload freight. This service involved close cooperation between the railroad and the truck line, as well as much interaction among marketing, advertising, sales, and operating people in both divisions.[26]

Vital in all this was the effectiveness of the sales staff itself in soliciting the traffic that the railroad was learning to handle efficiently. Frank Conrad, whom Jenks brought in as part of his original team, made sweeping changes in the organization and practices of the MP sales force. Conrad appointed eleven regional traffic managers and said that they came to headquarters much less often than previously, staying instead in their sales territories where they could now receive updated information. Technology aided immensely in this. In the late 1970s, traffic and

[24] *St. Louis Globe Democrat*, May 15, 1963, Feb. 26, 1966, DBJ clippings, vols. 1 and 2, MP public relations office; *St. Louis Post Dispatch*, Aug. 7, 1962, ibid., vol. 1.

[25] *Arkansas Democrat*, Sept. 1, 1965, ibid., vol. 2.

[26] MP Railroad, *Annual Report, 1972*, p. 8; Speech of Joseph Austin, "Rail Sales: A Creative Approach in a Changing Market," Dec. 1, 1972, copy in MP public relations office.

sales people were receiving special training from Bell and could exchange information through cathode ray tube (CRT) terminals without handling much paper. Also, air transportation made what was once a week's work, most of it travel, into a matter of a couple of days. One important result of improved efficiency was that the number of people employed in the Traffic Department declined from about 1,300 in 1962 to 630 in 1981, despite the merger into the system of several new railroads and a much greater density of traffic.[27]

In 1967 Joseph A. Austin came to the Traffic Department from the Operating Department to understudy Conrad and to take over his position as senior vice-president—traffic. Austin worked especially on developing an in-house training program for salespeople to help them develop more expertise in calls and to budget time better. He felt that the wrong people were often being promoted and began a management-by-objectives (MBO) evaluation program for quantifying performance. Austin allowed his salespeople to hold seminars for other carriers, since it seemed advantageous to have a similar system on connecting lines, and since it was perceived that the major competition came from motor carriers, not from other railroad companies. Foreigners were invited to the Traffic Department training program to learn about ICC regulations, U.S. commerce laws, and intermodal transportation. Also, representatives from the industries served by the railroad came to get education in traffic methodology. For the MP this sort of interaction paid off in increased traffic and less confused relationships with shippers.[28]

The sales training program made a difference in the attitude of salesmen that corresponded with a changed outlook on the part of managers throughout the system. As Austin put it once in a seminar in Wichita, a salesman once became a salesman, not with any training, but because the boss thought he had the right kind of haircut and smile. This untrained individual helped reinforce the poor image of transportation: "He slapped backs and he gave out cigars and he told dirty jokes. He begged and he

[27] Interview with Austin, July 23, 1981.
[28] Ibid.

pleaded and he wheedled for business." He might be called a "solicitor" rather than a salesman, and his approach was negative. He never completely learned the customers' or his company's products or operations. The training program changed that. It recognized that the modern railroad was complex and that the salespeople had to have a thorough understanding of how the railroad service could be adapted to a specific customer's needs. Said Austin, "You don't simply think such a salesman into existence any more than you can think a doctor, an accountant or an engineer into existence."[29]

Service innovation was useless, however, unless the traffic hauled was profitable. A railroad is a machine for hauling goods, but ultimately it is intended to be a machine for creating attractive financial returns for those who provide the massive capital investment it requires. At times in the past railroads were casual about profits. They were in a dominant position, and it was impossible to keep records that would determine profitability on certain kinds of annual movements of traffic, much less on individual cars and trains. Traditionally, the goal was to increase carloadings and ton miles without much regard for the now all-important statistics of revenue per ton mile and operating ratio, not to mention such presently calcuated statistics as revenue per carload by commodity. Some raw materials were carried at a loss in the hope of gaining the haul on finished products. There were no good statistics to present to regulatory bodies on what rates would be profitable. Obviously, in the 1960s that had to change. Joseph Austin, the MP senior vice-president—traffic, wryly notes, "We feel like after operating for over 100 years we've had all the experience we need. We need to make money."[30]

Making money on railroading involved at base two things: carrying a volume of profitable traffic sufficient to utilize the equipment fully and keeping operating expenses to a minimum through technological innovation and efficient management. The former involved primarily traffic, sales, and research people, while the latter involved operating personnel as well as

---

[29] Speech by Austin, "Rail Sales."
[30] Interview with Austin, July 23, 1981.

computer experts and policy makers. But when the railroad was thought of as a whole and as a profit-making machine, the cooperation of all these types was natural.

The goal of the company in the 1970s was to make a profit on every car coupled into. If research showed that a movement was not profitable, the Traffic Department recommended one or more actions. The movement could be made less expensive by using new operating procedures. For example, the carrying of chips and pulpwood was made more profitable by using larger cars and getting heavier loadings. Unit trains and faster turn-arounds were similarly economical. In conjunction with this, a better rate might be sought, either by application to the ICC, or increasingly, as regulatory legislation changed in the 1970s, by direct negotiation with the shipper for a higher rate in exchange for improved service. If the traffic was coming off a connecting line, the MP might try to get a better division on the haul. If none of these worked, the company was willing to abandon the traffic altogether. There was nothing sacred any more about statistics on pure gross traffic volume.[31]

General rate increases were critical in railroad revenue improvement since they had to be approved by the ICC and state regulatory bodies. As a result, general rate increases lagged behind changes in expenses. The computer helped to develop statistics necessary to correctly analyze rate matters, and the Traffic Department by the late 1960s developed an active statistical reporting section to assist in rate making. Thanks to their research work, President Jenks was able to note in 1967 that while several million tons of new traffic had been added that year, there was not a corresponding growth in net railway operating income. In fact, there was some evidence that inflation in wage and materials costs without a corresponding increase in rates was leading to a decline in net railway operating income and in revenue per net ton mile. Jenks told the ICC that the railroad had done all it could in the way of operating efficiencies, yet it had to reduce its capital outlays in 1967 by $25 million from the figure used in 1966. Shippers, meanwhile, wanted more specialized equip-

[31] Ibid.

ment and electronic railroading and would not benefit in the long run from a rate level so low as to prevent the railroad from making these improvements.[32]

The MP benefited greatly from the ICC decision in the Transcontinental Division case, closed in 1963. The issue was whether the trunk lines running to the Pacific were taking an unfair proportion of freight rates relative to those received by midwestern connections. The ICC decided that they were, an appeal by the transcontinental carriers to the Supreme Court failed, and beginning in 1967 several midwestern lines, including the MP, received a windfall payment for back abuses retroactive to 1963 amounting to about $45 million. More important, they were assured better divisions in the future.[33]

However, slow changes in national rate policy were only part of the picture. The MP created a team of experts in 1972, each specializing in two or more major commodity areas. During the mid-1970s the MP, the Santa Fe, and the Southern Pacific went before the Texas Railroad Commission arguing that they could no longer afford to carry aggregates for the burgeoning Texas construction business at a loss, as they always had. If better rates on sand and gravel were not forthcoming, the railroads said, these materials would have to be hauled by truck. The Texas commission permitted an increase in these rates, to the point of profitability. The rate increase on aggregates in Texas had the support of shippers and receivers of these materials. The MP was able to accomplish pricing innovation on unit trains. Reduced rates were negotiated on chemicals shipped in jumbo and superjumbo tank cars, while annual volume rates allowed chemical companies that could commit to shipping large volumes, such as 200,000 tons a year, reduced rates for such shipments. The Staggers Act, which became effective on October 1, 1980, permitted contract rates, which were similar to annual volume rates except that sometimes there was a specific service commitment from the railroad. There were also round-trip rates to eliminate the empty backhaul. Contract rates committed ship-

[32] Statement of Downing Jenks, June 1, 1967, Ex Parte 256, B. no. 2372, space 1150006, MP archives.

[33] The MP involvement in the case can be traced in MP Discovery Documents, secs. H and I, space 1150803B, MP archives, and in the contemporary business press.

ments to MP routes exclusively for specified periods of time.[34]

The second element of profitability, the control of operating expenses, fell to the Operating Department. No traffic manager could deny that his job was made easier by the fact that, for example, the MP developed one of the youngest freight car fleets in the country with one of the lowest bad-order ratios. Its 60,000 cars with an average age of ten or eleven years, and with only about 3–4 percent of them unserviceable at a given time, gave enormous flexibility in dealing with customers. Top management gave full support to operating people in their quest through the 1960s and 1970s to create a railroad that could operate with large tonnages at minimum expense in order to insure that whoever emerged from the stock fights as the true owners of the MP would benefit financially to the maximum degree. Operating and Traffic people met daily. Traffic informed Operating of those trains that were particularly sensitive and should have priority in operating on schedule, while Operating kept Traffic apprised of what they could and could not guarantee to shippers as the physical state of the railroad changed rapidly for the better.[35]

One important change in operating flexibility was the demise of the passenger train on the MP. Jenks understood that passenger service was impossible to maintain in the long run. In 1963 he noted in a speech that U.S. railroads had lost almost $400 million the year before on passenger service, and that 50 percent of intercity passenger traffic was carried by air, compared with 22 percent by rail. The MP was determined to maintain fairly high-quality passenger service on a reduced number of trains until the end came. Therefore, it took off all its oldest heavyweight cars and shopped the newer lightweights for refurbishing. Yet, in 1962 the company's losses on passenger trains went from the previous year's $9 million to more than $12 million.[36]

Statistics, however, were one thing—the nostalgia of Ameri-

[34] Interview with Austin, July 23, 1981.

[35] Ibid.

[36] *St. Louis Post Dispatch*, May 28, 1963; *Wall Street Journal*, May 15, 1963, DBJ clippings, vol. 1, MP public relations office; interview with John German, July 24, 1981, Saint Louis.

cans, including Interstate Commerce Commissioners, for the era of the passenger train was another. In 1963 President Jenks reported that the ICC had twice turned down the railroad's application to abandon passenger service between Saint Louis and Omaha, though that train lost $400,000 a year. Slowly, however, the trains came off, with the train-off hearings getting more emotional as it became clear that after over one hundred years the MP was going entirely out of the passenger business. In 1967 mail, passenger, and express revenues declined $2,874,000 or 12.7 percent compared with 1966. Six passenger trains were discontinued that year and four more were consolidated, for an annual savings of 964,330 train miles and $500,000. Applications were filed to discontinue eight additional trains, which together caused an out-of-pocket loss of $1¼ million annually. In 1968 passenger revenues were down 27.1 percent, or over $5¼ million, and fourteen more trains came off. As of December 31, 1968, all sleeping-car service ended. The railroad that year also stopped checking baggage, including "corpses and newspapers."[37]

In 1969 it came down to the Texas Eagle, one of the last two MP passenger trains, and emotion flowed freely. Witnesses at the train-off hearings yearned for the old days and criticized the railroad for allowing the train south of Texarkana "to degenerate to such a mess that no self respecting person wants to be caught riding it." The company was charged with setting unrealistic schedules and thus insuring the train would not succeed. "Maybe I'm too much of a romanticist," said one man. "I see a certain thing that was beautiful in the development of our country . . . I see it as something passing and I don't want it to pass."[38]

The argument of the railroad attorneys for abandoning Texas passenger service was concise. They pointed out that there was a lot of love for the passenger train and little patronage of it. In the five cities where hearings were held, with a population of

[37] *Wall Street Journal*, May 15, 1963, DBJ clippings, vol. 1, MP public relations office; MP Railroad, *Annual Report, 1967*, p. 3; ibid., *1968*, p. 4; *Daily Herald Press* (Palestine, Tex.), March 28, 1968, Alleghany clippings, MP public relations office.

[38] Comments of passengers and local residents can be studied in Railroad Commission of Texas, Docket 2098 RO, transcript of testimony, space 1150004B, MP archives.

over 1¼ million, only nine witnesses had actually ridden the trains in question during the preceding year. The projected loss for 1969 on those trains alone was $560,000. Mail had almost left the railroads, the military sent its inductees to Texas by air, and individuals took the bus even though the fare was higher and it had little romance about it. These arguments were decisive. In September, 1970, the Texas Eagle hauled seventeen passengers in two cars on its last trip. Observed a local editor, "The end comes like hair falling gently from a tightly wound chignon when the pins are removed. Freed from the tension of suspense and the wondering when, train men now smile easily, talking freely about the failing passenger service and the sudden death of the Eagle."[39]

The MP immediately began studying ways of abandoning its last passenger train between Saint Louis and Kansas City. In 1970 Congress created a quasi-public corporation, then called RAILPAX and later AMTRAK, which provided the answer the company was seeking. In 1972 AMTRAK took over the operation of the Saint Louis–to–Kansas City run, and the MP became, for the first time since 1849, an all-freight railroad.[40]

When John German came to the MP in September, 1961, as chief mechanical officer, not only did the railroad have passenger trains, but its freight operation was in enough disarray to throw doubt on the assertion that passengers were all that stood between the company and profitability.

In the first place, there was the matter of standardizing motive power. The MP and Texas & Pacific together had about 800 locomotives, ranging from 360-h.p. switch units to 2,400-h.p. passenger locomotives. There were forty-four different models made by six manufacturers. There was no system in the maintenance of these units. Every repair station might be called upon to provide parts or service for any one of the models. One of German's first steps was to assign certain points on the railroad repair responsibility for certain makes. Houston and Little Rock became the Alco experts and tried to keep parts and manuals on

[39] Applicant's Brief, July 6, 1970, and clipping from *Austin American*, Sept. 21, 1970, ibid.

[40] MP Railroad, *Annual Report, 1970*, p. 7.

hand, while Little Rock and Kansas City did all the service on
Baldwins. The second step was to re-engine worn-out units
whenever possible with GM EMD power, and then, as quickly
as financially feasible, to phase out all non-EMD types. The replacement program started in 1962 when the company phased
out 150 Alco 1,500-h.p. locomotives and replaced them with
one hundred new EMD GP18 1,800-h.p. units. German then
turned directly to the switchers, knowing that to get the railroad
operating in a modern way it would first be necessary to switch
heavier cuts of cars more rapidly than before. He purchased 140
SW12 1,200-h.p. switch engines, a few of which replaced Win-
ton 201A locomotives in service since 1937.[41]

German's idea was to standardize motive power as much as
possible in order to be able to "cascade" parts from newer to
older units, thus reducing inventory and cutting danger and
downtime resulting from mistakes in putting the wrong part on
the wrong engine. For a time the MP became all EMD. However, it was undesirable to be entirely dependent upon one supplier, and General Electric had introduced some test locomotives in the late 1950s. At first, the MP operating people thought
the GEs were noticeably inferior, but with the production of the
GE U30C, it was decided a new manufacturer had arrived, and
limited purchases began. Later, the line bought U23-B and
B23-7 four-axle units, and lately it has purchased some of the
B30-7A model. One advantage of the GE units in the age of
scarce energy was that their four-cycle engines used 3 to 5 percent less fuel than GM's two-cycles. Maintenance of the GE
units is centralized at Saint Louis and North Little Rock, though
crews throughout the system are familiar with their operation,
and they may be dispatched anywhere at any time.[42]

Many operating advantages in addition to ease of repair
came with standardization of motive power. The company now
has 2,000- or 3,000-h.p. units that can be coupled together to
form almost ideal building blocks for the traffic on the railroad.
The largest group of locomotives in 1981 were SD40-2s, differing from the popular configuration of that model all over the

[41] Interview with German, July 24, 1981.
[42] Ibid.

country only in the lack of dynamic brakes, which are not required on most MP grades. Second most popular were GP38-2s.
If necessary, a 1,500-h.p. engine, usually employed for local
freight, can be added to the road mix. On the main double-track
line running from the Gulf to Saint Louis, one usually sees the
EMD SD-40 six-axle series in two- or three-unit tandem, sometimes with a six-axle GE "U-boat" in the mix. The MP took the
lead in modifying its locomotives to make them safer, even prod-
ding the Federal Railroad Administration (FRA) to make certain
changes. Making any modification is easier when one design will
fit three-fourths of the fleet.[43]

It is probable that in the future locomotive types will be
even less varied than recently. The grades and condition of track
on the system will become ever more uniform, the signaling and
dispatching more precise (allowing for even train speeds and
fewer stops), and train weights more predictable. Unit trains
already make for shorter trains with heavier individual cars.
Shorter trains save on crew, as there are breaks in labor union
rules for trains less than 121 cars and again for trains less than 71
cars. With train operation that allows more frequent, shorter
trains with more uniform weights, chances are that the MP in
the future will tend toward European practice. In Europe, trains
are of uniform length and a sixty-car freight is large, which allows for precise assignment of motive power in given traffic
corridors. There are fewer delays when inadequate power is assigned to a heavy train or when horsepower is wasted with too
little tonnage. Crews will become experienced at handling a
train of given tonnage with a given power, and everything should
contribute to the "flow" that an operating manager craves in a
railroad system. The MP hopes one day to be able to run most of
its freights on a schedule as precise as passenger schedules once
were, and to eliminate the necessity for leasing motive power to
meet unexpected demands.[44]

Proud as the railroad was of its ability to repair and even
rebuild its own equipment, some of this was not paying off. Ger-

[43] Ibid.
[44] Ibid. Some of the author's observations come from a trip on the system taken in
Dec., 1979.

man found the Little Rock locomotive shops welding cylinder heads that very quickly cracked again in service, and the Marshall shop rewinding traction motors, which likewise had an additional life too short to justify the labor involved in repair. These practices were one symptom of a high-output but disorganized and nonstandardized shop system which German, with the help of Jenks and Lloyd, attacked at the roots.[45]

When German first visited the MP shops, they were, as he put it, "filthy, congested, obsolete, oftentimes in a state of disrepair." Like "Mr. Clean" Jenks, German felt strongly that cleanliness and order were the first steps in creating better morale and better productivity. Both Jenks and German had come from the Great Northern, where Jenks's father had insisted upon cleanliness everywhere on the railroad. German demoted several men for not keeping a neat shop and argued that the shop office did not have to be a place so salty that the floor was covered with tobacco juice from half-hearted attempts to hit the spittoon. The changes in work environment resulted in changes in dress among employees, and, according to management, in changes in attitude also. People in the shops began to see themselves as professionals, and they acted and produced accordingly.[46]

Shops and yard offices became standardized. Old buildings that had been added over the company's history and were not entirely functional for diesel maintenance were torn out and the layout of shops changed. German's prior experience indicated to him that it was most effective to have underfloor jacks on the repair tracks and to bring the cars to the tools and the men through a cable car mover system. While these systems were being installed, the orientation of shops was often changed. The MP traditionally had open-ended shops, and the orientation was usually northwest, southeast. This was fine in the summer but made things very uncomfortable in the winter. New and better lighting was installed, and various obsolete paraphernalia on the walls was replaced with safety slogans. The result was that pro-

[45] Interview with German, July 24, 1981.
[46] Ibid.

duction in these shops doubled with the same number of employees, and safety increased dramatically. In 1981 the MP was second nationally in railroad shop safety.[47]

The official statistic was that the company had about 9 to 10 percent bad-order freight cars, but German decided it was probably actually more like 13 percent. The road had many low-capacity ancient freight cars that seldom hauled freight at all. They just went from one repair track to the next. German retired cars that were not economical to repair and bought many new freight cars. The shops at DeSoto were capable of building cars, just as those at North Little Rock were capable of overhauling locomotives and those at Sedalia of refurbishing passenger cars. Here again, however, German decided that what could be done was not automatically what should be done. He assigned the DeSoto shops to the rebuilding of cars, something that could not be done reliably by outside vendors, and the company purchased new cars from the outside. The plan was that when the bad-order ratio got down to about 3 percent, which it did by the late 1960s, the DeSoto shops could be switched to building some new cars to keep the work load even and to put the outside vendors on notice that the company had this capability should the vendors ever give unsatisfactory service.[48]

Centralization and specialization was the order of the day in shops. The DeSoto shop became an open top car shop, with some activity in heavy repair of boxcars and building new cars. Palestine, Texas, became a secondary car shop, mostly devoted to closed cars. Sedalia, Missouri, became the passenger car and caboose and work equipment shop, and later, after retirement of the passenger cars, the multilevel auto car repair shop. The North Little Rock Pike Avenue shop became the focal point for all locomotive heavy repair, with Fort Worth a secondary heavy location, and Houston, Kansas City, and Saint Louis running repair shops.[49]

The air brake and wheel shops on the system came in for

[47] Ibid.
[48] Ibid.
[49] Ibid.

attention, too. The wheel shop machinery at all the locations was antiquated and hard to keep in tolerance with the Association of American Railroads (AAR) rules. The choice was whether to replace all this machinery or to put in a semi-automated centralized wheel shop and brake shop in one location. There the MP's luck in timing was important. These shops were worn out at just the time when significant new electronic technology was available. Therefore, instead of buying new equipment of the old design, the railroad replaced not only old equipment, but an old way of doing things. This had a leapfrogging effect, giving the MP an advantage over its competitors of the type that countries sometimes gain when starting a military establishment from scratch with the latest weapons systems.

In 1962 and 1963 German went around the country looking at the latest in automated wheel shops, and in 1964 a central wheel shop for the entire MP system went into operation at North Little Rock. It started in manual mode in July, and then on German's birthday, September 22, 1964, went into automatic mode. Downing Jenks chose that day to invite the media, railroad industry representatives, and board members to see the facility operating. It went into automated mode at 7:00 A.M., and the tour was at 9:00. That was confidence! A system air brake shop was built next to it, which for the first time on the MP handled both car and locomotive brakes under one roof. Car men and machinists worked side by side more efficiently than ever. Air conditioning later increased productivity at these sites an additional 10 percent. It could then be said that the central wheel and air brake shops increased production 50 percent with 50 percent fewer employees.[50] Furthermore, these centralized shops absorbed all the wheel and air brake work from the Kansas, Oklahoma & Gulf, the Chicago & Eastern Illinois, and other subsidiaries within the next twelve years.

Maintenance of way improved rapidly at the same time the cars and locomotives changed. There was constant heavy investment in literally rebuilding the rail line throughout the 1960s. Yard capacity was increased, the length of passing tracks was ex-

[50] Ibid.

tended, industrial sidings were revamped, and the Centralized Traffic Control (CTC) system was both extended and upgraded. The computer and the new inventory system helped greatly in organizing both the flow of materials and the work gangs on track projects. It was possible to go into one sector and renew crossings, turnouts, ballast, ties, and rail all at once with mechanized gangs. The material came when it was needed and in the form needed. For example, continuous welded rail arrived on special cars designed to deliver it in 1,440-foot lengths, and prebuilt panel rail sections could be put down for temporary routing of trains after a derailment or washout. Thus, the "sheer pandemonium" of previous track-laying projects, where delays in materials left track crews idle and trains on slow order for months at a time, was avoided.[51] By 1978, three sixty-man gangs laid 400 miles of new rail a year regularly. This was a 40 percent gain in productivity over methods used just ten years earlier. In 1971, 260 men had put in 1.2 million ties. In 1976, 180 men put in 1.5 million ties. Part of the reduction in manpower was due to the application of new technology, such as tie-tamping machinery, but more significant still was control of materials flow and organization of crews. For example, instead of working the three crews independently, the company operated two together, one on each rail. The effect was to much more than double the output of a single crew.[52]

This sort of reduction of the number of employees was a goal all over the railroad. Managers kept as close account of the ratio between the number of employees on the system and the gross ton miles of traffic as they did of the ratio of number of locomotives and cars to gross ton miles. In fact, operating with a compact staff was almost a fetish with Jenks and Lloyd, who had learned how to railroad with low funds and saw no reason to expand the staff in direct ratio to available money. German says of Lloyd simply but tellingly, "He gets more out of a nickel than anyone else."[53]

[51] Ibid.; author's observations on a system trip Dec., 1979.
[52] Kidder, Peabody & Co., "Missouri Pacific Corporation: Point of View," March 7, 1978, p. 13, MP public relations office.
[53] Interview with German, July 24, 1981.

It made no more sense to include large numbers of miscellaneous subsidiary corporations within the MP umbrella than it did to maintain different brands of locomotives. Therefore, in order to insure quick and standard actions throughout the system, several wholly-owned short-line railroads ceased their existence as independent corporations. Some had romantic sounding names—the Denison & Pacific, the Weatherford, Mineral Wells & Northwestern, the Abilene & Southern, the Natchez & Southern—and were dear to the hearts of rail fans and modelers. Jenks, however, was not interested in running a hobby railroad, and keeping all these separate identities was a luxury a modern railroad could not afford. When there were no compelling tax or legal reasons to maintain them, the small subsidiaries were eliminated.[54]

Also, the MP was busy in the 1960s adding some strategic mileage to its system to improve its operating options. The Muskogee Lines takeover of 1964, for example, involved three short railroads. The Oklahoma City–Ada–Atoka railroad was sold to the Santa Fe, while the Kansas, Oklahoma & Gulf at 203 miles and the Midland Valley at 335 miles were rebuilt and incorporated into the MP system, giving it a much better alignment in Oklahoma and advantageous connections with the Texas & Pacific in Texas.[55]

Similarly strategic was the acquisition of the Missouri-Illinois railroad, a 324-mile line operating in the lead belt region of Missouri and the coal mining areas of southern Illinois. There was some controversy in 1964 about the Missouri-Illinois, and the mining companies feared that the MP might abandon sections of the line to their disadvantage. At the same time, there was a serious strike on the Missouri-Illinois railroad. None of this stopped the MP from gaining and keeping control of that important mineral feeder line. In November, 1964, the MP in-

---

[54] To trace the corporate simplification moves, see J. H. Lloyd to C. D. Peet, Dec. 31, 1963, Bates 1595; Mark Hennelly to C. D. Peet, Jan. 15, 1964, Bates 1597; G. K. Weigel to C. D. Peet, Feb. 24, 1964, Bates 1602; M. Hennelly to Wm. Marbury, June 8, 1962, Bates 1610, all in space 1150803b, MP archives.

[55] *Tulsa Tribune*, Oct. 23, DBJ clippings, vol. 2, MP public relations office.

vested $6.7 million in this road, thus allaying fears that the purchase had been for the purpose of destroying it as competition to the Chicago & Eastern Illinois.[56]

Probably the most important purchase the MP made in helping the railroad operate better was the Alton & Southern. It was a switching railroad serving Saint Louis and had been owned since 1902 by Alcoa Aluminum Company. In 1965 Alcoa decided to sell the line, and both the Chicago & Northwestern and the MP applied to purchase it.[57]

Its importance lay in the importance of the Saint Louis gateway. Since no railway entering Saint Louis had direct physical access to any of the Mississippi River bridges, all traffic coming through the city on any of the seventeen trunk lines had to be carried on one of two belt railways—the Alton & Southern or the Terminal Railroad Association (TRRA). Saint Louis was one of the most complex switching districts in the country, and these two lines handled 2.5 million cars a year, 19 percent of which were from the MP. The trouble was that neither belt railroad handled them very efficiently. The history of the Terminal Association made it inefficient. It was an amalgamation of a number of small switching lines, most of which predated the major Mississippi bridges, and was so surrounded by the cluttered waterfront warehouse district that it would be hard to expand or realign. Both Jenks and Lloyd served on the board of the Terminal Association, and the MP controlled three-sixteenths of the stock. Still, thirteen other roads had input there also, and each had its own ideas about the best solution to the problem. The Alton & Southern had a better chance at efficiency, but under Alcoa management, it had not done well, especially since Alcoa abandoned its own Saint Louis plant in 1961. As of 1965 the minimum time to get cars across Saint Louis on these lines was twenty-four hours, and it could take as much as four days.[58] Control of the Alton & Southern would allow the MP to equip that

[56] *St. Louis Post Dispatch*, July 8, Nov. 17, 1964, ibid.
[57] "Brief for the Missouri Pacific Railroad Company" (F. D. 24075, 23935), A&S file, space 1150004a, MP archives.
[58] Ibid.

line with a modern electronic hump yard and to plan the pre-blocking of cars in such a way that the frustrating bottleneck at Saint Louis might be much relieved.

The Southern Pacific opposed the MP application for the Alton & Southern, as did the Terminal Association, which wanted indemnification for the business it was likely to lose if the Alton & Southern were improved and if the MP, which operated a full 25 percent of the trains into and out of Saint Louis, used it exclusively. The MP argued that its geographical location made it the logical choice to operate the line, and that it was financially capable of making the improvements needed while giving complete access to other users. The MP was even willing to share the Alton & Southern with the Southern Pacific, though the latter argued that it should have sole control since the MP would probably acquire the Chicago & Eastern Illinois. John Lloyd said that was like the sandlot baseball player saying that since someone else got to pitch yesterday, he should today. "They are in effect saying that even conceding that we [the Southern Pacific] monopolize the A&S and that will hurt MP, still MP won't be hurt nearly as badly if it gets the C&EI, because then it will be in a little better position to withstand the raids upon its traffic and the tremendous competitive disadvantage that SP–Cotton Belt will realize by its unique and favored position at St. Louis Gateway." MP attorneys argued there was no reason for the Terminal Association to get an indemnity since no new line was being created, and all that had changed was the aluminum company's going out of business.[59]

The MP was successful in acquiring the Alton & Southern, with first the Chicago & Northwestern and later the Southern Pacific sharing in the control. The MP took formal possession of the Alton & Southern in August, 1968, and immediately increased the capacity of its hump yard from 800 to 1,800 cars a day. But improvements in service were not spectacular immediately, since, as Jenks put it, it was hard to put enough ties in to hold the rails together, and the retarders in the hump yard were inadequate to hold heavy cars back when the winds were right.

[59] Ibid.

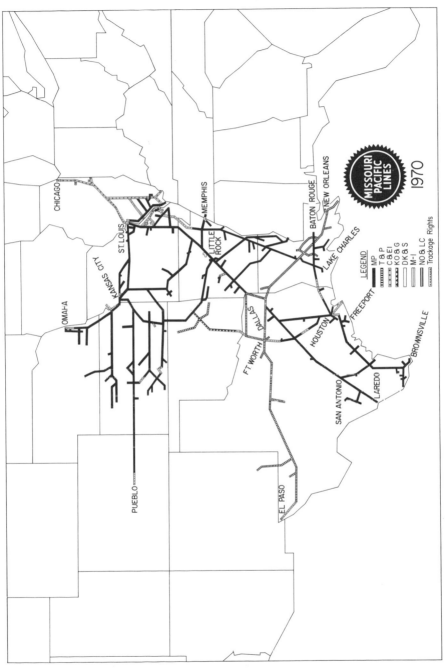

MISSOURI PACIFIC LINES

1970

LEGEND
MP
T & P
C & EI
KO & G
DK & S
M-I
NO & LC
Trackage Rights

CHICAGO
ST. LOUIS
MEMPHIS
LITTLE ROCK
BATON ROUGE
NEW ORLEANS
LAKE CHARLES
KANSAS CITY
OMAHA
FT WORTH
DALLAS
HOUSTON
FREEPORT
SAN ANTONIO
LAREDO
BROWNSVILLE
PUEBLO
EL PASO

FILE  B-6 -504 (1970 m )

In the first month of operation under its new management, the Alton & Southern had fifty derailments resulting from the poor condition of the property, an amazing figure for a 20-mile railroad operating at low speed. However, by January, 1969, westbound cars moved through Saint Louis on the Alton & Southern in two to three hours. The preblocking system instituted by the MP and taken up by other railroads meant less switching in the congested area and faster train building on the departure tracks.[60]

Jenks told an audience in 1969 that the type of work the MP was doing with its computers and yards in expediting traffic through a traditional bottleneck via the Alton & Southern was "far more than just another improvement," but rather "the beginning of a revolution."[61] In that he was prophetic. For while the 1960s were an era of massive capital improvements in the physical plant—rebuilding track, improving motive power and cars, modifying and standardizing equipment and shops—and the maximization of traffic and profit potential by applying all the rate-making and accounting techniques then known, the 1970s were dominated by strategies to apply a relatively new tool, the electronic computer, to the more effective and centralized real-time management of these resources. Jenks put it well in 1965, as computer technology was being applied for the first time on a large scale to rail management in controlling the MP's inventory. Speaking of the improvements that were modernizing the business of railroading, from unit trains to automated warehouses, he noted: "These are the railroads' tools of competition which in the days ahead will be honed to an even finer edge."[62] The operating men who came to the MP in 1961 did in ten years all the things for the company that experience had taught them would improve a railroad. More remarkable in a way was that they also were prepared to do in the next decade what no one had ever done with a railroad before, using computer technology with which they were in 1961 entirely unfamiliar.

[60] Speech of Downing Jenks, Jan. 22, 1969, in "Proceedings of the Trans Missouri-Kansas Shippers' Board," DBJ clippings, vol. 3, MP public relations office.

[61] Ibid.

[62] *Longview Morning Journal* (Longview, Tex.), July 11, 1965, ibid., vol. 2.

# CHAPTER X

# *Control and the Computer*

$\mathbf{I}$T was of great importance to the modern Missouri Pacific railroad that the company and the electronic digital random-access computer came of age at approximately the same time. The coincidence allowed a fortunate combination of managerial imagination with information and communications technology to achieve what complex and far-flung railroad systems had always to their detriment partially lacked—centralized control. The MP never went through the most primitive stages of the application of the computer to business. Though its first computer, ordered in 1958, did predate the transistor and so was bulky, balky, and produced heat, it was a true random-access computer with a number-crunching and data-handling capacity and speed far beyond the mammoth, semimechanical, glorified pocket-calculator type machines of a decade earlier. Because the MP started thinking of uses for a computer at a time when the computer was itself reaching maturity, its people never thought of it as solely an adding machine. Instead, the company started immediately to use the computer as a management tool, although only little by little. As the sophistication of both users and machines grew by leaps and bounds through the 1960s, the complete significance of the computer to rail management, eventually programmed into the amazing Transportation Control System (TCS) software, began to dawn on MP officers.

Interest in the computer predated the arrival of Downing Jenks. Russell Dearmont spearheaded the purchase of the first computer at the same time he was pushing electronically controlled hump yards. The study made at that time gave some general recommendations about what might be done with the computer, including obviously accounting, less obviously inventory control, and more obscurely still, control of operations. But people who were there at the time remember that ordering the first IBM RAMAC 305 was very much a shot in the dark for the company. Harold Hoffmeister invited Dearmont to a demonstration of new equipment by IBM at Endicott, New York, late in 1958. Dearmont was impressed and on the return plane told Hoffmeister to place an order for one of these machines. At Saint Louis, a committee of three was appointed to study how best to utilize it. IBM was taking little less of a risk than the railroad, as at the time of the MP sale it had yet to produce its first RAMAC 305.[1]

When the computer arrived August 1, 1959, the study committee made an important decision. It decided to devote the machine entirely to solving problems in materials and supplies. Even had the computer been inoperable, the preparations in this field necessary to even think about utilizing it would have worked a positive revolution in inventory control.[2] First, writing programs for inventory control required that the railroad catalog in some logical fashion all the materials it currently had on hand on the whole system. This had never been done before. Previously, inventory had been posted on wire recorders by the numerous warehouse managers and then sent into Saint Louis for transfer to large stock books. The information was usually at least sixty days old by the time this process was complete, and errors arose because it was tedious for clerks to listen to wire recorders all day while posting to ledgers. Using the computer required that each item be assigned a stock control number, and in assigning these staff people found that many items had never been listed anywhere before. It took two people two years to put the contents of the stock books on computer cards.[3]

It was learned that not only did the railroad still have many items relating to steam engines, but there was no standard sys-

[1] Interview with E. C. Pigeon and Robert Rathert, July 24, 1981, Saint Louis.
[2] Ibid.
[3] Ibid.

tem for determining the amount of material to be kept on hand.[4]

The AAR Inventory Classification System, initially employed, limited the ability to exploit computer potential. By 1967, MP people created a new Inventory Classification System. In doing this, they increased the number of classification categories from thirty-five to ninety-nine and organized the system so that like materials, regardless of intended end use, would fall together. The number of unique items cataloged in 1959 under the old 1880s AAR system was approximately 70,000. In 1982 approximately 22,000 were used on a much more extensive railroad. Each car shop had its own special way of building cars, often using lumber in exotic sizes which were unusually expensive and could not be used by any other shop on the system. When the new scheme went into effect, engineers created a standard method for building cars everywhere, using easily available tools and materials. This, combined with other factors tending to break down departmental empires, allowed the MP to be managed as a whole railroad with some standardized procedures. The purchasing and materials department was able to reduce its number of employees from 880 in 1958 to 202 in 1982. The idea was to substitute intention for history—to plan instead of react.[5]

Inventory was the first test of the computer. There was no extensive department in the railroad specializing in computer operation, and the purchasing and materials people had both the opportunity and the duty not only of writing their own software, but of selling computer control to a sometimes reluctant group of rail officers and employees. The first adjustments to the new inventory control were "traumatic," and both E. C. Pigeon and Bob Rathert, who were involved in running the system, knew at the time that it made fundamental changes in the level on the railroad where decisions were made. Warehouse managers in the field would henceforward not be able to order pretty much what they liked when they liked, nor would expensive

[4] Ibid.
[5] Ibid.

errors on their part so easily escape detection by officers in Saint Louis.[6]

Some of the first computer programs written after the initial categorization was complete were ones designed to control stocks on hand and reordering. In 1960 the department created a reorder point–reorder quantity book, which was given to employees. This gave them ranges and decision points, noting for example that when the stock of a certain item got down to ten they should order twenty-five. This went into effect throughout the railroad in 1962 and represented the first system of stocking and reordering that was more scientific than the guess of a warehouse manager. There was resistance. The computer, for example, determined that Palestine, Texas, ought to buy 1,800 gallons of gasoline at a time. The Purchasing and Materials Department got a call from a man in Texas who was having a hard time adjusting, as his department had always bought gasoline in 10,000-gallon tank cars. Also, it was difficult to get suppliers adjusted to a system under which the customer knew exactly what he wanted and exactly when and could keep track of just the kind of contributions each vendor was making to the materials flow. The result often was the installation of computer systems at the supplier's business and more careful control of the production processes there. It was no longer adequate to make vague guesses about how long things might take to produce and deliver because the supplier could no longer assume that the railroad had huge stockpiles, stored at its own expense, to take up the slack. The best guide to how well the railroad did this is the turnover statistic for inventory. In 1981 the MP averaged 70 percent monthly turnover of its warehouse stocks inventory value. Many railroads were happy with 25 percent.[7]

Naturally, also, the computer control system had an effect upon the method of storing material on the railroad. As in everything else, it promoted centralization and standardization. Four of the system's twelve warehouses were dropped immediately, and in 1965 a centralized system supply warehouse, known as a

[6] Ibid.; interview with Joseph Austin, July 23, 1981, Saint Louis.
[7] Interview with E. C. Pigeon and Robert Rathert, July 23, 1981.

material distribution center, was constructed at North Little Rock near the new locomotive repair shops and the brake and wheel shops. It had not been necessary since the days of steam to have water and parts available every fifty miles, but information processing before the 1960s was not sophisticated enough to allow much change. The North Little Rock facility replaced the old system of four district warehouses at Sedalia, Little Rock, Palestine, and Marshall, which duplicated inventory four times and were outdated. Again, the fact that the MP had not been updated in a while was an advantage. There was not much inertia about replacing the old warehouses, since they would have required an upgrading at considerable expense anyway. The Little Rock facility was built with room for 25 percent expansion in use of materials. By 1982 that capacity was filled and there were plans to increase its size.[8]

The design of the material distribution center both reflected and promoted changes in the railroad's way of doing things. In the early 1960s most of the unloading of materials at warehouses was done by labor gangs, often walking in file with bags on their shoulders. If a carload of five-gallon cans arrived, each man grabbed two and might walk a half-mile. This was inefficient, expensive, and added to the railroad's number of employees. The construction of the North Little Rock center was an opportunity for utilizing pallets and lift trucks in loading, unloading, and storing materials. The aisles were made wide enough to accommodate multiples of the standard 48' × 40' grocery pallet on which the railroad now demanded everything possible be shipped. Also, special packing methods were used to speed up loading and unloading. Railroad wheels, for example, were formerly shipped in open-top cars. They had to be put on the ground with a crane and then groups of strong men, called "rollers," set them on edge and rolled them to their storage locations. At the Little Rock Center it was required that manufacturers pack the wheels in boxcars stacked on edge. It was then possible to put a snorkel on the front of a lift truck and carry four or five wheels at a time. Again, suppliers at first balked but

[8] Ibid

found eventually this was to their benefit as well. Several innovations required by the MP from suppliers became part of those suppliers' advertising, and other customers took advantage of the new methods of packaging.[9]

Once the distribution center at North Little Rock was in place, it was possible to use the newer and more capable generations of computers being purchased by the railroad for ever more sophisticated inventory control applications. The most important of these applications was the EOQ (Economic Order Quantity) Model. Prior to its institution in April, 1966, inventory was completely counted once a year in July and the result was known four months later. Even then, it was not certain what individual items might be missing, but only the amount total dollar volume was off. The EOQ software was able to handle the 22,000 plus items and 55,000 item locations quickly and to make changes regularly. Reorder points and reorder quantities were established by the EOQ program and then updated automatically each month as trends in business and pricing changed. The program had the ability to recognize standard packages, price breaks on quantity, and to otherwise maximize value. Each Tuesday night a search was made of all 55,000 location items to determine if any had dropped below the reorder point. If so, the computer automatically reordered a quantity, Q, or a multiple of it. It took into account items owed to the center at North Little Rock, and also whether there was an oversupply of the item somewhere else on the system that could be transferred. The program then chose the vendors based on agreements stored in memory, and actually printed about 600 orders at an enormously rapid rate, ready for officers' signatures every Wednesday morning. Built into the program were ways of setting up a pipeline of orders so that cheap items were ordered in six-month quantities, but more expensive items, where storage is higher than shipping, were ordered more often and continued to flow in as needed and not too much before. The model also kept track of the performance of warehouse managers, and of vendors. It kept voluminous statistics with which reports were generated on the

[9] Ibid.

second day of each month. It compared an individual's performance with the same time last year and gave the turnover ratio by categories of parts. Officers and public relations people could use the statistics in speeches, and managers could see from printouts what areas were dragging down the overall statistics.[10]

Once the EOQ Model had proved its worth, the purchasing and materials people found further uses for the computer. However, increasingly, they had to wait for access to the machinery that had once been exclusively theirs, as other departments of the railroad underwent the electronic revolution.[11]

The recapitalization allowed the MP in the 1970s to pursue without interruption goals that Jenks, Lloyd, and Marbury and their management team outlined for it in the mid-1960s. Most broadly stated, these goals were computerized control of transportation, corporate simplification, and diversification. Of course, the team continued to concentrate upon improvement of physical plant and motive power as well as reduction of the work force (the last, aided greatly by the computers and the simplification). However, the upgrading of the railroad to work as well as any traditional railroad was, according to Downing Jenks, the easy part. The hard part, the part undertaken largely in the 1970s, was to make the MP into something it never was and which the conventional wisdom of the 1950s and early 1960s could never have expected it to be. Yet the revolution had to come to guarantee survival, not to mention success, in the atmosphere of railroad future shock that characterized the 1970s. It is to Jenks's everlasting credit that he recognized this early. "What would you do," he told his young ad hoc committee on computerization in 1966, "if you were creating a new railroad using computers?"[12] Jenks did not know the answer, but that he asked the question in that way was a piece of managerial brilliance that eventually had effects as overwhelming as the recapitalization itself.

The rail operating problem to which computer technology

[10] Ibid.
[11] Ibid.
[12] Interview with Wade Clutton, Dec. 17, 1979, Saint Louis.

could best be made to apply was communications. Lack of fast and accurate communication, and consequent lack of standardized procedures on the far-flung MP system, resulted in lack of current information and lack of control by officers in Saint Louis. It could be no surprise in the early 1960s, when to make a long-distance telephone call was a major undertaking and one often had to shout to be heard on a line from Little Rock to Kansas City, that it was difficult to keep track of real-time car movements along the railroad. Communication with yard offices in the field was through a relay office in Saint Louis and was done in a "contention mode" with different parties waiting for an open line in order to transmit information that sometimes was then garbled. There was a certain amount of automation in keeping track of cars, done mainly through the use of punched cards sorted by machine. However, these machines could at best tell Saint Louis where a car was twenty-four hours earlier, and the technology was not sufficient to get orders to a station consistently ahead of the arrival of the train to which they were meant to apply. Therefore, the machines provided history, even statistics for next year's annual report, but were not devices that could tell a shipper or yardmaster where a given car was at the moment or when the train carrying it would arrive at any point on down the line. Making changes in the speed or route of that train and others to fit real-time conditions was out of the question.[13]

A necesssary concomitant of a slow communications system combined with a slow data processing system was decentralized management. Wade Clutton, who was on the original team appointed by Jenks in 1966 to study the problem, put it very well. In those days, he said, when a car left the Dupo Yard (near Saint Louis) for Little Rock, "effectively it was leaving the Dupo Pacific Railroad and going to the Little Rock Pacific Railroad." All processes done in connection with the car at Dupo were repeated at Little Rock, just as if the car had been interchanged from a foreign railroad, and often the procedures were entirely different. For example, all yards had some means of identifying the

[13] Ibid.

At home in front of the Saint Louis arch, sporting the latest of the Missouri Pacific paint schemes. Engine #6044 is an EMD SD 40-2C, with 3,000 hp.

GE B30-7A motive power at Chicago.

North Little Rock yard. In the foreground is the intermodal terminal and piggy-back ramp, with the main classification yard in the distance.

Early cooperation—a Missouri Pacific–Union Pacific through train from North Platte, Nebraska.

Fort Worth Centennial Yard.

EMD SD 40-2 leaving Dallas with piggyback cars. The lead engine, built in 1974, was probably one of the last road engines painted in the full "modern classic" style introduced in 1962. The second unit is an EMD SD 40 built in 1971.

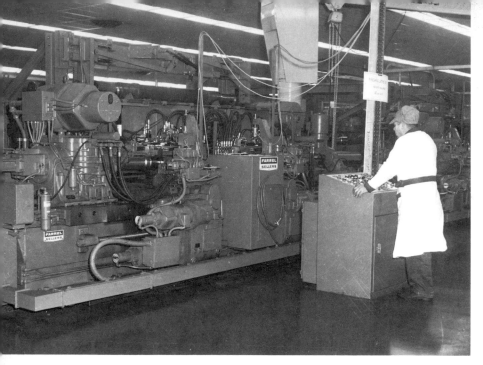

A finishing lathe for brakes at the North Little Rock shops.

Checking wheels at North Little Rock.

For more serious problems, a complete rebuild in process at North Little Rock.

Typical four-unit lash-up in the heartlands. A mid-1970s EMD SD 40-2 in the lead, complete with typical Missouri Pacific snow plow, and lacking, as usual, dynamic brakes. Second is a former Chicago & Eastern Illinois GP 35 (with dynamic brakes), built in 1964. Avoiding huge engines allowed the railroad flexibility in total power and running condition.

Engine #6044 leaves Saint Louis for open country, pulling, perhaps, with the aid of some lesser power, some of its parent pipeline company's goods.

Engine #3272, an EMD SD 40-2, in the lead with a load of trilevel cars carrying assembled automobiles.

Missouri Pacific grain hopper cars. The capacity marking is self-explanatory.

*Left:* Downing Jenks of the Missouri Pacific at the time of the Union Pacific merger in 1982. *Right:* John Kenefick, president of the Union Pacific and the combined system.

Western Pacific, Union Pacific, and Missouri Pacific engines poised for the big system future.

car destination and all classified blocks of cars going to the same destination on a single track so they could be placed in the proper position on the proper train. This was automated in the hump yards. But the designation code for a car going to Houston in one yard might be "H," and in another "19." The Houston cars might be classified on track 10 of the bowl at Little Rock and track 25 at Kansas City. When employees were moved from yard to yard, they spent six months learning a new system, and a good deal of their time after that trying to experiment with the local system in hopes of improving it.[14] All this took time away from straight production, that is, getting the maximum amount of traffic moved.

There was a similar and perhaps even more damaging decentralization in car distribution. Again, each yard acted autonomously. Often, empties were rapidly shunted back and forth between yards, only to arrive too late to meet the demand. Those in charge at the various yards always vigorously denied "stealing" or hoarding cars, but the practice was widespread and inevitable so long as it was impossible for anyone to "see" how such local actions affected the flow along the whole railroad. When a car arrived at a shipper's place of business, there was a waste of time while spotting instructions were worked out on the scene. Jenks and Lloyd saw all this, knew it was a problem, but could not entirely cure it. They could pitch a fit when they happened to run across an abuse, but they could not control the situation because there was no way of being entirely aware of it as it developed in hundreds of different places.[15]

Hope for change came in the early 1960s with the development of and ecstatic publicity for a rail computer application for car distribution on the Southern Pacific Railroad. It was a real-time computer system developed jointly by the Southern Pacific, Stanford University, and the IBM Corporation.[16] The idea was to use the techniques of "operations research" to build a large real-time model that would run on a first-generation com-

[14] Ibid.
[15] Ibid.
[16] Tom Dulaney, "Computers are Working on the Railroads," *Chillon's Distribution Worldwide* (April, 1979), reprint in MP public relations office.

puter—an IBM 650. Its first major application was to do sampling of the distribution of revenues on an interline basis. This was merely an extension of the accounting functions that had been assigned to computers for some time, and it failed because the error factor was too large for management to accept. A second application, however, was more revolutionary in that it attempted to apply computerization to operations by creating a model for the distribution of cars on the Southern Pacific. This failed largely because it was premature in terms of available communication-processing technology and because there was a misunderstanding about how much quality would be needed in the data to make it work effectively. Consequently, however, another joint effort known as TOPS (Total Operations Process System) grew up as a successful management information system on the Southern Pacific. It was the beginning, however modest, of systems designed to aid in planning, control, and evaluation.[17]

The impact of TOPS on the thinking at the MP and on railroads around the world was great. It would not allow officers to go to the golf course while it ran the railroad, as some press accounts led the reader to believe, but it was the first major experiment with computers outside purchasing and accounting, and it promised well. John Lloyd visited the Southern Pacific computer section in California and returned with a positive report about what it could do.[18] Eventually, the MP borrowed two elements from TOPS. First, it acquired the TOPS systems software at mere cost of reproduction for use in developing its own system. However, the MP computer group did not use the relatively limited TOPS applications software, but rather developed its own with third-generation technology and transportation control in mind.[19] Second, the MP eventually (1969) hired the man most responsible for the development of TOPS at the Southern Pacific, Guerdon Sines.[20] Sines proved as imaginative at making a revolution of the technology in 1969 as he had been in California in 1960 through 1966.

[17] Interview with Guerdon Sines, Dec. 17, 1979, Saint Louis.
[18] Interview with John Lloyd, July 12, 1979, Saint Louis.
[19] Interview with Sines, Dec. 17, 1979.
[20] Interview with Lloyd, July 12, 1979.

In January, 1966, just as the EOQ Model was going into effect at the new Little Rock distribution center, Downing Jenks called together a team of relatively young men provided by the various potential "user" departments on the railroad in order to create a "scoping study" on the design and potential impact of more serious operating use of electronic computers on the MP railroad. The Price Waterhouse Management Services Division was employed as consultants to aid this team, which gave interim reports regularly until its final recommendations were presented in 1968. The goal originally was to create something called a Management Information System (MIS), which it was imagined would operate much like the Southern Pacific TOPS system. However, Jenks and Lloyd did two things which in retrospect seem brilliant although at the time they may have been accidental or just intuitive. First, they drew the team from the user departments, and they happened to be young men who were not yet thoroughly enough indoctrinated in traditional railroad culture to know what could not be done. Second, they allowed the team to think creatively without any predetermined applications. In doing this thinking, the team decided what Jenks and Lloyd wanted was not so much information, but control. Why could the new technology not be used to centralize decision making through instant communication, thus standardizing procedures systemwide, placing responsiblity for operations design in the hands of specialists, and freeing field personnel to concentrate on production? When the final report of the MIS team appeared in 1969, it was obvious that what the MP had was no longer an MIS system, but a system that allowed top management to force things to be done, to control transportation. Therefore, in the summer of 1969, the name of the design was changed to Transportation Control System (TCS).[21]

The years 1966 and 1967 were devoted to selling the concept of control through computers, while 1968, 1969, and 1970 were largely taken up with designing a system, selecting equipment, and outlining strategies for implementation. In the ear-

[21] Interview with Clutton, Dec. 17, 1979. Clutton was the representative from the Traffic Department on that scoping study team.

liest phase, many persons laughed at the whole idea and regarded the study team as a hobby for management. Some of those who later were the greatest proponents of TCS felt this way before the step-wise implementation procedure began to demonstrate to them the practical capabilities of these transistorized creations of academics.

One special fear of traditionalists, as it is of anyone asked to depend on a computer for the first time, was how it would be possible to do without the security of papers that could be folded up and put in one's pocket, or without identifying cards which could be physically attached to the sides of cars. The team insisted that there could be no back-up paper, both because that would eliminate one of the greatest savings which could be brought about by computers and because if there were a fall-back procedure the new methods could never be effectively implemented among employees nor their virtues adequately tested. There continued to be a good deal of resistance, and one of the major problems of implementation turned out to be how best to orient railroaders to electronic media. But in an interim meeting of 1967 Jenks became convinced that TCS should be implemented and told the scoping study team that it would be. He had seen dramatic reductions in both inventory costs and employees through the application of computers to purchasing, and he saw more promise still in what the 1966 team was developing. When Jenks said it would go, all knew it would eventually be in place.[22]

The man more responsible than anyone else for the modular phased implementation program that was so important to the success of TCS was Guerdon Sines. Sines was a West Point graduate engineer whose father was a vice-president of the Southern Pacific. The younger Sines worked with the TOPS system from 1960 to 1966. While the MP MIS study was going on, he moved to the New York Central at the request of A. E. Perlman and then worked for the merged Penn Central. However, the problems associated with trying to interface the different computer systems of the Pennsylvania and New York Central

[22] Ibid.

Railroad, not to mention the difficulties integrating their differing management philosophies (so graphically outlined in postmortems of the merged line's bankruptcy) were not the kind Sines enjoyed. Therefore, Lloyd was able to hire him for the MP.[23]

Sines found the situation at the MP much more attractive as a base from which to make large contributions to computer applications. The MIS team had done its work well, although it had made the mistake of thinking that all of TCS could be put in place at once and turned on with some giant switch. Sines convinced them that, as Wade Clutton put it, they had "designed a cow to be eaten in one bite and if we didn't break our jaws, sure to God our stomachs would have exploded."[24] Sines directed the MIS team to divide it into digestible chunks, short term, easy to visualize and understand. This had the advantage of convincing doubters as the implementation went along as well as preparing them with the habits they would need for more subtle applications. There had been good preparation in the installation of second- and third-generation computer equipment and the kind of programming that would be needed for TCS. The MP was a pioneeer in using the RAMAC 305, a random-access system, and by the time Sines came in 1969, the people were fully up and prepared to use the new IBM 360 system. Sines's predecessor as chief of the computer section, Jack Heidenreich, had made the courageous decision to commit completely to the 360 and 370 rather than running programs in emulation of the old 7074, as many other users were doing. While most if not all programs retained the same concepts as before, they were completely reprogrammed in 360 COBOL, thus taking avantage of the full capabilities of the new equipment. The railroad's two 360/50 computers, with 212,000 positions and 512,000 positions of high-speed memory, respectively, and capabilities to receive from twenty-five message centers, were the hardware necessary to operate TCS as the planning team had envisioned it.[25]

Several important implementation reports were finished in

[23] Interview with Lloyd, July 12, 1979.
[24] Interview with Clutton, Dec. 17, 1979.
[25] Interview with Sines, Dec. 17, 1979.

1969. One was the so-called brown book, created with the consulting assistance of McDonal Automation. This defined the major systems in narrative and block diagram form and was sent out to a community of ten vendors for proposals. It was hoped that some company would be willing to share the costs of development, as IBM had with the Southern Pacific and with several airlines, in order to get entry into the industry. But no proposal was more attractive than the prospect of sticking with IBM and using at least the systems software from TOPS as a basis for new applications. This decision was made in the spring of 1970, shortly after the last report of the MIS scoping study—the "green book," the first of a series dealing with implementation—appeared.[26]

The TOPS software got the wheel reports into the MP's central computer and gave it a start in the important matter of keeping track of cars. But there was to be much more to TCS than there was to TOPS. Under the heading "General Flow," the 1969 "green book" report described a revolution in the way the railroad would run. There would be a series of customer service centers from which all waybill information would be input. Then car movement events would be reported as they happened in the field. The car files would be constantly updated with the latest events and would be always available to any user. From these files, batch programs would be created for the preparation of adminstrative reports, for statistical rundowns of all empty cars available in twenty-three different categories, and for the use of car distributors in making decisions on the basis of overall system need.[27] Thus, at this first stage, some of the most annoying problems having to do with car distribution would be addressed. The ultimate goal after some years was car scheduling, that is, being able to control the movements and arrivals of individual cars anywhere on the line fairly precisely and to tell a shipper not only where his car was at the moment, but where it would be at any moment in the future.

Procedures at the yard office changed also in stages. At this

[26] Ibid.

[27] Interview with Lloyd, July 12, 1979; MIS Scoping Study, Report of Task Force, Sept. 17, 1979, pp. 1–5, TCS office, MP Railroad, Saint Louis.

first stage the yard clerk prepared a list of car numbers that was keypunched and produced a Car Movement Control (CMC) deck which was then transmitted over the IBM 1050 communications system to the computer. The CMC deck would there be verified against the train's arrival and the conductor's freight train work order before being transferred to a Perpetual Inventory of Car Location (PICL) file. There were many codes to learn, but it was soon seen that the control this system gave was worth it. As was graphically demonstrated in a colored chart in the 1969 report, the computer would be able to "see" the railroad represented as a network of sixty-three reporting nodes with connecting links. Each node would have direct access to the computer for inquiry, updating, and forwarding through the teleprocessing system.[28]

None of this was inexpensive. The first phase, called for the moment MIS-1, called for forty-five customer service centers, the initial one of which was installed at Little Rock in 1968. A TCS center was established in Saint Louis. For implementation of MIS-1, the central computers also had to be upgraded. There was added 256K of core storage, 116M of disc storage, and a number of transmission control units, at a cost of $133,056 a year. IBM 1050 teleprocessing terminals cost $350 a month each, and there were to be eighty-one of them on fifty-six communication channels. Also, a training program would be required.[29]

Still, it was felt that labor savings alone would soon pay for the system. All car data relay work would be eliminated and telegraphic forces would be much reduced. In total, seventy work days a week and an annual savings of $122,000 could come from force reductions in the system's five relay offices. Another 121 work days a week or an annual savings of $192,000 could be expected from elimination of keypunching of conductors' wheel reports and interchange reports. Weighing the extra expenses against the savings, the 1969 report concluded that there would be a net cost of $256,000 a year for MIS-1, and a one-time in-

[28] MIS Scoping Study, Report of Task Force, Sept. 17, 1979, p. 6, TCS office, MP Railroad.

[29] MP Railroad, *Annual Report, 1968*, p. 4; MIS Scoping Study, Report of Task Force, Sept. 17, 1979, pp. 12–13, TCS office, MP Railroad.

stallation charge of $661,000.[30] While that might seem like a large figure, it was no more than a few 3,000-h.p. locomotives and promised a tremendous increase in the railroad's ability to handle freight and therefore to generate profits. In his 1969 statement to the stockholders, Jenks said that the ultimate TCS was "more complex than any commercial management information system now in existence" but would be the most effective. "TCS," he said, "may well be the most revolutionary development in railroading of this century."[31]

The succeeding phases of TCS implementation came up regularly, six to eighteen months apart, through the 1970s, each one more successful than the last. Yards and customer service centers were all tied into the information network in 1971, and the computers began to be used widely for simulation of actual yard operations and to analyze various scheduling opportunities for cars. The TRNG railroad, which existed only on the computer but which used authentic MP procedures entirely, allowed trainees to make decisions about service to several fictitious towns and see the results without leaving the computer terminal.[32] In 1972 the fourth generation of computers arrived with the replacement of three IBM 360/50s by two IBM 370/155s. Consequently, some non-TCS programs were added for payroll data reporting, computerized skill inventories for all employees, a computer tracing system for materials purchased, and a system to monitor labor and machinery expense in the maintenance of the way. There were simulations for optimum horsepower and tonnage ratios necessary to maintain given schedules, and programs to calculate fuel consumption by locomotives at various speeds and loads. The computers even aided the railroad in its political lobbying by making a railroad-barge cost analysis and pointing out hidden costs in using barges instead of railroads. Most significant, though, was the success with which TCS handled the job for which it was originally designed: moving cars over the road. The MP reported in 1972 that car hire had been

[30] MIS Scoping Study, Report of Task Force, Sept. 17, 1979, pp. 16–17, TCS office, MP Railroad.
[31] MP Railroad, *Annual Report, 1969*, Jenks's statement.
[32] Ibid., *1970*, p. 9.

reduced by $9.1 million that year and that foreign cars remained on the MP railroad nearly 2 million fewer days than the year before, thanks largely to the control given by TCS.[33]

At the end of 1971 Sines's input led to a much more sophisticated report than ever before. "TCS Implementation/Development Strategy" outlined a means of implementation that it was hoped would produce the greatest economic advantage while maintaining technical feasibility and operational practicality. It described in considerable detail a step-by-step multi-million-dollar procedure that would make the MP into an almost wholly computerized railroad by 1980.

TCS-1, also called MIS-1, has been described. Using IBM 1050s and Model 35 teletypes as input devices, it established a data base for the car movement cycle that was more complete than ever before. It provided automatic forwarding of train consists and car movement cards to downline terminals to drive local car control systems and improve car tracing capability. Initial cutover of TCS-1 at Kansas City was November 17, 1970. Full implementation was accomplished on February 20, 1972.[34]

TCS-2, 3, and 4 represented the staged implementation of the most advanced car control system in railroading. TCS-2 had no effects in the field and consisted of installing the systems software and file organization packages acquired from the Southern Pacific. TCS-3 made the field modifications to take advantage of TCS-2's computer modifications. Central to TCS-3 was the upgrading of waybill reporting and installation of CRT terminal devices at customer service center locations to operate the waybill system. It also involved the installation and field testing of the first stage of the Yard and Terminal Subsystem (YATS), which introduced CRTs and minicomputers for the clerical effort required to collect car identification, switching, and track location information. TCS-4, which was cut in overnight with full management backing in the middle of the 1975 recession, completed everything needed for complete reporting and car distribution.[35]

[33] Ibid., *1972*, pp. 8, 11.

[34] Transportation Control System, Implementation and Development Strategy, Sept. 27, 1971, revised Aug. 15, 1972, pp. 41–42, TCS office, MP Railroad.

[35] Interview with Sines, Dec. 17, 1979; Transportation Control System, Imple-

The waybill system (to be called AUTOBILL), which was a major part of TCS-3, did away with the need to enter repetitive information, as this was stored in the computer. Many shipments from industry were very similar each time and almost all that had to be entered was the car identification and its weight. The computer even knew the date. A repetitive waybilling code (RWC) allowed a shipper to call a customer service center clerk and say, "I am releasing your car—IC56201 loaded for Denver, pattern number 563 with 82,500 pounds." No further information was necessary. The number of strokes to produce a waybill was reduced by 75 percent in this way, and input delays were minimized.[36]

The YATS subsystem dominated yard offices from the time of its implementaion. In its first implementation stage (concurrent with TCS-3) it replaced Yard Car Control (YCC) by moving the PICL card box into a local computer file, provided computer-supported classification work-order generation, and gave data for yard management.[37]

The phased installation of YATS, one of the most complicated subsystems of TCS, well illustrates Sines's philosophy of implementing things carefully and in digestible bites. Before anything, yards were given what was known as ZTS (Zone, Track, Spot Numbering System), a uniform location code without which any of the computerized control processes would be impossible. ZTS located cars by assigning them a seven-digit number, the first two of which represented the zone, the third through the fifth the track, and the sixth and seventh digits the spot. Following implementation of ZTS, YCC and ICC could be implemented using the card systems and PICL clerks sorting inventory cards in boxes. Finally, the yard was ready for the full electronic YATS methodology. Implementation of YATS required two teams. The first team, consisting of two men, spent two weeks at each yard performing pre-cutover and training tasks.

mentation and Development Strategy, Sept. 27, 1971, revised Aug. 15, 1972, pp. 42–49, TCS office, MP Railroad.

[36]Transportation Control System, Implementation and Development Strategy, Sept. 27, 1971, revised Aug. 15, 1972, pp. 43–44, TCS office, MP Railroad.

[37]Ibid., pp. 46–48.

The second team of four men arrived at the yard prior to cutover time and provided six weeks of training and shift coverage for clerks and yardmasters. This was quite a task, considering that YATS was planned initially for twenty-three YCC locations.[38]

Implementation of TCS-4 promised to be even more difficult than YATS had been, as it included not only the first stage of YATS, but the cutover from all of TCS-2 and 3 as well. TCS-4 provided the final sophistication in reporting on cars to the central computer as well as the real-time monitoring for the reporting of scheduled events. It was designed to provide the data base necessary for the extension to TCS-4.5 (Car Distribution), TCS-5 and 6 (Car Scheduling and Work Orders), and TCS-7 (the Management Information Exploitation and Science Phase). Exploitation of the data base from the reporting system would allow management science computer techniques to be used to distribute cars throughout the railroad.[39]

As it happened, the one-time cutover of TCS-4 on November 30, 1975, involved the most intensive training program ever instituted on the MP railroad, and the largest such single computer project, other than the implementation of the American Airlines system, ever attempted in transportation. It involved training for the 9,000 people who would be using it every day and an eleven-week training program in Saint Louis for a 260-member implementation and field training team. It was done during a recession and while the MP was recovering from financing its recapitalization.[40] For by 1975, there was no more scoffing at the men in the computer section.

TCS-5 and 6 provided for car scheduling and the generation of work orders. Although it had been planned this way in 1971, the MP received a boost in developing this phase from a $5.5 million grant from the FRA for an automated car-scheduling system for the railroad industry as a whole. The FRA in making the award commended the MP for its pioneering effort with TCS thus far and pointed out that while other railroads had spent as much money on computerization, only the MP had accom-

[38] Ibid., pp. 34–36.
[39] Ibid., pp. 48–49.
[40] MP Railroad, *Annual Report, 1975*, p. 11; interview with Sines, Dec. 17, 1979.

plished all steps necessary "as a foundation for precise scheduling of individual freight cars, loaded and empty, from dock to dock."[41] TCS-5 would account for 30 percent of the car hire savings attributed to TCS as a whole. When sufficient confidence had developed, the scheduling would be extended from major yards and associated industrial areas to the rest of the railroad served by local trains. This phase was designated TCS-6. The wholesale closing of small stations it allowed permitted clerical reductions estimated to save over $2 million annually.[42]

The last two phases of TCS implementaion, 7 and 8, were management exploitation–management science phases, with 7 concentrating on the generation of executive and middle-management controls and 8 upon accounting. Neither required extensive field implementation, but each did allow much closer cost accounting on individual shipments to find out not only if the railroad was carrying a lot of freight, but to obtain information on what cars were profitable and how profitable they really were.[43]

By 1978, when car scheduling was working and working well on pilot sections of the MP, management was able to print a series of booklets explaining a virtually complete TCS to shippers and a very impressed railroad community. Along the way in implementing the phases of TCS, the major goals had been even further subdivided, and the spinoff of "bells and whistles" useful to the railroad in some way was enormous. One major system or subsystem after another represented such original research and development that they were rail industry firsts. The AUTO-BILL system was a first, as were YATS and the car-scheduling and car-distribution capabilities of TCS. So was the generalized inquiry feature of the TCS computers, which allowed the manager to ask anything he wanted about the status of the railroad.[44] The MP departments, far from being skeptical about TCS, were by the late 1970s putting a tremendous load on Sines and his as-

[41] MP Railroad, *Annual Report, 1975*, p. 11.
[42] Transportation Control System, Implementation and Development Strategy, Sept. 27, 1971, revised Aug. 15, 1972, pp. 50–54, TCS office, MP Railroad.
[43] Ibid., pp. 55–57.
[44] Interview with Sines., Dec. 17, 1979.

sociates by constant demands for more programs to further aid their respective operations.

The capabilities of TCS gave managers a great deal of confidence in their ability to manipulate the railroad and allowed them to scoff at skeptics who were still wondering "whether a railroad can operate in that disciplined an environment." It seemed to MP people that the real question was how railroads ever operated without that disciplined an environment. Assistant to the Vice-President—Operations W. F. Hildebrandt in a speech before the Southwest Shippers Advisory Board in June, 1978, quoted a statement concerning what railroads needed that almost exactly corresponded to what TCS provided. Railroads needed: the most effective use of motive power; the regulation and reduction of speed to the lowest standard consistent with the exigencies of business; the means of controlling the movement of rolling stock, that the greatest amount of service may be derived therefrom; and the reduction of dead weight and an increase in useful load. That statement was made by an officer of the Erie Railroad in 1854![45] In providing more predictable, reliable, and efficient transport, TCS was not revolutionizing the goals of rail operation, only the means used in attempting to realize them. "Why are you so confident?" a reporter asked Hildebrandt. He answered without hesitation:

> I've worked with various subsystems of our TCS since the early days, for the past seven years. It works. It has already paid for itself. We came into the benefit side of the cost/benefit ratio four or four-and-a-half years ago, based strictly on car utilization, car-day savings. Car scheduling is the final, or at least the latest, phase of the system. To a great extent, it ties all the other pieces together, particularly from the user's standpoint. We're confident that the technology works. We deal with a computer system where the uptime is in the 98%-to-99% range—and my automobile is not that reliable. We have highly disciplined input from the field. What this adds up to is that you can make decisions with a high degree of confidence, management decisions, operating decisions. You don't look at the system and then check it against

---

[45] W. F. Hildebrandt, "Car Scheduling: 'What's in it for Me?'" MP public relations office. See also Robert L. Barley, "Freight Car Scheduling," ibid.

something else before you make a decision—we got out of that mold several years ago. That may sound overly simplistic, but I think it's very important in terms of reassuring other people that it works. Take an operating officer from another railroad: We have to start with his believing, with us establishing our credibility. Yes, this hammer does have a handle. Yes, when you swing the hammer, the head doesn't fall off. Yes, the hammer hits the nail.[46]

Indeed, the MP had made the hammer head with the upgrading of its physical system and traffic capabilities. The computer was the handle, and it fit perfectly.

[46] *Railway Age*, Aug. 28, 1978, pp. 23–24.

# CHAPTER XI

# The "Mop-Up"

THE recapitalization not only allowed the Missouri Pacific management to concentrate on realizing the most far-reaching goals in reform of the physical plant and operating practices of the railroad, but also opened the way for corporate simplification and strategic merger. At the same time young managers for the railroad's new age emerged regularly from the Management Development Program that Jenks had made one of his first priorities upon coming to the company.

Mississippi River Corporation was more than the great "What Is It?" that provided Marbury and his successors with a corporate vehicle for large financial schemes. It also supervised operating companies in the fields of oil and gas exploration, gas transmission, and the manufacture of cement. Here too the management abilities of the Jenks team were evident, and the activities were profitable despite difficulty predicting the moves of political forces in those highly regulated areas. As late as 1964 the official line at Mississippi was that in the future the gas pipeline, exploration and production of oil and gas, and the investment in the MP railroad would all be about equal in their contributions to the parent company's income.[1] As it happened, the cement business was marginal, and the most important role of the pipeline and oil and gas profits was in providing capital for MRC's moves in the railroad field.

Least successful of MRC's major nonrail ventures was its oil

---

[1] *Wall Street Transcript,* June 29, 1964, MRC clippings, MP public relations office.

and gas operation. This was so primarily because during the 1960s oil and gas prices were unattractive and exploration was on the decline precisely at a time when MRC was in need of capital for its purchases of MP stock. It did invest with some success in wildcat wells, often along with major oil companies. However, its accountants found that gas and oil prices were too low and exploration and production costs too high to make the pre–energy crisis drilling business very exciting. In 1966 more than half the wells drilled were dry, and in Louisiana, where it would be convenient to find production close to the Mississippi River Transmission Company (MRTC) pipeline, gas wells were often going to 15,000 feet and costing $1.5 million each. Therefore, beginning with the sale of Milwhite Mud Sales at the time of Mississippi's first big purchases of MP stock and through the 1960s, the company slowly dismantled the exploration group that Marbury had put together in the 1950s. In January, 1968, Marbury announced that MRC was selling a part of its remaining oil and gas exploration operation. Holdings in Kansas of the Natural Gas and Oil Corporation, a subsidiary of River Corporation, which was in turn wholly owned by MRC, brought a net gain after taxes of $686,000. Bids were asked for West Texas Properties.[2]

Ironically, in light of the tremendous increase in exploration activity following the OPEC embargo only five years later, MRC took a loss in its overall 1968 selloff of oil and gas subsidiaries of $336,000. Marbury and Jenks, however, were not ones to put all of their money on one roll of the dice. In May, 1973, Jenks was able to announce that MRC had sold Natural Gas and Oil Company, too small without its Kansas holdings to operate independently, to Ada Oil Company of Houston for $17 million in cash. Meanwhile, MRTC maintainted its own exploration subsidiary, and some joint exploration ventures continued.[3]

Cement was a logical field for MRC to continue in, as the company had property near the Mississippi River where large amounts of sand were available and where there was access to

[2] *St. Louis Post Dispatch*, May 27, 1965, Jan. 17, 1968, ibid.
[3] *Wall Street Journal*, May 24, 1968, *St. Louis Post Dispatch*, May 13, 1973, ibid.

energy from the pipeline in the quantities and at the cost that might make a large-scale cement business attractive. MRC's subsidiary River Cement built a large plant thirty miles south of Saint Louis at a cost of $30 million and by the spring of 1965 produced at a rate of three million barrels of cement a year. It distributed its product by means of its own barge fleet as well as by truck and railroad. In 1968 the plant was expanded to a five-million-barrel annual capacity and in 1973 was again enlarged, to a capacity of 6.9 million barrels a year.[4] The innovative engineering that went into River Cement's large plant seemed to pay off in an ever-increasing volume of business.

Some of the plans for River Cement were frustrated, however, by a series of run-ins with the Federal Trade Commission (FTC) over acquisition of ready-mix concrete companies. Stewart Concrete & Materials Company, the MRC subsidiary that controlled River Cement, purchased three ready-mix companies in 1963 and 1964. This led to a complaint by the Federal Trade Commission that Mississippi River and others were "aggravating the trend toward vertical integration between suppliers and consumers of Portland cement" and thereby decreasing competition in violation of the Clayton Anti-Trust Act. The FTC argued that when River Cement began construction of its large producing facility in 1963 it purposefully purchased ready-mix companies to provide a market for the output.[5]

Marbury had never been fond of regulatory agencies, and he turned the ire he had formerly reserved for the Federal Power Commission (FPC) on the FTC. He said that River Cement was just now getting into the business of the production of cement and singling it out would only compound the competitive problems in the industry. He called for a complete investigation so that all members of the cement industry might be treated equally by the regulatory agency. Marbury said that many cement producers controlled ready-mix companies through extensions of credit and direct financing and that MRC was only

---

[4] *St. Louis Post Dispatch*, June 7, 1965, March 28, 1973, *Wall Street Journal*, Feb. 6, 1968, ibid.

[5] *Wall Street Journal*, March 24, 1965, *St. Louis Post Dispatch*, July 18, 1966, ibid.

doing openly what had been done secretly in the industry for years. Besides, some degree of vertical integration made economic sense, he argued, and increased competition by allowing River Cement access to distant markets that might otherwise be barred to it by covert agreements between established producers and ready-mix companies.[6]

The FTC was not impressed by these arguments. In 1969 it ordered MRC to divest itself of its three ready-mix companies. The commission concluded that River Cement used its power to avoid price competition. MRC appealed to the courts, but in January, 1973, the U.S. Court of Appeals in Saint Louis upheld the FTC's decision.[7]

By this time the ready-mix companies were a financial burden as well as a legal headache. However, selling them, as was done in 1972, compromised the overall plan, and left MRC management looking for a good way out of the cement business. River Cement was sold in 1979 to the Italian firm of IFI International SA for $78 million.[8]

MRC's gas pipeline subsidiary, MRTC, became involved also in its share of regulatory squabbles. However, because of its historic hold on the business of supplying natural gas to Saint Louis, it was much less a mixed blessing than any other MRC nonrail property. Laclede Gas Company of Saint Louis, which Marbury had once tried to control, had begun mixing natural gas with manufactured gas in 1932 and by 1949, when MRTC finished its second pipeline into Saint Louis from Louisiana, had switched to straight natural gas purchased from MRTC.[9] This monopoly on the Saint Louis gas supply was the source of the promise and the problems of the Transmission company in the 1960s.

Beginning in 1962 Saint Louis industries began trying to

[6] *St. Louis Post Dispatch*, July 18, 1966, ibid.

[7] Ibid., and March 23, 1972.

[8] Ibid.; Missouri Pacific Corporation, *Annual Report, 1979*, p. 3. Interestingly, one of the first things the corporation considered doing with the money was getting back into the oil exploration business. *Wall Street Journal*, Oct. 17, 1979.

[9] *St. Louis Post Dispatch*, Nov. 30, 1969, MRC clippings, MP public relations office.

obtain an increased and more regular supply of gas. They brought a case before the FPC proposing that other pipeline companies be allowed to make contracts for the Saint Louis supply. The major applicant for that business was the Oklahoma-Illinois Gas Pipeline Company, which thought of building a pipeline into Saint Louis. However, a consortium of Natural Gas Pipeline Company, Trunkline Gas Company (a subsidiary of Panhandle Eastern), and MRTC made a counterproposal that the FPC in 1965 decided was more in the public interest than the Oklahoma-Illinois plan. MRTC made agreements with the fourteen largest Saint Louis industries to increase its supply by 100 million cubic feet a day starting in the fall of 1966, set interruption temperatures lower than before, and make firmer supply contracts. MRTC increased its underground gas storage in Illinois at a cost of $1 million in 1965 and $2 million more in 1966.[10]

The FPC was not unanimous in approving this plan. Commissioner David Black said that the commission's acceptance of the three-company consortium plan was the result of deception by Panhandle Eastern, which had first proposed to build a competitive pipeline into Saint Louis and then at the last minute had thrown its support to the MRTC consortium. The three-company scheme gave no new line, but only allowed MRTC to buy gas from the other two companies until it could expand its own supply.[11]

The industries of Saint Louis, however, needed more gas from whatever source. Air-pollution studies indicated that Saint Louis industry, long run on high-sulphur Illinois coal, must switch to gas to meet the requirements of new clean-air legislation. Both the industries and MRTC were upset by the FPC's suggestions that the whole matter be reheard in five years. Without long-term arrangements, the pipeline company said, "both the gas supply and the financing of pipelines would be thrust into chaotic conditions."[12]

The industrial necessities of Saint Louis held sway for the

[10] Ibid., Nov. 12, 1965; *St. Louis Globe Democrat*, Nov. 18, 1965, ibid.
[11] *St. Louis Post Dispatch*, March 1, 1966, ibid.
[12] Ibid., May 18, 1966; *St. Louis Globe Democrat*, April 6, 1966, ibid.

next few years over the hesitations of the FPC. Strict air-pollution regulations took effect in Saint Louis in October, 1968. The FPC cut corners because industrial customers were "beating on Laclede's doors to see if they would get firm gas supplies." In the spring of 1968, MRTC was allowed to bypass the hearing examiner and appeal directly to the FPC with a plan to increase the Saint Louis gas supply, and in the summer of that year it got approval to install additional pipeline capacity and storage facilities.[13]

The regulatory agency then approved MRTC requests to increase rates in order to finance the improvements. Not surprisingly, Laclede Gas opposed the rate increases. A Saint Louis newspaper observed that while "the Laclede Gas Co. . . . speaks of Mississippi River Fuel Corp. as Damon spoke of Pythias, or Huntley of Brinkley, when it is being pressed to seek a second wholesale gas supplier, [it] now says in opposing Mississippi River's proposed increased rates that they 'may well be unjust, unreasonable, unduly discriminatory, and preferential.'" Laclede, however, was wholly dependent upon MRTC for its supply, and the 450,000 families, businesses, and industries using gas in Saint Louis would have to pay whatever MRTC demanded and the FPC approved.[14]

MRTC did gain regular rate increases in the late 1960s and early 1970s. In 1971 it contributed largely to a 30 percent increase in the earnings of parent MRC and became more actively involved in exploration for new gas than it had been in several years. In 1974 MRTC, which had been 82 percent owned by MRC, became a wholly owned subsidiary. In 1977 it contributed 26 percent of the net income of the Missouri Pacific Corporation holding company. In 1979 it had a net income of $32.6 million on revenues of over $524 million. Increases in net income of over 30 percent a year were not unusual for MRTC in the energy crisis–deregulation period of the late 1970s and early 1980s. It remained a working part of the Missouri Pacific Corporation long after most of the historic elements of Marbury's empire were ab-

[13] *St. Louis Globe Democrat*, June 29, Aug. 16, Sept. 5, 1968, *St. Louis Post Dispatch*, March 8, July 31, 1968, ibid.
[14] *St. Louis Post Dispatch*, July 31, 1969, ibid.

sorbed and even after the corporate disappearance of Mississippi River Corporation itself.[15] It provided the holding company with the kind of diversification that was attractive both to its own stockholders and to any potential merger partner desiring more than a railroad in a corporate package.

Now that there were no B stockholders to worry about, corporate simplification came in planned steps. Most important were the full merger of the Chicago & Eastern Illinois and the Texas & Pacific into the MP system (the so-called three-way merger) and the change of the name of the holding company from Mississippi River Corporation to Missouri Pacific Corporation. The three-way merger was approved by stockholders in October, 1974, and the name change came in June, 1976. The discarding of the old name was a joy to Jenks, who was forever finished with explaining that his railroad was not controlled by a barge company. The change, he said, "reflects the fact that we have become a major railroad holding company." Jenks became chairman of the board of the new MP Corporation and Thomas O'Leary its president. John Lloyd was president of the railroad company.[16]

This time the MP expected little trouble from the regulatory agencies. There was relatively little, but two surprising issues did crop up. There was a request that the Rock Island be included in the MP system. Fortunately for the MP, that was denied.[17] Also there were lawsuits filed by Palestine, Texas, which was trying to preserve its rights to the system-wide shops guaranteed it in a nineteenth-century contract. A victory by Palestine could have endangered the railroad's mechanical simplification, but that victory was not forthcoming.[18]

In December, 1977, the MP stockholders approved a plan of consolidation that made the MP railroad a wholly owned sub-

[15] *Wall Street Journal*, Oct. 6, 1971, March 7, 1974; Kidder, Peabody & Co., "Missouri Pacific Corporation: Point of View," March 7, 1978, p. 16; Missouri Pacific Corporation, *Annual Report*, 1979, p. 12.

[16] *St. Louis Globe Democrat*, May 28, 1976, MRC clippings, MP public relations office.

[17] *Journal of Commerce*, May 11, 1970, 3-way clippings, ibid.

[18] *Palestine Herald Press*, May 26, 1976, ibid.

sidiary of Missouri Pacific Corporation. The corporation already wholly owned River Cement and MRTC. The consolidation also provided 100 percent ownership of seven remaining subsidiaries of the rail corporation, thus simplifying considerably the filing of reports. The ICC approved all this in the fall of 1978.[19] So at last it was time to think of the future, a future in which a good deal more control could be exercised by centralized management than in the days of the vacuum tube and the B stockholder.

From the time Jenks arrived in 1961 great emphasis was placed on the MP's management training program. There were several reasons for this. It was clear, for example, that outstanding managers were required for the centralized management style that Jenks preferred and developments in computers made more possible. Also, railroading in the future could not be so much a traditional occupation laced with mystique and special techniques as before. It would be a big business, more like other contemporary big businesses than like historic railroading. This required that the company compete with other large corporations for the most skilled managers and allow them to move quickly to executive levels. This was in contrast to the usual rail policy of gleaning managers from among older men, often without college degrees, who had started with the railroad as brakemen forty years earlier. Jenks, himself a rail president before his fortieth birthday, was not sympathetic to the idea that mere time-serving was of any benefit. He was convinced that outstanding managers were the key to the success of the railroad and that the company needed to recruit young graduates from colleges and universities in the area served by the MP and then motivate them strongly with opportunities for rapid promotion and large salary increases.

There had been a training program in the late 1950s, but it had been limited. There were only five trainees in 1959 and 1960, whereas in the early 1980s there were thirty-five to forty at a time. Jenks had run the training program at the Rock Island with success and had informed his top people in February, 1961,

---

[19] *Traffic World*, Sept. 29, 1978, ibid.; Proxy booklet, Nov. 3, 1977, in blue merger book, MP public relations office.

that training was to be high on their list of priorities and was something to which top managers should devote a significant proportion of their time. The training program was first instituted in the traffic and operating departments but spread quickly to most departments on the railroad. Careful records were kept on retention, since training involved a substantial investment of time and money in a young person. As the program developed, retention improved. By 1982 slightly fewer than six hundred persons had begun the training program since 1961, and more than three hundred were still working for the railroad, many in top positions.[20]

A major goal of the Management Development Program was to acquaint future mangers with the way each department of the railroad interacted with others and contributed to the overall success of the company. Richard K. Davidson, in 1981 senior vice-president of operations though under age forty, had begun working for the railroad as a brakeman/conductor in 1960, earned a history degree, and entered the MP Management Development Program. During his training he worked in various departments, including sales, and found his perspective on the railroad entirely altered. "I thought the world revolved around a certain division of the railroad," he later said, "and that the superintendent was God." Through the 1960s and 1970s, thanks partly to the training program there was lots of migration between departments at the MP, and there were regular contacts among officers who had perhaps first become acquainted in the training program. The interaction was especially fertile between the traffic and operating departments, with a significant number of officers starting in one area and moving to the other. One express purpose of the training was to acquaint the trainee with key people he or she would need to know in all departments and to ensure that if one career choice turned out to be a dead end, a bright person would know where else on the railroad to look for the right kind of challenge.[21]

In addition to gaining this general acquaintance with peo-

[20] Interview with Paul Morey and Ray Breedlove, July 23, 1981, Saint Louis.
[21] Interview with Richard K. Davidson, July 23, 1981, Saint Louis.

ple in various departments, each trainee received a sponsor. To ensure that each person the MP bet on as a senior officer had a "significant level friend," each was assigned a sponsor who was an officer below the vice-presidential level. This sponsor kept track of the career of the trainee after the formal training was over. The sponsor was available to discuss professional or personal problems.[22]

The training itself became ever less like college classroom work and more like a co-op experience, combining academic instruction and field work. In the beginning the training was about one year long and consisted of a general orientation to the railroad tailored to the kind of work the trainee wanted to do with the company. Later the so-called general orientation phase, which all trainees went through, was cut to about eight months, but the total training time was increased to twenty months. The last twelve months were divided between different types of work experience. For six months the trainee served as an assistant general foreman in a mechanical department facility and for six months as an assistant roadmaster in a maintenance-of-way area. People headed for some departments received only general orientation. All of the operating management trainees, however, went through the one-year hands-on experience. Since about two-thirds of trainees are operating department trainees, a high percentage of people in the program share a similar training background.[23]

That much of the training was designed to be hands-on should not hide its academic elements. The ubiquity of the computer on the modern railroad required formal training in TCS (Transportation Control System) procedures and by the Information and Control System Department. There was a classroom session on safety and the book of rules, usually held at Fort Worth. The company in the early 1970s established a full-color in-house television training center, the first railroad to do so. At the end of 1972 the video training section had completed seventeen productions and had nine underway. Also, the company of-

[22] Interview with Morey and Breedlove, July 23, 1981, Saint Louis.
[23] Interviews with Morey, Breedlove, and Davidson, July 23, 1981, Saint Louis.

fered employees tuition aid to get formal academic training in job-related areas, while middle-level managers were sent to seminars at outstanding schools of business. Chief among these have been the Transportation Center at Northwestern University at Chicago, where Jenks was a trustee, and the mid- and advanced-level management development programs at Harvard.[24]

Trainees typically spend a large proportion of their time observing railroading throughout the system. Spending 50 percent of training time away from Saint Louis and out on the line was not unusual. Trainees rode trains, observed the switch shanty, and absorbed the atmosphere in yard offices. Richard Davidson's first day in the training program in 1965 was spent serving as a conductor during an unexpected strike. Shortly thereafter there was a flood in Texas. Mr. Jenks called Saint Louis and ordered all the trainees to the site. Any who felt this was beneath the dignity of those being groomed as executives were surprised to see Jenks and Lloyd wading in the floodwaters along with them. It was clear that the MP manager, for all his education and general business skills, would be required first and foremost to have a gut feeling for the way a railroad operated day to day.[25]

The schedule for Operations and Maintenance-of-Way Management Development trainees in the general orientation phase was varied and rigorous. In 1980, for example, after one day of introduction to the training program, the trainee proceeded to two days of Intermodal instruction, learning about containerization and sources of traffic revenue and getting experience with equipment distribution, customer service, and tracing. Next came Accounting, where operating trainees spent eight days and maintenance-of-way people three. Of the eight days, five were an assignment to a station auditor to assist in the actual audit of a station. There followed twelve days of instruction in the working of Information and Control Sytems, ten days of rules and safety (including riding yard, bowl, and hump engines and attending a

[24] Interview with Morey and Breedlove, July 23, 1981, Saint Louis; Missouri Pacific Corporation, *Annual Report, 1972*, p. 12; *St. Louis Globe Democrat*, DBJ clippings, vol. 2, MP public relations office.

[25] Interviews with Morey, Breedlove, and Davidson, July 23, 1981, Saint Louis.

safety investigation), and five to fifteen days learning the functions of Equipment and Operations Control people. Ten days centered on the mechanical side of the railroad (most spent in intensive observation at the North Little Rock shops), and three to ten days were spent in Engineering (including signals, communications, architecture, and even utilities). Ten days were devoted to freight traffic and work with a sales manager, and then various briefer periods dealing with labor relations, economic research, personnel, industrial engineering, purchasing and materials, law-tax-claims, contracts-leases-land, and explanation of the management-by-objectives programs by which managers were evaluated. Sales, Customer Service, and Accounting training programs varied in emphasis from this pattern, but no specialization neglected any phase entirely.[26]

The success of the training depended not only on the quality of the program, but on the quality of the people who entered it. Therefore, much attention was paid to recruiting. Employee records were examined to see what persons might be invited to enter the program. The goal was to attract the most outstanding college graduates, especially those with degrees in engineering, to become the operating-oriented managers of MP's future.

One of the first things Jenks did on his arrival in 1961 was to call Joseph Austin in the Operating Department; Joseph Savage, the assistant chief engineer; and Ray Breedlove, the manager of Personnel, and tell them to turn all their work over to assistants so that they could go on an intensive recruiting sweep to area universities. The three took a business car and spent eight weeks on the assignment. They had a film on the modern railway industry and invited professors to dinner in order to try to convince them, and their students through them, that railroading was no longer a backward industry. The tradition of involving top officers in recruiting efforts continued. Those who were not in the field recruiting were likely to become involved in the final evaluation of the best training-program candidates, who were then brought to Saint Louis for an interview.[27]

[26]Training Schedules, 1980, Personnel Department, MP Railroad, Saint Louis.

[27]Interviews with Joseph Austin, Morey, and Breedlove, July 23, 1981, Saint Louis.

It was important to try to isolate the qualities that the MP wanted in a manager. Most candidates had good grades, so the keys were leadership ability, attitude, and a scientific orientation. Recruiters looked for a pattern of leadership and were interested in everything from extracurricular activities and volunteer work to previous employment. The potential manager should be enthusiastic enough about a rail career to be willing to accept its special hardships, including long hours, travel, and the frequent relocation that was part of the MP management philosophy. Perhaps the guidelines missed the brilliant eccentric, but this was considered justified since railroad managers spent most of their time dealing with people and sheer brainpower without good social adjustment could be counterproductive.[28]

One way of familiarizing college students with a railroad career before graduation was the MP's Co-operative Education/ Tuition Assistance Program. After completing the freshman year, students in fields desirable to the MP could be selected to work alternate semesters for the railroad. After the first work period they were eligible for tuition assistance from the company.[29]

Especially in the 1970s this program concentrated on industrial, civil, mechanical, and electrical engineering majors, along with those in computer science. As the flyer passed out at colleges put it: "The MoPac's need is for engineers who also have the ability to manage our railroad operation. We want to talk with engineering majors about the opportunities available for people to make careers as generalists, dealing with technical problems, perhaps handling some pure engineering work, but normally moving along career paths toward general management."[30] It was a simply stated goal, but finding individuals who fit the description was difficult.

The spectacular gains of the MP in both structure and function in the years following recapitalization did not go unnoticed in the rest of the country. Rail analysts at New York investment houses applauded each of the MP's accomplishments and ad-

[28] Interview with Morey and Breedlove, July 23, 1981, Saint Louis.

[29] Ibid.

[30] Missouri Pacific Railroad, "Missouri Pacific Railroad's Co-operative Education Program," MP public relations office.

vised any investors who were not impressed enough with the company's income statistics that it indeed had bright prospects for the future. "Missouri Pacific has the best management group I know of," wrote one analyst. "It is the only company I know about where I don't know of any strategic or tactical mistakes." Naturally, not only analysts and small investors were watching the MP. It was widely believed that the "urge to merge" movement, which had been interrupted when the Union Pacific, after thirteen years of negotiations, backed away from the ruined Rock Island in 1975, would inevitably reappear. If anything, conditions favored even fewer large systems in the West than Jenks had predicted in the 1960s, and no large railroad wanted to be left out. At the corporate offices of the Union Pacific Railroad, merger kits, consisting of plastic overlays showing the "fit" of various railways with that line's system map, had been in heavy use. Particularly worn were the transparencies showing the nearly perfect end-to-end mesh of the amazingly strong and diversified Union Pacific with the equally strong if not quite so diversified MP. There was good understanding between the management of the two roads—the mutual respect of masters of their trade—and the Union Pacific people said among themselves that if and when the time was right the company could move quickly toward a marriage with the MP with a minimum of courtship.[31]

However well the management of both roads may have understood the possibilities (Jenks had suggested merger with the Union Pacific in the 1960s), the actual announcement on January 8, 1980, that the two had agreed in principle to merge took the financial press by surprise. This was so especially because the trend in mergers had traditionally been to join relatively strong railroads with relatively weak ones, both to ensure the survival of the weak and to maintain a government-induced competitive balance. These potential partners, however, were two of the largest and strongest rail-based corporations in the country.

The Union Pacific had since 1969 carried out a diversifica-

---

[31] *World-Herald* (Omaha), n.d. [March, 1981], *St. Louis Business Journal*, March 9, 1981, *Business Week*, March 9, 1981, UP-MP clippings, MP public relations office.

tion program, particularly strong in energy, without running up a huge debt, without diluting stockholder equity, and, particularly unusual, without the "helter-skelter" panic buying typical of diversifying companies. In energy, for example, it worked with Standard Oil of Indiana at first in developing its massive land grant–based mineral rights and only slowly shifted to its own exploration companies. When it was ready for an integrated oil company, it bought Champlin Petroleum for $240 million in cash and had one full-grown. On its own, Champlin in 1977 would have ranked 240th in the *Forbes* list of the 500 most profitable U.S. corporations. The Union Pacific railroad ranked 64th on that list and first among railroads. Like the MP, it was in "splendid" physical condition, having benefited from $3.6 billion in capital improvements over the decade. The Union Pacific and the MP had the highest traffic densities in the industry and a good mix of bulk commodities. The merger would give the Union Pacific new outlets on the Gulf for its coal and increase its average haul, which at 711 miles already led the industry.

Would the combination be too large and collapse with management problems? Not a chance. The plan was to leave both roads autonomous, though coordinated, and even to retain the original names Union Pacific and Missouri Pacific. It was then thought that both would be subsidiaries of the new corporation Pacific Rail Systems, Inc. However, things coordinated so well that eventually, after the merger approval, the holding company concept was abandoned and the roads were operated using common officers for both companies. Jenks was his usual matter-of-fact self in explaining it: "We will keep two separate profit centers to avoid getting a railroad that is too big to handle. By keeping them separate, on merger day everyone will go to work as usual. Keep in mind that these two railroads fit together very well. UP runs its railroad about the way we run ours, the condition of the properties is very similar, and the lines will function well from the start." [32]

Others responded less calmly. "Things are starting to happen again," wrote the *New York Times*. An analyst in Chicago

[32] *Forbes*, June 1, 1977, *Business Week*, July 14, 1980, ibid.

commented: "This is the world's greatest merger. The Union Pacific is a landholder of great magnitude, with a big natural resource play. And the Missouri Pacific is a well-run, gold-plated railroad." Surely here, finally, was the immense, serious western merger that would bring about either the concentration predicted since the ICC study of 1920 or nationalization or both. Proponents and opponents alike (though with different tones in their voices) called it the "Mop-up" merger. Said one observer of the proposed 22,000-mile giant: "It's like combining the Pittsburgh Steelers and the Dallas Cowboys."[33]

That the country's ninth-largest railway (Union Pacific) and its sixth-largest (MP) would choose to negotiate a merger over the late-1979 holiday season was anything but a whim or accident. There had been a great deal of what the military might call contingency planning going on at the two railroads for nearly ten years. "We had been good friends for a long time," said James Evans, the head of the Union Pacific Corporation, "and there were indications that the Missouri Pacific would favorably entertain an offer of marriage by us." In fact, when talks between the two corporations commenced, agreement was reached in only two weeks. It was a question for some time not so much of whether but of exactly when.[34]

The creation of the Burlington Northern in 1970 had been a sign, but no one was sure exactly what it was a sign of. The final collapse of the Rock Island did not by itself portend much, for, as Downing Jenks put it, everywhere the Rock Island went someone else went there and did it better. It was a different matter when the Southern Pacific moved to acquire part of the Rock Island, as it did in 1979. In December the ICC, after a short and efficient consideration, approved the Southern Pacific's purchase of the Rock Island's so-called Tucumcari Line. That saved the Southern Pacific four hundred miles in reaching the Midwest compared with its former circuitous route via the Cotton Belt (Saint Louis Southwestern) and made it a real threat in the trade territory of the Union Pacific and the MP. Similarly threat-

[33] *Chicago Sun-Times*, Jan. 9, 1980, *New York Times*, Jan. 9, 1980, *Wall Street Journal*, Jan. 9, 1980, ibid.
[34] *Washington Star*, April 22, 1980, ibid.

ening was the Burlington Northern's application at the same time, approved—even with some court delay—only a year later, to merge with the Saint Louis–San Francisco. This created a 28,000-mile system with single-haul service from the Midwest and the Gulf to the Pacific Coast.[35]

These moves were discouraging from a competitive standpoint, but in a different way they were encouraging to the Union Pacific and the MP. Even before the election of Ronald Reagan as president there was a conservative turn in the country. Encouraging the trend, a group of statistics showed that if something did not change by 1985, railroads, excluding the government-subsidized Conrail, would fall $13 billion to $16 billion behind in generating the funds necessary to replace track and rolling stock and repay debt. There were only two ways around this—subsidize the railroads and thus in effect nationalize them or deregulate them, freeing them to find their own level of profitability through mergers, marketplace pricing, and reduction of overhead. There were strong signs of movement along the second course.[36]

The Rail Revitalization and Regulatory Reform Act (4R Act) passed in 1976 limited the time that could be spent by the ICC in making a decision on rail merger applications to thirty-one months. The Southern Pacific application for the Rock Island and the Burlington Northern merger with the Frisco were tests of this timetable, and in both cases decisions were made promptly, well in advance of the deadline. By contrast, the merger that formed the Burlington Northern had taken nine years and the Rock Island case thirteen. This streamlined procedure was encouraging to railroad companies, which in the inflationary economy of the 1980s would have to pay as much as $15,000 an hour for attorneys for each hour hearings continued. There were signs also that the ICC now favored end-to-end mergers over the parallel mergers common in the 1960s. Perhaps most important, the ICC seemed to have abandoned at least partially the idea that weaker railroads had to survive and be helped by

[35] *Washington Star*, April 22, 1980, *St. Louis Post Dispatch*, March 13, 1981, *Transport 2000*, Sept.–Oct., 1980, *Business Week*, July 14, 1980, ibid.

[36] *Business Week*, July 14, 1980, ibid.

stronger ones. In the Burlington Northern–Frisco decision handed down in April, 1980, the commission wrote: "Railroads do not have a proprietary right in the future to the traffic they have carried in the past. . . . Indemnity may be viewed as a reward for being unable to compete in the marketplace." Further moves by the ICC early in 1980 to lessen the paperwork required for mergers (reducing the application involving the MP to a mere twenty-six volumes and 4,300 pages) and exempting certain kinds of transactions from regulation altogether further encouraged the Union Pacific and the MP. Said James Evans of the Union Pacific: "The Balkanization of the railroad industry, so that it has to be both competitive and cooperative, is not the most efficient way of serving rail transportation needs. What is essential in the public interest is not the preservation of small rail carriers." The time was right to bring out the dream plans— the things you would do as a rail manager if all restrictions and all protections were suddenly removed and if it were each corporate alliance for itself with no quarter from others. ICC Chairman Darius Gaskins, Jr., said in June, 1980, "We don't have a master plan for the railroads."[37]

The plan that came forward was actually larger than the first public announcements revealed. Its other element was inclusion in the new Union Pacific system of the Western Pacific. Two weeks after the news of the deal between Union Pacific and MP became public, the Union Pacific offered twenty dollars a share for the 1.26 million shares of Western Pacific A stock it did not already own. During Union Pacific's planning the Western Pacific had the code name Tiger, while the MP was Silver Spike and the Union Pacific, in honor of the alma mater of its president John Kenefick, was called Princeton. The Western Pacific's seventeen hundred–mile system had a main line running from a Union Pacific connection at Salt Lake City to San Francisco, thus giving the merged system direct access to northern California, which it would otherwise have lacked. By March the Union

[37] *World-Herald* (Omaha), March 8, 1981, *Washington Star*, April 6, 1980, *Transport 2000*, March–April, 1981, *Arkansas Gazette*, Sept. 28, 1980, *Railway Age*, July 14, 1980, *Houston Chronicle*, April 23, 1980, *Business Week*, June 16, 1980, *Journal of Commerce and Commercial*, Aug. 26, 1980, ibid.

Pacific was successful in buying more than a million Western Pacific shares for $20.9 million in cash. Potential objections by Union Pacific shareholders to expansion in rails or by the MP shareholders to the exchange ratio did not materialize. All the railroad boards approved the merger, the Union Pacific split its stock 2 for 1, and on September 15 a formal application for the Union Pacific–Missouri Pacific–Western Pacific combination was filed with the ICC. The MP shareholders were to get 1.1 shares of Union Pacific Corporation common stock and .275 shares of that company's $7.25 Convertible Preferred Stock. "They think long term at UP," a writer at *Forbes* had concluded in 1977, "and no one seriously believes that the heirs of Edward H. Harriman would ever give up hope of one day running a coast-to-coast railroad that is not part of a nationalized system."[38]

Naturally, there was not universal joy among other western railroads at the merger prospect. Harry Dimmerman, the vice-president—traffic of the Missouri, Kansas & Texas, told his regional people in a meeting: "If I was to give you the worst possible news I'd be telling you what I'm going to tell you." He then informed them that the Union Pacific, the Katy's best freight connection, was combining with the MP, the Katy's biggest competitor. "It's a real serious thing for us." Also seriously affected was the Denver & Rio Grande Western, which connected with the MP at Pueblo and with the Western Pacific at Salt Lake City and predicted that the merger could cost it 40 percent of its freight volume. The Chicago & Northwestern, already in perilous financial condition, feared being bypassed by the Union Pacific on the haul from Omaha to Chicago. The Burlington Northern worried that a Union Pacific proposal to placate the Chicago & Northwestern by joining it in building an extension of the Chicago & Northwestern into the Powder River coalfields of Wyoming would threaten Burlington Northern's traffic there. The Santa Fe and the Southern Pacific were not much heard from immediately because the two were themselves trying to

[38] *Kansas City Star*, Jan. 21, 1980, *World-Herald* (Omaha), n.d. [March, 1981], *Wall Street Journal*, Jan. 22, Feb. 26, 29, March 4, April 21, 1980, *U.S. Rail News*, Jan. 22, 1980, *St. Louis Post Dispatch*, Sept. 15, Jan. 8, 1980, *Forbes*, June 1, 1977, *New York Times*, Sept. 16, 1980, ibid.

work out a merger involving, like the Union Pacific deal, a stock exchange worth more than $1 billion. Public announcement of talks came in May, and the talks collapsed in September, 1980, just after the Union Pacific application went to the ICC. Then the anti–mop-up rhetoric, especially from the Southern Pacific, heated up considerably. In November the Southern Pacific filed a suit in California charging that the Union Pacific merger plan violated the Pacific Railway Acts of 1862 and 1864 and asking triple damages for traffic diversion. While the Union Pacific argued that it was vulnerable if left out of a merger—for example, it would be the only one of the four major western railroads (Southern Pacific, Santa Fe, Union Pacific, and Burlington Northern) without a Gulf connection—Southern Pacific spokespeople were not very sympathetic. Chairman Benjamin Biaggini characterized the Union Pacific as "embarassingly rich." "Union Pacific is already a dominant force in the rail industry west of the Mississippi River and is the country's richest and most powerful railroad." By March of 1981, when the ICC hearings on the Union Pacific–Missouri Pacific–Western Pacific consolidation began, rail opposition in varying degrees of intensity came from the Santa Fe, the Burlington Northern, the Denver & Rio Grande Western, the Chicago, Milwaukee, Saint Paul & Pacific, the Illinois Central Gulf, the Kansas City Southern, the Missouri, Kansas & Texas, the Soo Line, and Conrail. Most of the objections could be satisfied by the granting of trackage rights, though that was certainly not the case with the demands of the Southern Pacific.[39]

The Union Pacific deal, though, would not only affect competing railroads in the usual way mergers did, but it would set off defensive consolidations that would change the national rail picture permanently. The Federal Railroad Administration (FRA), for example, had been pouring money into the weaker

[39] *Washington Star*, Jan. 9, 1980, *Journal of Commerce and Commercial*, June 23, 24, 1980, April 6, 1981, *Salt Lake City Tribune*, Sept. 16, 1980, *Kansas City Star*, May 19, 1980, *Wall Street Journal*, Nov. 26, 1980, *Kansas City Times*, Sept. 16, 1980, *Chicago Tribune*, Jan. 9, 1980, *World-Herald* (Omaha), July 16, 1981, *Locomotive Engineer*, March 13, 1981, *Traffic World*, Feb. 23, 1981, Southern Pacific press release, March 3, 1981, ibid.

midwestern rail systems for some time and was uncertain the Union Pacific move would be consistent with its efforts. One federal official commented: "We had hoped the healthy railroads were going to move into the Midwest and help us solve the problem by picking up viable pieces of the unhealthy railroads. I don't know . . . whether the U.P. is going to be part of the solution or part of the problem." In September, 1980, there were nine major railroads in various stages of mergers. In the East the Chessie Systems line and the Seaboard Coast Line were in the preliminary stages of creating what became CSX Corporation and a 27,000-mile-long railroad. This almost forced the Norfolk and Western and the Southern Railroad to merge, which would leave three systems in the East (CSX, Norfolk Southern, and Conrail). One man was led to predict that by 1990 "you could hold an AAR [Association of American Railroads] meeting in the corner booth of your favorite restaurant."[40]

While the changes kept people excited, there were those who saw them as ultimately dangerous and therefore did not see the Union Pacific's opening shot as the masterstroke so many considered it to be. There were negative comments from states that perceived that part of the policy switch was a virtual elimination of the railroads' historical government-imposed obligation to "serve" assigned territories in return for protection from intrusion by other companies. With open competition there was likely to be a trimming of branch lines and a concentration on bridge traffic, leaving many communities isolated and increasing the trend toward metropolitanism and industrial concentration.

Also annoyed were those served by the "weaker" lines, which would perhaps be left out of the merger movement with no compensation and would be requesting government aid. "It may be champagne time for . . . directors but not necessarily for taxpayers." What about the subsidies, including land grants, that had been given railroads over the years in return for "public service" functions? Would these be written off? In the spring of 1981 Congressman John Dingell of Michigan and the Water

[40] *Chicago Tribune*, Jan. 13, 1980, *Christian Science Monitor*, Sept. 17, 1980, *Wall Street Journal*, June 3, 1980, *Chessie News*, Oct., 1980, *Railway Age*, July 14, 1980, *Arkansas Gazette*, July 14, 1980, ibid.

Transport Association pushed this last argument rather hard to the ICC, insisting that the Union Pacific, the MP, and the Western Pacific submit estimates of the value of lands given them and that these estimates be used in evaluating the merger and setting future rate levels. "It is unacceptable," said Dingell, "to have government aid diverted from its main objective of benefiting the ultimate public which the railroads serve." Present to some extent in all the broad objections was the fear of corporate power that had led to the creation of the ICC in the first place nearly one hundred years earlier. The railroads argued that their position in transportation as a whole was nothing like the dominant one they had enjoyed in 1887, but the critics thought the new merged companies would be powerful enough to oppress. "No matter how well intentioned management may be," wrote an editor in Arkansas, "the absence of competition virtually guarantees intolerable arrogance." That arrogance, he thought, would lead eventually to demands for re-regulation or nationalization. The other possible scenario was that the new "corporate monstrosities" would drain off rail profits to finance other enterprises undertaken by holding companies and allow the railroads to fall into disrepair. Again, nationalization would be the likely result.[41]

The hearings on the Union Pacific merger began before the ICC on March 3, 1981. Witnesses for the applicants could hardly deny that the Union Pacific and the MP were at present well run and financially stable or that Pacific Rail Systems, Inc., the merged concern, would exercise great power. Thomas O'Leary of the MP estimated that the total assets of the merged company would approach $9 billion and that it would have a consolidated debt-to-capitalization ratio, conservatively, of 39 percent. A Union Pacific marketing officer testified that the new combination would be able to take $160 million in gross revenues from competing railroads in the third year following the merger. The thrust of the argument, though, was not so much that the merger would save money and eliminate duplicate facilities (the most common tack in the parallel mergers of the 1960s), as that without such a merger both the Union Pacific and the MP, however strong they might appear in 1981, would shortly lose out in the competition among giants that was forming in the rail industry. The Union Pacific could not in the future depend upon gateways to the north and south as it had done, but would have to control lines running there. Intense competition would be created under the opportunities presented by the Staggers Rail Act and by other mergers. The Union Pacific, left alone, was unique in the West in not being able to join with the CSX, Conrail, or Norfolk Southern to provide a two-carrier coast-to-coast service for shippers. Its competitors in the west (Burlington Northern, Atchison, Topeka & Santa Fe, and Southern Pacific) all could do this. The Western Pacific was even worse off in this regard, as shippers using it required four railroads for a coast-to-coast journey. If the ICC denied the merger application, the Union Pacific would probably de-emphasize its rail operation to the detriment of the public. So might the MP. Such a situation, said Mark Hennelly for the MP, "may be the last hurrah for [UP] and the last hurrah for [MoPac]."[42]

Actually, there was never any great chance that the merger would fail to be approved, though there was considerable discussion about what conditions to attach, if any. The Department of Justice expressed "concern" about possible anticompetitive effects of the merger but remained neutral. The Department of Transportation (DOT) came out in favor of the merger but agreed with Justice on certain conditions and added others of its own. The DOT felt the Burlington Northern should be well protected in the Powder River, the Denver & Rio Grande Western should get trackage rights from Kansas City to Omaha and to points in Texas, and the Southern Pacific should have trackage rights from Kansas City to Saint Louis. The only government agency to come out against the merger regardless of conditions was the ICC's own Office of Special Counsel. The OSC thought the merger would cause a competitive threat to the rest of the industry while providing little benefit to the public. Most of the

[42] *Washington Star*, March 3, 1981, *St. Louis Globe Democrat*, March 13, 1981, *Traffic World*, March 9, 23, 1981, July 26, 1982, *Dallas Times Herald*, March 10, 1982, *Journal of Commerce and Commercial*, Sept. 2, 1981, ibid.

$106 million-a-year benefits estimated by the merging roads were, said the OSC, merely transfers of resources to the applicants from other railroads. The merger would actually cost the public between $9 million and $10 million a year and would mean that the Denver & Rio Grande Western, the Katy, and the Southern Pacific would be severely damaged—the Denver & Rio Grande might not even survive as a viable competitor. Opinion among the commissioners, however, as shown by comments during the hearings and by the eventual 5-1 vote of approval was overwhelmingly favorable to the basic idea. ICC chairman Reese Taylor told an opponent of the merger at the hearings, "The fact is that competition really ought to be enhanced by the creation of a single system to compete with you."[43]

On September 13, 1982, the ICC announced the approval of the merger of the Union Pacific, MP, and Western Pacific. Trackage rights for the Denver & Rio Grande Western, the Katy, and the Southern Pacific were attached as conditions, but the commission generally took the merged roads' side in the issue of access to the Powder River Basin coalfields. ICC chairman Reese Taylor commented that it was "another major step in the restructuring and revitalization of the nation's railroad system, as was envisioned by Congress in the Railroad Revitalization and Regulatory Reform Act of 1976, and the Staggers Rail Act of 1980." Vice-chairman Reginald Gilliam was more specific. He concluded that the commission's decision was the first phase in reordering and modernizing the railroad system. He pointed out three special ramifications. First, Gilliam said, the country was now "clearly and irreversibly embarked" upon a new era of total transportation companies that would be the forerunners of the type of integrated transportation networks (rail, motor, air, and water) that Jenks had talked about in the early 1960s. Second, combinations such as the one just approved would stimulate others, probably including moves of the large eastern systems to consolidate with western systems. "Such is the nature of healthy, dynamic business competition." Last, the Union Pacific decision was a benchmark in the federal relationship with the railroads.

[43] St. *Louis Post Dispatch*, Feb. 4, 1981, *Sedalia Democrat*, July 23, 1982, ibid.

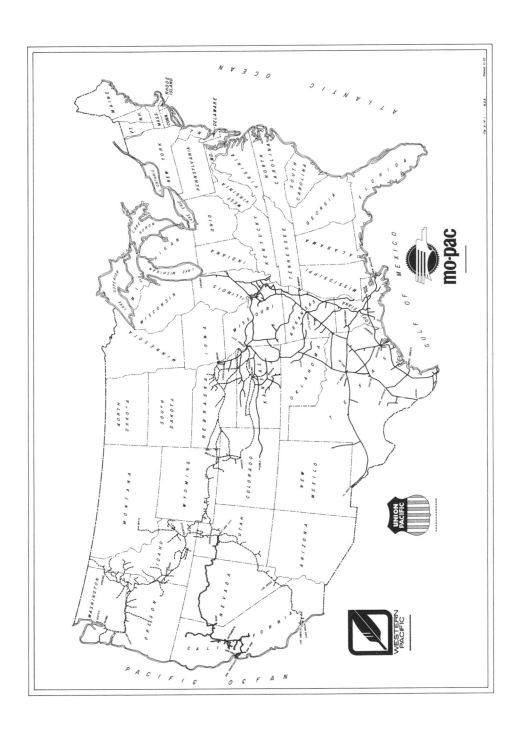

"Railroad management and initiative is appropriately assuming primary responsibility for the structure, operations, and pricing mechanisms of the new system." The role of the ICC in the future would be only to guard against abuse of market power and potential monopolistic activity.[44]

"What the commission is doing is creating impregnable fortresses," was one analyst's response. "My God, it would be easier for me to start an automobile company and compete with General Motors than a railroad to compete with what the commission is creating." The Southern Pacific sued to delay the merger. Suits were also filed by the Santa Fe and the Kansas City Southern. Early in December these and several other suits were rejected by the U.S. Court of Appeals for the District of Columbia Circuit. The Southern Pacific appeal to the Supreme Court failed on December 22, and with that decision the merger took effect and the lately reborn Missouri Pacific railroad reached the goal its managers had wished for and worked for directly since 1961.[45]

The Missouri Pacific, pulled from the crisis of an almost interminable receivership, modernized, and negotiated out of its oddball financial status, was in 1983 an object of pride. Downing Jenks was proud with special reason in May, 1982, when he rose to announce to the MP annual meeting, the forum where twenty-six years earlier the newly independent company's groups of claimants had so strenuously battled, that those battles were over and larger ones joined. There was a pall of sadness over the celebration, as only a few hours earlier the president of the MP, James Gessner, had died of a heart attack at age fifty-one. There was comfort in knowing that the merger was exactly what Gessner, like so many of his colleagues, had long hoped for. In a speech in 1975, when he was vice-president of operations, Gessner had put the MP ethic succinctly and well:

[44] *Wall Street Journal*, Sept. 14, 1982, *Business Week*, Sept. 27, 1982, ibid. The statements of the commissioners and the complete decision in the case are in Finance Docket No. 30,000, 366 ICC 459.

[45] *Business Week*, Sept. 27, 1982, *Traffic World*, Nov. 22, 1982, *Kansas City Times*, Jan. 28, 1983, *New York Times*, Dec. 10, 1982, *St. Louis Globe Democrat*, Dec. 11, 1982, UP-MP clippings, MP public relations office.

I don't believe we can any longer afford the traditional ways and traditional thinking that pervade our industry. Railroading today possesses little or no mystique. It is not an art based upon personal genius or intuition. Railroading is first a business. . . . All of us have a choice. We can fight change and cling to the traditional methods of performing our function. Or, we can welcome change as an opportunity to develop a railroad system the like of which has never been experienced in our industrial society.[46]

The recent history of the MP has demonstrated the benefits of a matter-of-fact engineering approach and of an openness to innovation and change. It also shows that the best of traditional railroading, notably pride in craft, has and will remain. Downing Jenks once wrote a historical article for a series published by *Nation's Business* in which he quoted Thomas Allen, the president of the Pacific of Missouri, the MP's predecessor. In 1849 at the Saint Louis groundbreaking for the construction of the first mile of what would become the Missouri Pacific system, Allen said, "The railroad is a noble and profitable work, reflecting the highest credit upon its projectors and its finishers."[47] Allen was the projector, but it remained for the team that arrived to work with William Marbury just over 110 years later to take the place in Missouri Pacific history as the railroad's ultimate finishers.

[46] *St. Louis Post Dispatch*, May 26, 1982, *Railway Age*, March 31, 1975, ibid.

[47] Downing Jenks, "Missouri Pacific: The Blueblood Who Brought Rails to the Rugged West," *Nation's Business*, Jan., 1973, DBJ clippings, vol. 3, MP public relations office.

# Index